THREE MARRIAGES

lies I've lived by

MAGDALEN BOWYER

THREE MARRIAGES
lies I've lived by

ISBN: 978-0-9938552-0-7

Cover art "Angel With a Star II"
by Hermann Edler, edlerfolkart.com
Photography by Marlow
Author photo by Patrick J. Adams
Design and layout by Lighthouse24

to my husbands

dangerous friends each
holding a mirror
reflecting
the Big Pain in me

I know I was your dangerous friend, too.

to my son, Matthew Kent
I had you for me
to have someone to live for.

to my son, Gabriel Adam
I had you for something larger than me
to have something to surrender to and trust.

"*Every reader, as he reads, is actually the reader of himself. The writer's work is only a kind of optical instrument he provides the reader so he can discern what he might never have seen in himself without this book. The reader's recognition in himself in what the book says is the proof of the book's truth.*"

~ Marcel Proust

"*From the broken heart comes a heart that can recognize and identify with the pain of others. A wound such as that must not be wasted or buried in self pity, but brought into the light and examined, reflected upon, and used as a lens through which the lives of others are better understood.*"

~ Caroline Myss

"*You do not become good by trying to be good, but by finding the goodness that is already within you, and allowing that goodness to emerge. But it can only emerge if something fundamental changes in your state of consciousness.*"

~ Eckhart Tolle

This is a story of the female search for love – a search inspired by the notion that opening a deeply personal space in one's life creates a place from which understanding may emerge. Using the process of emotional recall, the author moves in, out, and around her story to contextualize it both as personal narrative and social construction. The story is told through real and composite characters, and collapsed events. It is not a historical document, nor a work of invention. It is a transcomposite narrative.

Prefatory Note

When reading this work, let it be a mirror for your own journey.

We are the stories we tell. All stories are partial and situated. If we bend back in on ourselves, reflexive learning can lead us to look more deeply at our interactions with self, with others and with our world. We can explore, celebrate and reveal the relational moments we live.

Every scene in this story is ethnographic. The cast of characters is comprised of myself – "I" and "she" and finally "you" – and Kent – my other "I/eye" and "you" – along with composite fictional characters that I've created to embody the essence of my story and real characters whose names and other identifying characteristics have been changed.

"Marlene" is the name my parents gave me at birth, "Maha" is the name my third husband bestowed upon me and "Magdalen" is the name my soul revealed on my fortieth birthday.

ONE

Crossroads 1985
ENSPIRITING WIDOW-HOOD

When women unwind our veils, our winding sheets, our attention is at first fixed upon the unwinding. The task which next becomes visible, before us and around us, is the task of seeing / sensing / Self-moving in the directions which our dis-covering senses open out to us. This Self-conscious, Self-directed movement is springing free. As we do this we inspirit our Selves, freeing the life force that has been frozen, reified, fetishized.[1]

---

[1] excerpt from Mary Daly's *Gyn-Ecology: The Metaethics of Radical Feminism,* page 339

Muse

Last night
you spoke with kindness
and we were patient with each other

inhale

a mess of living between us
heart fragments spilled on the floor
each tenderly touched
making us naked and whole

what is this life if not
heart break and heart ache?

what courage we have
to still show up and breathe
risk a place we call home

exhale

There is nothing sexier than trust.

I met the love of my life when I was eighteen on the summer solstice in Cypress Hills, Saskatchewan. We performed the marriage ritual on the next summer solstice under a tree in the Cypress Hills Park. The Heron Farm on the banks of the Notukeu Creek became our home. My young husband died before our fifth summer solstice together. Today, twenty years later, I am carried down the passage where those memories linger. And I remember him waking up one Sunday morning awash with affection. He lit a smoke, stepped into his knee-high rubber boots, and headed out the porch door. He had this walk. His feet turned slightly outward. He lumbered with his long legs, loose ankles, and relaxed hips. I could always *hear* him walking. He hit his stride across the yard to the fencepost where the rain gauge was nailed. He checked how much rain we had, poured the water from the glass tube onto the ground and then set it back in its place. He stood there for a long while smokin' and thinkin' wearing nothin' but his rubber boots. Man, he lived free. He loved the prairie. He loved me.

• • •

What is this life if not
heart break and heart ache?

It is open doors of trust
that hinge upon
attentive, caring arms
gentle and strong
holding two heart beats
in a dance of contentment.

It is lovely conversation,
the tangle of bare feet,
wet, warm breath on your neck
and heat rising in our bellies.

Life is coming home
again and again
I find me
when I love you.

The conjugation and (sometimes) adverb unless, with its elegiac undertones, is a term used in logic, a word breathed by the hopeful or by writers of fiction wanting to prise open the crusted world and reveal another plane of being, which is similar in its geographical particulars and peopled by those who resemble ourselves.[2]

I was widowed at the age of 23. My pilgrimage has been a search for the sacred. Life has demanded I walk hand-in-hand with others on this journey. Detaching when endings arrive. Embracing when beginnings present. Each time my heart cracks open, I am changed

---

[2] excerpt from the novel *Unless* written by Carol Shields, page 314

forever. At times leaving myself behind, I meet myself again and again. Through dis-identification and dis-location and dis-placement I have learned what it means to connect with myself. Life has demanded I stay open. I'm still trying. This is part of my story.

Unless you are asked to tell your story.[3]

• • •

Felhomaly. The dusk of graves. With the connotation of intimacy
There between the dead and the living.[4]

My place is still here even though you are not and I try to convince myself of it every morning upon waking. The smell of your skin is on the bed sheets and the pile of your dirty clothes is on the floor in the laundry room. How can I wash away what remnants of you may remain? The evidence that you were here, you did sleep next to me. Your overalls are full of grain dust and the cuffs of your pants hold the dirt of yesterday's labour. To put such remains in a washing machine with soap and water will unravel the threads of my life. How can I forget? This is our world. Don't tell me it no longer exists. It is here. I have proof.

Last night I opened the bottle of dark rum you kept on the top shelf of the kitchen cupboard. The alcohol flushed my cheeks. The first one was slow going down. Hard for one who doesn't favour the burn. But within a few moments, the warmth flooded my body and it was good to feel the heat. I lost myself in images of what should have been and the smooth liquid fell easily down my raw throat. My tears washed me with a grief too tangible to be consumed in the harsh reality of one who is not drunk. I swallowed the next dose more easily. This is what it comes down to, what I can bear.

---

[3] Dialogue spoken by the character Reta Winters during the stage play *Unless* adapted by Carol Shields and Sara Cassidy as seen at the Belfry Theatre, Victoria, BC on November 12, 2005.
[4] excerpt from the novel *The English Patient* written by Michael Ondaatje, page 170

There is never any way to predict which day will be good. The slightest provocation and I am right back to the beginning with no sense of time having passed. I'm transported to seeing you walk across a field of wheat, your hair as gold as the grain ready for harvest.

Prairie storms remind me I am still alive. Shocking my senses back into the physical world, the thunder is loud in my ears, the lightning bright in my eyes. The wind blows through my skin and bones. My body is a place I once knew and now I must make mine again, somehow, without your touch. Yet, I feel your presence. As though you have gone around the corner of the house into a different room. I know it is there, but I cannot find it.

I am still with you in whatever space you have hidden yourself. I can't name it but I know I am living it. I keep this place sacred, safely hidden from anyone who may want to destroy or invade it. I won't go out at night. I stay on the farm and tend to the chores. Your family watches me. My family has all gone home. Since we met, home for me has been with you. I feel untouchable. It's easy to be alone with you because everyone is most comfortable when they don't see me. I only remind them of their loss. They would rather live in denial than face the pain of losing the promise of what your life meant to them. It seems an easier way to live.

I am isolated. I don't yet see it, but I am beginning to feel the alienation. I am becoming an invisible woman.

• • •

Who can tell what will happen when a woman is unlinked from the chain of familiar living by being consumed in the foreign land of dying? I sit by your grave and I know, we knew, this was the way it would be for us.

I remember your twenty-sixth birthday. And in my remembering I see the clues to the ending of your life. You said to me you couldn't imagine us growing old together. Lying in your arms, I asked you to tell me your birthday wish. After a long pause you replied, "I wish for a long and happy life for us together."

Smiling, I nestled my face in the nape of your neck.

"I wish for our first child and I wish if either one of us ever has to go, we'll go together because I can't bear the thought of living without you."

How sweet and unforgiving your wishes live in my memory.

Now I bring red roses to your grave and my imagination fails me. How long has it been since I stroked the blond hair of your forearms or watched the sunlight dance in the blueness of your eyes? When did I hear your lingering voice call to me across the field of wheat and feel the warmth of your breath on my neck? How can I tell the people who call me widow, I still dance with my dead husband in the twilight?

• • •

Open

No more chocolate kisses,
I want the taste of you.
Breathe open
my heart's yearning
to be seen.
Tell me
touch me
part these lips
drink desire
quench this soul thirst
warm and wet
right as rain.

Candy left in the dish the day you walked out the door remains. Some part of me expects you to appear in the kitchen doorway at any moment. I feel you will come back if only I solve this puzzle, unlock this mystery. Where will I find the key? You are just a heartbeat from me.

The trees are in their full summer bloom. The grass still needs to be cut; the cows need to be fed and watered along with the chickens, turkeys, ducks and geese. The wheat in the field was destroyed by hail and the insurance barely covers the damage. I am up every day at sunrise tending to the chores on this farm that has sustained your mother and father, your grandmother and grandfather, generations living the rural life. I'm keeping your dream alive. The dream of children and farming and long life.

Our dog Sadie has been obsessed looking for you. Her eyes hold a sadness that pierces my heart and I don't know how to console her. You never liked Sadie sleeping in the porch. You worried she would become accustomed to the warmth and then she would be unable to withstand the cold winters. But she whines and whimpers in the dark so, I let her inside. I feel better knowing she's not the only one crying in the dark and her presence in the house is welcome. One morning, when I opened the porch door to let her outside, she refused to leave.

Sadie pushed past me and came into the house. She checked every corner, under every chair. She wandered into the bathroom and then the laundry room. I watched, not wanting to disrupt the ritual. Without hesitation, Sadie was in the dining room next to the piano and through the rest of our house. Her pace quickened. She panicked. In our bedroom, she began to howl and I felt as though my feet were nailed to the floor, my spine tingling. A few moments later, she returned to me with a look of despair. I tried to calm her by stroking her neck but she wanted to go outside. I opened the door and Sadie crossed the yard towards her doghouse where she stayed all day. And we both cried into the night.

The next morning, as I was on my way to the barn, I checked Sadie's bundle of straw inside her doghouse. She was gone.

I haven't seen Sadie since. I know she is looking for you. Sometimes I imagine the dog has found you and it is all I can do to keep from walking out of the yard and into the fields to find both the man and the dog. I sense you are waiting for me. Will walking out the front door, never to return, bring me freedom? And what am I trying to free myself from? Something is keeping me bound to this old farmhouse. I am afraid if I walk out the door, I will perish as the two of you have and yet, I want nothing more than to be with my husband and our dog wandering the wheat fields bodiless. Wait for me. Please take me with you.

• • •

Desiderium

Trade my pillows in
for real flesh and skin
to fold myself into
a cradle.
The featherbed warm
when it's cold outside
and cool in the hot summer nights,
but I prefer the heat of love.
To taste the salt on your back
move my fingers through
soft brown curls of your chest
my tongue tender
to lick your ample earlobe
before lips kiss to have and hold
skin pulse
feet, legs, arms, hands
tangle our hearts
make home here.

This Sunday morning
with only pillows and feathers
hot tea the liquid on my lips
words the fire of my passion
no voice, no dance, no salty sweet of you
just me
slipping beneath the covers
eyes folding down
conjuring you between
my body and my dream.

We savor love there.

My body is heavy as rock and I do not want to leave this place of dreaming yet the telephone will not stop ringing.

"Hello?"

"Yeah, I'm here. Who is this?"

"It's Maureen from the hospital. I need you to come into town right away." I feel the beating of my heart in my chest.

"Something's happened. What is it? Kent? Is he okay?"

"Just come to the hospital and we can talk."

"No. Tell me now, Maureen. Is he okay?" Only silence from the other end of the phone. "What's going on? Just tell me!"

"I can't. Trust me, just get out of the house and drive to the hospital. We will talk when you get here. Just do it. Okay?"

"Damn it, something is wrong with Kent. He's gone, isn't he?" Again only silence.

"Please, we're waiting for you."

"Fine. I'm on my way." I hang up the phone.

My mind races backwards in time. I'm standing at the door saying goodbye to you and you look at me in a way that puts distance between us. I am flooded with the feeling of wanting to reach out to you, tell you not to leave, but I don't move forward. Instead, I watch as you turn and walk out the door and there it is, in black, block letters above your head, the word "A C C I D E N T." It is there, lingering and time seems to stop. We are both motionless, sensing there is nothing more to say. Each of us knows the other's love. Then you were gone. I slowly go over to the porch window to wave goodbye and you look at me in the rearview mirror of the car as you drive out the yard. You wave goodbye to me and I see your hand moving through the car rear window.

There are times when I know something, but I don't fully understand what it is I know until the time has come to pass. Feeling drained of energy, I walk through the kitchen, go to our bed and lie down.

It is the telephone that woke me from my slumber.

Now I know I must rush into town as I grab my sweater and fumble with my shoes. Time is rushing. As I step outside, I wonder why you drove my car and not your truck. Turning the key, I glance at the fuel tank indicator to see the needle on empty. "So, you didn't want to take the time to fill the truck with gas," I murmur out loud to you.

Pulling up to the gas tanks on the other side of the yard, I remember the first time I met you. Having just graduated from high school, I was working at a gas station for the summer at Cypress Hills Provincial Park. You and your best friend were at Cypress camping for the weekend. I filled your car with gas and forgot to put the gas cap back on. You returned again to get your gas cap and then again several times to talk with me until my boss was angry with you and asked you to leave. I smile now when I remember him toasting the bride and groom on our wedding day. He said he was embarrassed at the way he tried to interfere with fate. He never imagined those two young kids would fall so deeply in love.

Since the first time we kissed, we felt a sense of urgency. Our friends always watched with envy as we did most everything together. We bonded and nothing could distract us from our attraction and commitment to one another. Yet, some deep undiscovered part of our love waited for the written hand of fate to tell its story. My hands are shaking now as I grip the steering wheel of your truck. This is what we have been waiting for. This is the moment. This is it.

There is something in the human spirit willing to move forward despite unrelenting fear. I drive until I come to a place along the road, only a couple miles from our home, where there are people and vehicles. And I see the car, poppy red, in the ditch. I stop the truck. A haze seems to descend upon me and everything begins to move in slow motion. Someone is knocking. I roll my window down and meet his eyes with caution. Luke is insisting I move over and let him drive. Obediently, I slide to the middle of the seat and allow him to take control of your truck. Before I realize what is happening, Dwayne opens the passenger's door and moves in to sit next to me on the other side. I now understand what a kind and generous gesture this was.

"We'll take you to the hospital. Everything will be okay."

I do not speak. What can I possibly say to make these men understand I knew this was going to happen a long time ago? I have placed myself on this journey and now I will have to summon the courage to keep walking. This is the day to change my life forever in ways I'm not able to even imagine yet.

• • •

No one will speak to me. There are no words for me. They just want to move me to another room or to another person. I am desperate to hear the words he is dead, but no one offers such a gift. Instead, they stay inside their own hearts frozen by the knowledge they are privileged to have. The silence makes me suffer the most. Only the words will bring me comfort because only the words will name what I am feeling. I am offered a glass of water and two small white pills. I take the tranquilizers, hoping these people in authority have some small miracle planned to rescue my now numb body and racing heart. Years later I will recall the taste of metallic substance on my tongue. The taste of pain.

The doctor has tears in his eyes. The edge of my vision is blurring with the edge of your life. I seem to float between two worlds, seen and unseen, oblivious to what my husband's death will mean for my life.

"Please, I need to see him," I plead.

"It really isn't necessary. There is nothing you can do," replies the doctor.

"But I need to see him."

The doctor glances despairingly to the nurse on duty. Finally, an acknowledgement that you are here and I have the right to be next to you. "I don't want you to stay long. You have to understand he is on the stretcher in the emergency room. There was nothing anyone could do. He was gone when they brought him to us."

I nod my head and there is a moment of doubt. I know there is no turning back now. I hesitate, but I must be left alone with you. I am desperate to see your face, touch your skin.

The nurse turns the knob on the wide ER door and pushes it open. I catch a glimpse of familiar blue jeans. "I want to be alone with him. Just leave us alone." She hesitates, but hears the resolve in my voice. She quietly leaves the room.

I walk forward. You lay still on a stretcher a few steps in front of me. Your eyes are closed and I feel a sense of panic. I want to see what you were feeling the moment you took your last breath. Your eyes would have said something. How dare they close your eyes. What have you done? What happened?

Your arms are resting beside your body, palms facing outwards, twisted and mangled even though not a scratch is visible. The wounds are deeper than your skin. Shoeless, the toes of your right foot point toward the floor. Your left foot is still in your shoe and points in the opposite direction. I calmly unlace your one shoe and remove it from your foot. Holding it to my belly, I promise I will find its mate.

I imagine the dancing blue ponds of liquid, the eyes that have watched me sleep for almost five years. Placing my hands on your face, I gently lift your eyelids, one at a time, and search for a sign of life but your pupils are vacant. Empty eyes. You are not here. I am stunned to see the slivers of glass in your eyes and a wave of nausea creeps into my throat as I lay my head on your chest. Listening for your breath, I hear a gurgling deep within your body. A surge of hope pulses through my heart. But as I look into your face, feeling your chin on my nose, there is a gush of blood seeping from the corner of your mouth. Your lips are red, I know you are broken. Smelling the salt of your skin, I know there is nothing I can do to put the pieces of my dead husband back together again.

• • •

There will come a time when I view these rituals of tending to the dead as bizarre and even harmful. The two days that followed my sojourn with you in the ER were filled with mundane tasks. Tasks that kept me from feeling the reality of what happened. What changed? At night, I lay my head down on the pillows of our bed, my eyes closing, and I see the way I slipped my hands under your clothes to touch your skin as you lay on that stretcher. I expected the reassurance of your desire for me as I softly stroked your cock, but you didn't respond. At the time, it seemed the most natural thing to do.

Drifting into sleep, I awake in the mornings feeling as though you are here with me, very close, and I sigh with relief. It has all been a nightmare. Then my mother enters the bedroom with a list of things I need to do for your funeral.

You were limp, broken and silent. I left you there. Alone. And I began walking the path set out before us when I walked away from the hospital on that warm day in May. Taking those first steps away from you, I thought how neither of us had realized that the last time we made love, would be, the very last time we made love. Still, it is your skin I miss the most.

• • •

Sweet Body

Damp with longing
we discovered our pleasure.
Ravenous loving
we opened each other.

I heard the dark descending
lover, lover, lover
you vanished
and left me the night.

When they took me to your body,
I lay my head upon your heart.
black blood bruised bones broken

The beauty of us rippled,
became a memory overnight.

They said you were going fast. They said you came over the crest of the hill and they said you saw the other car coming towards you on your side of the road. They said the accident was inevitable; you tried to get out of the way by steering the car into the ditch but there wasn't enough time. They said you felt no pain. You died instantly, they said.

I wondered if you thought of me. I said I always knew this was going to happen.

• • •

The man at the funeral home reassures me of the quality and service they will provide. The coffin is lead-proof and rust-proof. I hadn't even imagined what would happen to your body when it lay six feet below the ground. Suddenly, I am flooded with horrible thoughts of maggots and water and dirt and weeds and I'm sure I'll vomit if I don't excuse myself to sit down on a nearby chair.

After what seems like an eternity, I leave the funeral home with my parents and images of blue satin pillows and dressed up dead bodies dancing in my head. I'm consumed with decisions about what you should wear, and flowers, and music, and guest lists, and schedules, and food and the list seems endless. I stop for a brief moment of clarity and realize how much planning our funeral is like planning our wedding. And it is ours because in time, I will see how a part of me died with my husband. For many years to follow, I will be the walking dead among the living.

• • •

Being judged can feel like being dead. You become invisible to others. I felt alienated from my community, my family and a whole way of living. I could feel people watching me from a distance, saying nothing to me yet bringing to life words and stories all around me. Stories that seemed to protect others while implicating me with some field of expectation. I couldn't imagine anyone wanting to hurt me, but it happened insidiously over a short period of time. I was left to spend more and more time alone. People we once called our friends didn't make much effort to visit. Nor did they invite me to the occasions we had once shared as couples. It was as though I made them feel uncomfortable. During this time it was difficult for me to see the truth of what was happening because it was too painful. All of my women friends were distancing themselves from me and I didn't understand why. I was no longer part of a couple and I sensed they feared me. Perhaps they felt as vulnerable as me, but we had no common ground on which we could meet. I was in a field alone. I was not wife. I had become widow.

I longed for the company of women during this time, but if my women friends did not fear my situation then they seemed to envy it. There was the sense they didn't want to end up like me, without a husband, but there was also a sense they wished for the freedom that I suddenly had because now I was free from marriage. I loved

Kent, this is the truth. But I wasn't crazy about marriage and its traditional expectations. Kent knew this about me before I did. I remember him reassuring me that we didn't need to stay on the farm forever. He could see I wasn't satisfied with being a farmer's wife. He told me we would remain together regardless of what we decided to do or where we decided to live because I was the most important person in his life. I realize now the power of his words and the sincerity of his love. He was the real deal.

• • •

Women living in patriarchy do not have the right to self-determination because we are schooled to believe love is outside of us. Self-worth becomes something to be determined by others and not something generated from within us. We want others to love us and we spend our lives searching for someone else to give us a sense of our value.

I met Kent a month after I graduated from high school. As class valedictorian I gave a speech to an audience of several hundred people and received a standing ovation from my classmates. What I wrote then reveals to me now the yearning of my 18 year-old self for approval and love. Here's part of what she spoke: *Even though we are seemingly at the stage in our lives where we need to be individualistic and most independent adults, perhaps there is even more to this seeming 'search.' Underneath us lies the need to be wanted, needed, and loved by that extra special someone. Time may be essential, but even so the day will arrive in which we will be singled out simply because we are who we are.*

Getting married a year later, I felt I had succeeded in securing love for the rest of my life. When I was widowed, I was thrust once again into the emotional uncertainty that haunted me as a heterosexual female living in patriarchal culture.

• • •

Those first weeks after Kent's death, I was unconsciously making the transition from having a physical relationship with my husband to having a spiritual relationship with him. No one told me that death doesn't end your relationship with someone you love. That the bond between you doesn't die. I wonder how much easier this transition may have been for me had someone spoken this truth out loud. Instead, I struggled with strong physical feelings until a close friend, he too in his grief over the loss of Kent, touched me.

It was innocent in its beginning. We were both grieving the loss of someone we loved. This someone was the bond between us. We shared our grief through physical touch. And in a moment of clarity, he and I realized we had the power to make Kent's wish come true. We could give Kent his longed for legacy – a child. If our intentions were honourable, perhaps the power of the universe would create through our joining a son to carry the essence of Kent into another lifetime.

I felt alive with purpose and my body found solace in the arms of a man who had known Kent since early childhood. The desire between us felt beyond us. Some compelling force held us in each other's arms. It was Kent touching me, moving his body over me. It was Kent's breath I felt on my neck. His murmurs came to me from beyond the space and time I was limited to. I connected with him in a realm full of peace, fulfillment, and possibility. Awakened to the energy swirling within me, I expressed my deep love for my husband while in the arms of his guardian. A man who was moved to love me briefly. In that moment, we conceived a legacy. Kent's child. My child. I was released back into the world after having contained my passion, my longing, my desire. He gently let me go and I re-entered the physical life a changed woman. I knew in our moments together that my life had shifted and there would be no going back to the old places. Everything was new. A brilliant light had found the darkness in my being and illuminated new possibility for who I would become, how I would live, and what I would give to the world. I was pregnant with new life. And nothing in my world would ever be the same again.

• • •

And if you're lost enough to find yourself . . . [5]

---

[5] A line from the poem *Directive* written by Robert Frost

The experience of death is the experience of ending. People enter a period of transition and require time to process death, to react to ending. As a young widow in a social reality that lacked mythic imagination, I did not possess the tools of passage rituals as a way of understanding the changes death had thrust into my life. Mine was an unconscious and unritualized experience. William Bridges discusses four aspects of the ending experience that are useful in considering my journey through tragedy: disengagement, disidentification, disenchantment, and disorientation. There is no natural or normal order through these aspects just as there is no right or wrong way to progress through the five-stage sequence that Elisabeth Kübler-Ross identified: denial, anger, bargaining, depression, and acceptance. The point is that we must let ourselves and others enter the stage of transition and respond to the changes in the ways best for us. Every person is unique and will uniquely process grief, but process is the key and considering endings are part of life, I was ill equipped to deal with Kent's death.

Death disengaged me from the context in which I knew myself. I didn't just lose my husband. I lost my role in our family, my sense of belonging in our community, my patterned way of living. As a daughter of patriarchy, my husband was my mirror. I had yet to develop a strong sense of myself from within myself. When he died and I became a widow, I no longer recognized the reflection of myself as seen through family, friends, and community. I lost my way of self-definition. My greatest distress was that I didn't know who I was anymore.

I started to walk with one foot in the spirit world where I sensed the presence of my dead husband and one foot in the physical world where I was still called upon to participate in life in tangible ways. But the immensity of my feelings confused me. How was I to trust the pain of my grief and still be open to the world? In a world of social identities, I was now widow and I wasn't sure what that meant.

Being in limbo between what felt like two worlds, I hadn't separated completely from my old identity. Sensing that what I knew to be my world was no longer real disenchanted me. A lifetime consists of much disenchantment and significant transitions often begin with it. However, an element of time is usually required to see the disenchantment as a meaningful stage. Mine came as a shock. A sudden and terrible accident. And it was the catalyst to move me into transition. On some level I needed to believe that marriage was forever, that my husband would always be with me and this belief protected me from the contingencies of life. The disenchanted experience brought me to a place in my life where I was called to look below the surface of what I knew to be true. The sense of my life moving in a certain direction broke down. My confusion and don't-know-who-I-am feeling deepened as I became disengaged, disidentified, and disenchanted.

With Kent's death, my reality was a matter of questioning which way was up, which way down, which way forward, which way backward. How would I orient myself and move on with my life? I was in unfamiliar territory. I was disoriented. My plans for the future were destroyed. I lost power and direction as the essential arrangements of my life were endangered. Disorientation affected my sense of place and my sense of time.

• • •

It rained the day Kent's body was lowered into the earth. She held her head high feeling the black hat she had been given to wear and allowing it to impose dignity at a time when she felt utterly miserable. Looking to the sky, the clouds over her danced their promise of rain. And it was there, suddenly and brightly, streaming across the grief of the day with colours so vibrant it was shocking. Seeing the rainbow, her mind made the connections; she had written about a rainbow in her valedictorian speech using the metaphor to contain the promise of life beyond high school; the rainbow on the day she met Kent; their wedding invitations in a rainbow theme; the rainbow fabric from which her mother sewed the bridesmaid's dresses. These colours painted on sky embodied the spirit of new life for her. And on this day of death, she was gifted with a rainbow while standing in the graveyard preparing to bury her husband. She knew instantly in her heart it was a message for her. He was watching her. He was the light of rainbow and it made her still. Still enough to hold the promise, hold her body, hold her thoughts and look beyond what seemed to be happening.

Hope poured through her starting at the top of her head and flooding from the soles of her feet into the wet earth she stood upon. Somewhere deep within her, she knew everything was perfect and Kent would never leave her. Then the casket was lowered into the ground, slowly and with care.

The relief was momentary. Soon enough everyone had something to say and some way to explain what she should do next. Why couldn't these people just be quiet? Everyone was talking and nobody was listening. She drove Kent's truck home to the farmhouse, an entourage of family and friends not far behind her. The house was soon full of noise – voices and food and drink. It made her sick the way people here always turned to alcohol on any and every occasion. Their vision was distorted because they never allowed themselves to see or feel clearly about anything. Least of all, about death. What was it about living in this environment that caused men and women to instill fear in their children? And the attitude of poverty seeped into all the corners of their lives. There was never enough of anything: the right weather, the good crops, the proper teachers, the trustworthy people. Not enough food, not enough time, not enough money, not enough room in the house. She was sick of the poverty mentality surrounding her but when she looked around the house it was filled with baskets and bouquets. Their little farmhouse, the place they called home, was brimming with hundreds of flowers. Such abundance amidst the emptiness left in her life by his absence seemed bizarre in a way she couldn't quite put her finger on. She loved flowers. She celebrated every occasion with flowers, especially roses. And now her house was literally full of flowers. The perfume permeated the threads of her curtains, the threads of her thoughts. And now she cried because she realized Kent had become an occasion in her life. Just a passing love, a short trip, a weekend visit. He had come and he had gone. All that was left were roses and tears. She sat on the floor with her hands over her face and cried until the night became morning. Family and friends took turns holding her as she crumbled in their arms.

Day was indistinguishable from night as she slipped into her darkness. Anyone watching from the outside would have thought she was handling this unfortunate mishap in her life just fine. In fact, she was to be admired for her strength and her ability to bring comfort to others. But there was no heart that could see her truest moments, her darkest fears, her hours alone. All the people around her had lives to return to. They carried on. And there was an unspoken expectation that she would pick up the pieces left for her and do the same, quietly and without disruption to anyone else's life.

• • •

Aunt Clare was willing to see more than the others. She insisted on visiting her when all the others had left. She stayed for a week which gave her the opportunity to sit and listen and watch this woman who had lost her husband. It was her age that concerned Clare the most. She was too young, married too briefly to be able to withstand the shock that should only come when one is middle-aged. The two women together tried to find routine to put back in her life – the farm chores, the household work, the afternoon coffee break with neighbours. They baked bread and they sent thank-you notes. With Aunt Clare's guidance, she was able to pay the outstanding bills and set up a budget which helped her feel a renewed sense of control. It was comforting to smell coffee brewing in the kitchen upon waking in the morning and it was hopeful to not be left alone. These were days she would remember with gratitude for an aunt who was willing to set aside her own life temporarily to allow her to be fully present in her niece's life. They laughed and cried together and, in truth, this was all she needed – a soul to share her grief with, someone who could stay beside her until it washed over and through her. But it all ended when Aunt Clare packed her suitcases, loaded the car, and drove down the same road Kent had taken when he left the farm. It was another goodbye and it broke her heart, again.

• • •

The soul is an abandoned girl,
lost in the wilderness, and crying out for
the home that she has lost.[6]

---

[6] Spoken by the character Sefadhi in the novel *Abandon* written by Pico Iyer, page 40.

The archetypal wilderness is a place where we meet ourselves. It brings up images of aloneness, isolation, and danger. This is a place where fear rises up and we are tested. Confronted with our own terror, we may discover the strength and truth that lives within us. Widowhood was my first place of wilderness. It was wilderness because I was isolated and could not be reached by the outside world. It was an experience I would ultimately face alone. It was as though a veil descended between me and the rest of the world.

• • •

One afternoon, when she was cleaning Kent's desk out, there was a knock at the door. It was Sophie.

"What a nice surprise." Sophie greeted her with open arms as though she had visited a hundred times.

"I wanted to see you." She loved the way Sophie made no excuses and spoke with honesty. She felt attracted to the woman in a way that made her feel she'd known her a long time, even though she had only met her through her husband. Kent and Sophie had gone to school together and their parents had been friends for many years. She noticed how well put together Sophie was. Her white nurse's uniform crisp. Her auburn hair falling loose on her shoulders. Her face fresh and bright with make-up applied like a professional. Suddenly she was aware of how she must look in dusty jeans and Kent's flannel shirt.

"I'm happy to see you. Come in."

Gesturing towards the kitchen table, she walked to the counter and started to make coffee. It was refreshing to have Sophie in her kitchen because they seemed to have so much in common. They were the same age when most of the women in her life now were the generation of their mothers. Which wasn't a bad thing but the older women had lived on the farmsteads for years and were seasoned in the country way of living. She always felt like the new girl, the one who didn't know the way things ought to be yet. "Your time will come," the older women always teased or, perhaps, it was a warning. Neither she nor Sophie had children, but that was just a matter of time. All young couples were trying to get pregnant. It was part of the expectation around getting married and living on the family farm. There would have to be a new generation of farmers to live on the land when their parents and grandparents were able to retire. Both women worked outside of the farm in small neighbouring towns. Sophie had an advantage over her though. She had been born and raised in this community. She knew all the rules.

"I'm doing evening shifts this week so, I thought if I left home a little earlier today, I would have some time to stop by and see you. How're you doing?"

"Oh, some days are better than others, but mostly I am keeping busy doing all the work around this place. I never knew we had gathered so much stuff in the last few years. I've been putting some things off, I suppose I just don't want to do them, but Aunt Clare keeps calling to check up on me. I feel guilty when I'm not doing what I said I would. You know, cleaning closets, going through old boxes. I have so many things in this house that aren't even mine. Stuff that was here from Kent's family before we even moved in and I keep skirting around all of it, but between you and me, I'd love to start tossing and burning!" She notices how at ease she feels with Sophie and how she speaks of things with her that she never mentions to anyone else.

"I know what you mean. My mother-in-law left everything in the farmhouse and nobody ever asked me if I wanted any of it, it just became part of the package I married. Then again, I shouldn't complain. The woman did die and who am I to say I don't want her stuff around?" Pausing, Sophie realized what she had just said. "Oh damn, I didn't mean to be insensitive. It's just that I don't think of my mother-in-law dying in the same way of Kent dying. I'm so sorry."

"No need to apologize. At least you'll talk about it. Everybody else seems to act like nothing ever happened and what the hell is my problem? Why don't I just get on with things? Sometimes I feel as though I will lose my mind if I don't hear someone at least say Kent's name."

"It must be horrible," Sophie says quietly.

"Well, I don't want you to feel sorry for me. That's the last thing I need. But I really get tired of everyone pretending like nothing happened. Why can't people just acknowledge the truth?

Instead they walk around it, not wanting to upset anyone and it all makes me feel like I'm crazy. Like I have no right to want to cry or scream or talk about my husband. The hell I don't! Oh, Sophie, I don't mean to take this out on you, but everyone else makes me feel like I should just leave and pretend nothing ever happened. What does that say about the last five years of my life? That it can just be swept under the rug because nobody wants to look at it?"

"Of course not," Sophie tried to comfort her, but she was interrupted.

"You know, I get the feeling people just want me to be like them. And I'm not sure what the hell that means."

"This is all such small town stuff. Everybody thinks they know what is best for everybody else. You've always been the new wife here – the woman from somewhere else. It's no fault of yours that Kent didn't want to marry anyone from around here. He found you. You were perfect for him and he knew it. All the rest of us were a little bit jealous because we all wanted what you guys had."

"And what was that?"

"Each other," Sophie stated without hesitation. Both women knew they had just shared a little bit of truth about their lives and there was a feeling of understanding and closeness between them because of it. "Never mind anyone. They have all been driving me crazy for years."

Feeling lifted, she watched as Sophie opened her cupboard doors, took two mugs and filled them with fresh coffee. She loved the way this woman just made herself at home and never expected to be waited on. There was more she wanted to tell Sophie. Taking the mug of coffee Sophie was handing her, she thought about what had happened yesterday. She knew if she didn't share it with someone she would simply die inside. And so, with relief to have this woman, this friend near her, she began talking again. "Kent's father came by to see me yesterday."

Sipping hot coffee Sophie asked, "How is he? Mom said she and Dad haven't seen much of Kent's parents lately. Guess this has all been hard on them, too."

"Yeah, I guess so. They don't have much to say to me. When Kent was here, they were always around, but now that he is gone they never come over. Maybe it's just me, but I get the feeling they kind of blame me for what happened. Like somehow, it's all my fault." Sophie nodded her head as though to understand what she was trying to say. "These people were always on Kent's case, especially his dad. We, or should I say Kent, could never do anything right."

Sensing her hurt, Sophie tuned in more closely to what it was her friend was trying to tell her. "Look, I went to school with Kent and I know how hard his dad was on him. I remember Kent having to feed the pigs before going to school and his dad not letting him clean up before getting on the bus. All us kids used to tease the heck out of him because he smelled like pig barn. Isn't that just awful? Kids can be so mean."

"Yeah, well so can some fathers."

"Sure, but you have to remember, Kent left the farm when he left school. He did what he wanted to do. Went to trade school. Started his own business. It wasn't until he met you that he decided he wanted to come back to the farm."

"I know, Sophie. And I remember well the day he told me he wanted to return. But it wasn't his father he was coming back here to; it was the land, the farm. He felt disconnected being away from it and I can still see him sitting on the sofa with tears in his eyes looking at some photos his sister had sent him during harvest one year. It was then I knew I would have to follow him back to the farm if we were going to have a life together and I just couldn't imagine a life without him. There really was no choice. It was the way it had to be, but believe me, there have been many times when we both regretted ever coming back to farm. Kent told me once, when I couldn't find a job, that he never wanted me to feel trapped. That we did not have to think of doing this our entire lives. If we wanted we could travel, we could study, we could do anything as long as we were together. My happiness meant so much to him, Sophie, and I just wilt inside when I try to imagine having a life without him."

"I'm so sorry this has happened to you guys."

"I know. But it has. And here I am. On this farm. And it seems ironic that there were times when I couldn't wait to leave, to work or study and now that there is nothing keeping me here, I can't bear to go. I never really knew this until yesterday."

"What happened yesterday?"

"Kent's dad came over. I could tell he had something on his mind. He drove into the yard and came straight into the house. He had a good look around, but didn't have time for coffee. And then he let me have it. I wasn't prepared for what he had to say."

"What did he want?"

"Basically, he asked me how I was planning to contribute to the farm now that Kent was gone. I was shocked. What could I say? I have always had to work outside of the farm to feed and clothe us because we have yet to see any income from this place. Everything that comes from the farm must go back into the farm, that is the family policy. This man didn't come into my home to thank me for all I'd done to support his son and our life here. No. He wanted to make sure I wasn't going to stick around and take something I have no right to. I'm sure he's relieved he hadn't signed over the land lease to us. We're still renting it from him. I guess in his mind, I have become some kind of threat now that Kent is dead. Can you believe this?"

"Yeah, sounds like something he would do. Look, don't take it personally. My parents have been friends with Kent's family for years, but my father will be the first to tell you when it comes to business, Kent's dad pulls no punches."

"Great. So, my husband is dead and I'm getting kicked off the farm. Now I understand how Kent felt that day I watched him chase his father into the combine. His dad ran into the cab and slammed the door on Kent's face only to have Kent spit at him on the window. He was so pissed. I remember telling him he was being unreasonable, but what the hell did I know? I had no idea. Guess I'm learning it now. I can't help but think there will be more surprises yet to come."

Sophie laughed. "Don't take it all too seriously. Just do what is best for you right now. If Kent were here, he'd tell you the same thing. Just take it easy."

"Maybe you're right. Meanwhile, I don't hear Kent's mom or dad knocking on my door offering to help me pack their son's belongings or clean out his closets."

"Never mind. I'll help you."

"You're sweet, but believe me, this is not a job you want to do. I appreciate your kindness. I feel better just talking about some of this stuff. Some days I feel if I try to hold anymore inside me, I'm going to burst."

Glancing up at the kitchen wall clock, Sophie says, "Look at the time. I have to go or I'm going to be late for work."

"I really needed this break, Sophie, thanks for listening."

"I want you to know you're not alone. Just remember what Kent would tell you if he were still here."

"What's that?"

Smiling, Sophie mimics Kent by opening both arms for a hug and says, "Lighten up, woman!"

Hugging Sophie, she promises she'll try to do just that.

As she walks to her car, Sophie calls from over her shoulder, "I'll call you tomorrow. Maybe we can do something together this weekend."

"Okay," she called back. She felt a renewed sense of hope as she watched Sophie drive out the yard. Maybe there would be life after all this cleaning out and cleaning up.

• • •

She shouldn't have gone. She knows that now. But at the time it seemed like a good idea.

Luke had been calling to check on her. She appreciated his tenacity and imagined he felt an obligation to Kent. It was one man taking care of another man's wife because of the friendship they had shared since childhood. Luke and Kent had many things in common but a different way of living. In Kent's opinion, Luke was less than honest and drank too much but he never let it get in the way of their companionship. The two boys grew up together and became men together. The men were neighbours willing to help one another out. They depended on each other. They played hockey together. Talked cattle business together. Drank mickeys of rum while sitting in the truck overlooking an open field and cursed their fathers together. They were kindred spirits and when Kent died, Luke felt lost.

Luke's wife was expecting their third child and when she gave birth, he called Kent's wife to share the good news. The pride in

Luke's voice pulled on her heart in a way she couldn't explain. He was thrilled and wanted her to join him and the guys for a little celebration Friday night. She hesitated but was overcome with a feeling of responsibility. She should go to represent Kent. Luke needed her to do this. She accepted the invitation with trepidation.

She really didn't want to be with a group of guys, so she waited until late Friday night to get in the truck and drive over to Luke's farm. With any luck, the guys would be gone or going home soon and she could make her guest appearance and leave quietly having fulfilled her duty of Kent's wife. She was lucky. A few of the guys were outside, standing around their trucks, saying goodbye when she pulled into the yard. Luke was delighted to see her.

Shortly after her arrival, everyone went home and she and Luke were left sitting on the step drinking beer and gazing at the stars. It was a beautiful prairie sky full of glitter and the light of a waxing moon. The summer air was still and cool. Silence surrounded them and they began to talk.

"I always imagined one of the best moments of my life would be telling Kent I was pregnant. Now I know it is never going to happen. It kills me inside."

"Look, I still can't believe he's gone. I keep expecting him to drive up the road. Even tonight, when I saw his truck, for a moment I thought I saw him but then I realized it was you. It's too weird. He's gone but he's still here."

"I know. Where does it end? I mean, what the fuck happened anyway? I feel like I'm in a dream world sometimes and I just can't connect to anything real."

Luke closed his eyes for a moment. "I miss his laugh. Shit, we used to laugh so much. I remember the time we stole barbed wire from old man MacKenzie. Couldn't afford to buy it, needed to go fencin' so we thought we'd borrow some from the neighbours. Kent was scared shitless when he thought MacKenzie was followin' us. Man, I just howled!"

"You guys! Kent was never really up for all of your antics, you know."

"Yeah, I know. But we never hurt nobody. Just havin' fun."

"You were a bad influence on him."

"You wish."

"Tell you what I wish. I wish he was here right now. Sitting between us and drinking his beer, even telling his stupid jokes. I miss him so much. And every day it gets worse. Who the hell said it would get better with time? Every single day I live without him kills me a little more inside. Like I don't know who I am anymore. He's gone. And I have nothing. Luke, you don't know how lucky you are. Three children. Kent and I have been trying for two years to get pregnant. Why didn't it happen? Besides being alone, I feel like I've let him down. I never gave him the one thing he wanted most in life and now he's dead. His parents will never have a grandchild from their eldest son. We look like losers. I look like a loser. What the hell else is there?"

"It's just not fair. You shouldn't be so hard on yourself. Every time I drive down that damn road, I see his car in the ditch and I wonder what the hell happened, too. He was a good driver. Traveled that road hundreds of time. Why him? Why now? None of it makes any sense."

"What am I gonna do without him, Luke? He was my whole life. I have never felt so alone. Every night I lay awake hoping he'll come to me. I have no idea how I expect it to happen but it's like I'm searching for his presence. To think I'll never see his face or touch his skin – oh, God! – it's just too much." Heavy with grief, she felt Luke reach out to her. Putting his arm around her, he drew her close, wanting to comfort her. "I can't even cry anymore. Sometimes, I just wish I could cry."

Luke was whispering now. "It's going to be okay, I promise."

She allowed herself to feel the strength of Luke's arms around her. His muscular chest made her feel protected. As she closed her eyes, she imagined it was Kent's heart she felt beating against her face. It was Kent's breath she felt warm on her forehead. It was Kent's lips gently kissing her cheeks, her nose, her chin.

"He'd want me to be here for you. I loved him. He was the best friend I ever had. I'll do anything for him. Anything." The moistness of her lips invited his desire. "Let me make love to you. Let me give you the child and it will be Kent's."

Hearing the words startled her and she started to pull away. "What are you talking about?"

"Why not? No one would have to know. If it happens, we know it was supposed to be. If it doesn't, well, maybe I can have the chance to make you feel better. So you are not alone. It is the one thing you and I can give him. His legacy. I know it's what he wanted. I know it's what you want right now."

"I want to be pregnant, now, instantly. Sure. It feels like I've been trying to get pregnant forever. Maybe there is something wrong with me."

"Trust me. There is nothing wrong with you. You are a beautiful woman, Marlene, and Kent loved you more than he ever thought he could love any woman. You deserve to have a child from him and he deserves to have a child to carry on his name. We can do this. You and I. It can be our gift to him." His crystal blue eyes searched hers for permission to fulfill what he understood to be his responsibility to a dying friend. They could make new life possible. There was hope. "Let me show you how much I care. Let me show you."

Closing her eyes, she tried to remember what Kent's face looked like. She feared one day she would forget. Holding Luke's hand, feeling his aliveness, she felt her dead husband's presence. He was with them. He was smiling. He was encouraging. This was the presence she had longed for and she knew it was right. This was the right thing to do. This would be a gift to her only love from his two best friends. She opened her eyes to Luke's face and nodded her head in approval. No more words were necessary. They kissed long and passionately. Both of them were crying now.

Somehow, on that night, there was a union of souls. A moment filled with grace. It was above and beyond the three human beings involved. It would take years to re-member the beauty because they were surrounded by people who only understood black and white conventions. Anything between was cause for shame and dis-grace. It would take years to restore the balance in her life, to remember the gift, to cherish the blessing. Until that time, most of her energy would be spent trying to survive, to maintain a sense of dignity in a world that places more importance on the human order of things than on the divine order of things. In her moments of despair, she would feel the weight of widowhood as she became the woman no one wanted to be with and she would carry alone the challenge of being a parent. How quickly she had been made to forget the intention behind the action. How quickly everybody made her feel she was a wicked woman. A strange woman. A marked woman.

• • •

The world is alive within and around me. I feel full and now have a mission. I expected when you died that you would be out of my life forever. My head tells me our marriage is over. People ask me what I am going to do now that you are gone. In fact, they were asking me at your funeral. But my heart knows different. We still are. We haven't ended at all. I wonder sometimes if we are closer in death than we were in life. It is as if we have a direct line of communication between your world and mine. You are my bridge. I am yours. And we are no longer bound by constricting notions of time and space.

At night I dream. In the morning the boundary that should separate my dreams from the skin covering my body seems to have dissolved. I feel you making love to me and I know you are holding me this morning. I am aware of a warmth that is purely you and it fills me with great peace at times when I need comfort most. If you are not in your body, where are you? Now you are here. What will happen if I leave this house, leave our farm? What will happen if I pack your treasures away out of my sight? Will your sounds cease to fill the empty corners of this room? If I drive out of this yard, never to return, will you follow me? Or will you stay behind? If you are not in your body, where are you?

You are with me.

One Sunday afternoon with music filling our little house, I felt your arms around me, holding me. We swayed to the rhythm of the melody, our bodies melded together through an eternal moment. Even through your passing to the other side of this invisible veil between us, you have never left me alone. You are present in this hour as I write this story. And I am speaking to you in my holding, my containing of all we have meant to each other. I see the challenge clearly now. To have and to hold this love between us, to create and to sustain this desire we possess for each other by living it from a higher place. This is a place of knowing and, I tell you, it is such a relief to understand you never really died at all.

• • •

My relationship with Kent did not end. It was simply transformed. Grief tore my heart open, and I no longer experienced Kent as a separate body. It was the essential connection joining us that remained. We melted together and truly became one beyond the identities of who we had been to each other. Vulnerable and exposed, I was learning the deep lesson of compassion.

• • •

She had driven home in the early hours of the morning – the morning after she'd been with Luke during stolen moments away from family, friends, and any sense of responsibility to the every day, visible reality of their lives. When the telephone rang shortly after 10 a.m. it startled her. Gathering herself out of slumber, she picked up the phone. "Hello."

"Hi, it's Sophie."

"Hey, good morning. How are you?"

"Good. The guys are getting the machinery ready for harvest. Looks like it may be early this year. And I don't have to be at the hospital today so, I was wondering if maybe you and I could get together later."

"Sure. Sounds great. Why don't you come over here and we can have lunch. I need time to bathe though. I'm still in bed."

"That's unlike you. You okay?"

"Yeah, I'm fine. But I'd love to have your company."

"I have a better idea. Why don't the two of us drive into the city, have lunch at Mario's and do a little shopping. I think we need a change of scenery."

"I think you're right. I don't have anything keeping me here, that's for sure. I'll get ready and call you before I leave. I'll pick you up and we can take my truck."

"Good. Take your time and I'll see you when you get here."

"Okay, see you later."

As she hung up the phone, she felt a warm sensation run from the tops of her thighs, through her breasts and out the top of her head. It was a delicious feeling. The thrill that comes from being physically open to sexual energy. She felt more alive this morning than she had felt for weeks. And she had the strongest sensation that Kent was just above her, hovering over her shoulders as she waltzed into the bathroom and started the water for her bath.

• • •

Her body had lost its sense of how to function. Her internal clock settings were skewed. The male body she'd been physically in sync with no longer interfaced with her female body. The woman longed to be touched by the man. In desperate moments she'd pull one of his shirts from the closet and bury her nose in its cloth. She needed to smell him. Where was the rhythm of the dance they moved to? The beat was gone. The music had ended. No warning. No preparation. Suddenly her body was on its own. Lost.

• • •

It was a relief to get to the city. It was a different pace of life, the urban life. Traffic, noise, people – a welcome change from the silence of the farm. She felt the urge to make herself new and she began to buy clothes. Sophie encouraged her and there was a sense of abandon in choosing items without even looking at the price tags.

She felt controlled in her carelessness. What could possibly matter? The one true thing in her life was gone. All the things that had once glued her life together no longer held any meaning for her. Everything seemed trivial in the afterglow of death. Including money. The insurance company had paid her a few thousand dollars and it made her feel like she'd been paid for the loss of her husband. It was absurd. She didn't want the money because of the way it had come into her life. When he was alive, she and Kent had been careful in their spending and they'd lived by a closely followed list of priorities. Whatever the farm produced went back into the farm including payment for leasing the land. All living expenses were paid by her salary from her job at the bank. After the accident, she'd decided to take a leave of absence and now she wondered if she'd return to work. She had some savings and she couldn't imagine pulling herself out of bed in the morning to go to a job she agreed to do only to make ends meet on the farm. It all seemed rather pointless. Her motivation had been buried six feet under the ground next to her husband's coffin.

It was fun to spend the day with Sophie. They talked long and deep while eating, shopping and driving. At the end of the day both women felt nurtured. Yet, it was the empty house she still had to go home to alone. And it was dark. She had left in such a hurry she hadn't remembered to leave on any lights. She managed to settle herself into bed and say a prayer of thanks for this new friend in her life.

• • •

The next time she drove to Swift Current, it was for a doctor's appointment and a pregnancy test.

She bundled her purse and packages as she looked up to see the nurse gesturing towards Dr. Russell's office door. She entered the room and sat in the chair across from his desk. The nurse closed the door and she waited.

When Dr. Russell finally opened the door, it startled her. She'd slipped into some other world which seemed to be happening more frequently to her lately. She looked up as a short, stout, middle-aged man extended his hand and introduced himself to her. As he sat in his chair he said, "The pregnancy test result is positive."

She woke up. "This means I'm pregnant?"

"Yes, you are pregnant." She knew the doctor was still talking because she could see his lips moving, but she'd been transported to some place outside of the office in which she now sat. This was the moment she'd anticipated sharing with Kent. She'd played and replayed everything she would imagine it to be in her mind and now it was before her. And she felt nothing. She was numb. She came back to the conversation in time to hear Dr. Russell telling her she had options.

"Excuse me? What options?"

"Well, I'm aware of the fact that your husband died recently and I'm guessing this pregnancy occurred after his death. Am I wrong?"

She slowly shook her head.

"So based on this information, I'm telling you that you have options. If you don't want to carry this pregnancy to term, we can make certain arrangements for you. It would mean a drive south of the border, but I can take care of everything. If cost is a concern then perhaps the man involved with you would be willing to take the financial responsibility. I'll give you the necessary details."

Only half realizing what the doctor was suggesting, she replied, "That won't be necessary."

"Well, you have some time to think it over. Adoption is also a possibility you may want to consider," he continued.

"No, you don't understand. I want to have this baby."

"Is the father involved in your decision?"

"Yes and no."

"What do you mean?"

"I mean, he'll know about the pregnancy, but I don't expect him to get involved. It's rather complicated."

"I see. Is he a married man?"

"I'd rather not say."

"You know, people make mistakes. But God expects you to learn from these mistakes. He will forgive you the first time, but not the second time. Do you understand what I'm saying?"

"Yes, of course I do," she replied obediently. But inside her was a voice screaming at this man, this ignorant man, this man who knew nothing of her or her life. How dare he judge her and dump his punishing God upon her. She kept herself in control and allowed this man to feel as though he were guiding her, teaching her something. That somehow he knew better what life was about and she was just a grieving widow who had taken refuge in the arms of a married man only to be impregnated with a bastard child. She, according to him, had committed a sin and she would need to ask for forgiveness. Funny though, none of this was a part of her reality. It didn't touch the part of her that knew this pregnancy was a blessing. There would be new life and it was already living inside her body. Dr. Russell would never understand the inner workings of a woman like her.

• • •

She wasted no time sharing her good news. She wanted everyone to feel the excitement she was feeling. Now she had something to look forward to and something to share. It was Luke she told first. And his response had been not much more than a smile. She reassured him it was between the two of them and she expected nothing from him in terms of emotional or financial support. She understood that he had a family to take care of and this was the best she'd hoped for. A baby to love. A baby to carry Kent's name. A legacy for her deceased husband.

She never said it was Kent's baby. She never said it wasn't. She let everyone believe whatever they wanted to believe. And they wanted to believe. Her family was loving and supportive in every way. Kent's parents seemed pleased their son had left them the hope of a grandchild. This is what they had counted on from him. He needed to carry on the family name and the family farm. She felt she had finally done something right and good for Kent's parents. Now they'd accept her. There was light to cast out the darkness of grief. There was something else to focus on. Birth instead of death. This baby was a gift.

She returned to work at the bank. Kent's dad harvested the wheat his son had planted in the spring. Life started to feel as though it had rhythm again and it was the heartbeat of the child within her body that gave her a sense of purpose. She had to eat to nourish the baby. She had to sleep to keep a strong body for the baby. She had to be calm for the baby. Everything was for the baby and it pulled her out of herself long enough to look around and decide it was time to leave the farm. With winter coming, it would be lonely and cold and isolating to remain so far from town. She started to look for a house to rent so she wouldn't need to worry about winter driving and getting to work during the inevitable stormy weather. And there would be many storms to come.

• • •

She rented a small two bedroom house on Maple Street just a five minute walk from the bank. She was ready to leave the farmhouse still and silent. Sophie helped with the move and she called her parents once she was settled in her new home. The new space felt clean and full of promise. There was much to be thankful for. And much she longed for.

While Kent was alive, they had enjoyed many friends. Weekends were filled with dances, parties, pot luck suppers. Winters were for curling and hockey, getting together for card games. The prairies were unforgiving in the winter, but the weather brought people together. Families had to stay home and entertain themselves. If the roads were good enough to travel, neighbours spent time socializing. The winter months offered people the opportunity to play together – in spring, summer and fall, people worked together. Winter was for fun. And if the roads were blocked with snow, the men and women would commute by snowmobile. The long nights and short days gave one the feeling of hibernation, but with light and sound and sun because there was always big prairie sky. It was the one thing you could count on.

This winter would be different. She searched the sky for answers in the hours she spent alone. No visitors. No invitations. Everyone else's lives remained unchanged by the tragedy of her life. And there were whispers that some people doubted she was carrying her deceased husband's unborn child. She started to feel the stares when she was at work and then when she was shopping at the grocery store. Women whom she considered friends were growing more cold and distant from her. In time she would see she was mourning the loss of her husband and losing the nutrient of community – her sense of belonging. She was growing bigger every day; her ability to sleep soundly every night sustained her. She looked forward to quitting work for maternity leave as she imagined having the time to wallpaper the baby's room and shop for the things she would need. Her willingness to deny the gossip and the silent arrows slung in cruelty allowed her to believe she was where she belonged. And her new friend Sophie was her grace.

Even though they worked in different towns, she and Sophie spent their free time together and when that wasn't possible because of Sophie's husband, they were on the telephone talking for hours. It made life bearable. Sophie joined her for birthing classes as her partner. With spring promises whispering in the wind, the big storm approached and hit with such ferocity that it could have knocked her out of her bubble had she not so carefully built walls of protection around her heart.

• • •

Kent's mom and dad knocked at the door one evening, unannounced as she was finishing her supper.

"What a surprise. Come on in."

Tension immediately filled the air as they entered the house. This would not be a friendly visit. "We want to know who the father is. If it were Kent's, then you are overdue. And we don't believe that to be the case."

Taking a deep breath, her instincts were to remain calm and clear. "I understand. But I don't want to discuss this right now. I've been feeling low the last few days and the doctor has advised me to take it easy. I'm sure you'll appreciate how upsetting this is for me. Can we agree to have this conversation at another time?"

"Absolutely not! We are here now and we demand you tell us what the hell is going on." Kent's father was clearly distressed. Her immediate response was to move away from him and protect herself.

"Please, don't do this now. I just need some time."

Now Kent's mother spoke and with force. "You are a disgrace to our family, Marlene. If Kent were alive today he would be ashamed of you. You have been unfaithful to your marriage and we'll not have any part of it."

She was beginning to feel defensive. "I have never been unfaithful to your son."

"We don't believe you. Look at you. You are forever married to our son and look at you," she continued.

These words were stinging and all she could think about was protecting her baby which meant keeping herself calm. She didn't want to engage this anger – not here, not now. "I believe if Kent were here he would ask you to leave. I loved your son. Always have, always will. But he's gone and I'm alone. I don't want to jeopardize my health. I'm due any day and I ask that you just give me some time. Please try to understand."

"To hell with you. Who do you think you are?"

"This is really hard for me to say, but you leave me no choice. I want you to leave. Please leave."

With indignation written all over their faces they marched to the door, walked through it, and slammed it closed behind them. She never realized it would be the last time she'd see or speak with Kent's parents.

• • •

A few short weeks after the birth of my son I realized I no longer belonged in the place Kent and I had cultivated as home. It was time to leave. And leave I did. This set a life-long pattern of mothering and studying as I enrolled in college because planning a class schedule meant I had the flexibility to work around my breast-feeding schedule. Getting a job would mean daycare for my son and I wasn't prepared to do that. I learned early on how to find creative ways to function and survive in this world as a lone mother without having it cost me time with my child. Becoming a mother allowed me to redefine my place in the world.

Once again, I had someone to commit to and my life's energy was invested in this commitment. The stigma of being a single parent was lessened by the fact that I had been widowed. I engaged the self-identity of lone mother by being motivated to create a new life and take care of my child in a responsible way. For some reason unknown to me even now, I understood that even though the social role of mothering has low public value it had and still has high moral worth for me personally. Motherhood transformed my self-conception and I became strong through my maternal identity. I was changed and I could make new sense from my life. I was anchored in the world. This was now the guiding metaphor through which I could integrate my biography. I didn't realize at the time that I had just traded one mirror for another – the one held by my husband for another held by my son. Each reflection would illuminate a part of my personhood that was given the opportunity to grow. It would not be without pain. However, inner guidance comes through relationship and being my son's mother was now a place of learning discernment.

Motherhood has been my greatest spiritual practice; a practice which came to me through intense grief. Genuine love leads us to be more fully who we are. Motherhood potentially fosters personal growth. Through the death of my beloved husband, my identity was challenged. It was the beginning of coming home to me.

• • •

As a woman living in the modern world I was identified with patriarchal culture and alienated from my own feminine soul.

Patriarchal dominance began in the third millennium B.C. and it is the patriarchal domination that has suppressed the feminine voice in history. Not knowing our own history has been a significant means through which women have been kept subordinate. Women along with men have preserved our collective memory, which has been the link between generations. Acknowledging this allows us to understand patriarchy as a complex collaboration manufactured by men *and* women through the ages. It is a system that had not always existed. Therefore patriarchy can, and will, end. An essential part of this process is the reclamation of the feminine voice to liberate both men and women's economical, political, and social rights. Without making the inner connection of lost voice with this outer historical context, I could not become whole. This process would require me to sacrifice my identity as a spiritual daughter of the patriarchy and engage in a descent into the power and passion of feminine energy that has been in exile for five thousand years.

I was constricted and demeaned as whorish and because I was ungrounded as a daughter of the patriarchy, my erotic feminine energy was demonized. I was disobedient in my duty bound role as widow and my passion cut off from my dream as my instinctual patterns were frustrated.

In my disobedience, grief was a spiral journey into the depths of my soul. Today the journey continues as I make the connection between self as constructed by patriarchal society and self as informed by spiritual awareness. In my ceremony of grief and desire, I threw off the alienating ideological "hood" of widow-hood.

Kent Elwood Sonder
September 21, 1957 – May 22, 1985

Our wedding day, June 20, 1981
(Photograph by Murray & Lorraine Senicar)

Forgive me
if you are not living
if you beloved, my love
if you have died
all the leaves will fall on my breast
it will rain on my soul all night, all day
my feet will want to march
to where you are sleeping
but I shall go on living.[7]

---

[7] extract from Pablo Neruda's poem *The Dead Woman* translated by Donald D Walsh and spoken in dialogue between the characters Nina and Jamie in the film *Truly, Madly, Deeply* written and directed by Anthony Minghella (1991)

TWO

Crossroads 1988
WANDER-LUST

Every once in awhile in a woman's life
she's got to pack her bags and hit that trail
she's got to bid farewell to the ones she loves
she's got a case of wanderlust and she's got to set sail.[8]

---

[8] lyrics by Connie Kaldor in her song titled *Wanderlust,* album *Vinyl Songbook,* 2003

Woke up at 4 a.m. Wide awake. Wandered through the house to see if there was a reason I was awake. I could find none. Last night while reading in bed, I heard forceful wind moving outside. The house groaning. Two bright flashes of lightning. Hard rain. And this morning the grey has lifted. There is the sun. Something has cleared. Shifted. Left. Gone.

I went back to sleep after I woke up at 4 a.m. And in dreamworld I was driving a red Ford 150 truck. It reminded me of when you died in our red Dodge car and I was left the red truck to drive. It felt like freedom then and it was feeling like freedom now. Driving fast down the road I could go wherever I wanted because I had no-one to answer to. Nobody cared where I was or what I was doing and I felt free. In dreamworld I was driving down roads and going to places I've not been before. Driving. Driving. And suddenly I drive off the edge and the road disappears. And I am falling, falling, falling. And I hear the words: FREE-FALL. I feel it in my body. A deep, deep letting go as the road falls away. I see the curve of the earth. I'm high above the ground. There are trees and buildings and land below me. The colors murky brown and soft. There is a thrill and a hint of fear but it leaves my body as I allow myself to fall. I am weightless and I know not when I'll land but I'm not thinking that. All I'm thinking is free-fall, free-fall. And feeling it in my body.

Moving under the force of gravity, this story is my parachute.

Forty-three years old, and the war occurred half a lifetime ago, and yet the remembering makes it now. And sometimes remembering will lead to a story, which makes it forever. That's what stories are for. Stories are for joining the past to the future. Stories are for those late hours in the night when you can't remember how you got from where you were to where you are. Stories are for eternity, when memory is erased, when there is nothing to remember except the story.[9]

• • •

---

[9] excerpt from the novel *The Things They Carried* by Tim O'Brien, page 38

She glanced over her shoulder one last time while she moved through the front door. She couldn't be certain, but she felt this moment may be her final leaving from this place, this home, this marriage. Ahmed was loading the suitcases into the Mercedes. The children were sleepy-eyed knowing well enough they were embarking on a journey into the night. They'd be sleeping again soon in the first class seats that recline into beds on the British Airways flight taking them to Europe. She scanned the majlis wondering if she could fit anymore into her bag without causing suspicion. And in her mind's eye, she was going through the rooms in the rest of the villa to make sure that she had all that she held dear. But she was overwhelmed with the knowing that she couldn't take it all. It would have to remain here and her focus would need to be on the children and on herself. She was careful to not raise any concern. If her husband suspected even for a moment the truth of her thinking, he would not allow her this leaving and there would be nothing she could do. Her fate would be sealed. She would be powerless to choose otherwise. And along with her two sons, she would be subjected to her husband's expectations in every area of their lives. It was time to go. This was a window of opportunity and it required that she walk through the door without looking back one more time. Leave it. Let it all go. Just walk away.

She could feel the cool brass door knob in her hand as she stepped into the heat and humidity of the desert night. Pulling the door closed, she felt a stab of panic and she had to catch her breath. This was not going to be easy. The anxiety rising from her belly was causing her arms to tremble. She couldn't allow herself to think too much right now. She just needed to move through the motions. All she ever wanted was love and security; at times it seemed like she might be consumed with the disappointment of never getting what she needed. She could hear herself thinking of all the reasons she could not return to this place. Her eldest son was growing into adolescence and she sensed it would be a dangerous time if he were to live here in a country where teenagers were thrown into jail for what in other parts of the world would be seen as normal teenage behaviour. And this was a fight she had no power to engage as a foreign mother. Her youngest son was now three years old and this would mean his father's desire to 'arabize' him would drive a wedge between the two boys because her eldest son was not his "blood" child having come from an earlier marriage that ended when her husband was killed. This fact alone meant that he lived on the edges of the family, never really fully accepted. The wise woman in her knew he would be ostracized and rejected on many levels, and probably was feeling so already in ways she wasn't aware of. She couldn't bear to cause this beautiful boy such anguish. These two boys who came into the world through her body and her soul would be brothers in every sense if she could just break away from the oppressing forces bearing down on them here. Surely she could think herself out of this mess.

Walking down the marble steps of the veranda, she could feel the night air moist on her flesh, her black silk abaya clinging to her arms. *Walk away. Just walk away.* She could hear her inner voice guiding her footsteps. *Don't think too much. Just walk. Look ahead, not back. It's all going to be okay because I'll make it okay.* These were her mantras. Looking up into the night sky she could see the Little Dipper and she remembered a young girl sitting at her bedroom window looking out at that very same asterism wondering what life would have in store for her. That younger version of herself was thousands of miles away on the Canadian prairies in a place she knew was home. In contrast, the sand beneath her feet in this moment had called to her over the years while she had tried to make it home, but she felt as though she had failed. She was not welcome to be herself here. Her children were estranged here. There was no reason to stay. To say that he loved her had lost its meaning. Love is more than feeling, he had once told her. It is action. Well, she was ready to take action towards a different kind of love. Not the love that is expected in a patriarchal marriage; the kind of love that is supposed to give a woman physical and emotional security. This love, she had learned, was an illusion. There was something else she was pursuing and she intended to hold it in her grasp. This was something deeper that stirred within her and had nothing to do with what her husband could and could not give her. This was about something she was giving to herself. And she knew the first steps had started many months ago. This night was just following through on that vision so she had to keep walking towards Ahmed who held the door to the Mercedes open to her. It was time to leave.

• • •

Her Arab lover had been the net that appeared when she was ousted from her home, her marriage, and her life as the wife of a teacher in a Canadian college system being built in the Persian Gulf.

It was her second marriage.

She had known when Dan proposed that she was not ready to marry again. Being widowed had become a comfortable identity; she had learned what it meant to be in the world as widow. But when Dan asked for her hand in marriage, there was the real possibility of another life with another man.

Her first steps toward that reality were tentative because she just didn't want to go there again. This man and their relationship had nothing in common with her first experience of being married. All the ingredients she had with Kent were missing with Dan. Maybe that's why she needed to talk herself into this opportunity. *If this man is willing to love me, shouldn't I be grateful?*

When he pulled out the diamond ring and said, "Marry me," she was strangely surprised. She knew she didn't want it. She was just beginning to get her life back on track. First year of college complete. Inspired to continue her studies, she could actually imagine a life for herself and her son. She remembers her internal response being, "Oh, shhh-it." Yet she heard herself say aloud "Yes" to his plea. Then she watched herself put the ring on her finger.

At that moment, a small voice deep within her cried *no, no, no... this is not the place I want to go! Not with this man and not in this way!*

Still, she justified her agreement by telling herself that it would be a long engagement. What harm could come from saying yes and seeing how things unfolded from here over time?

What she didn't see coming was a blatant lie.

A few weeks after their engagement, Dan announced that he'd applied for a job in the Persian Gulf. It was a dream of his to work overseas and this was the opportunity he was waiting for. He'd be teaching with the Higher Colleges of Technology in Abu Dhabi and he wanted her and her son to come along with him. The only way for that to happen, according to Dan, was for them to be married. The sooner the better.

A native of Trinidad, Dan seemed to have a laid-back approach to life. In the beginning he was easy, soft and generous. It appeared that his friends and family loved him and loved having him around. He lubricated social situations with his wide interests and ease of conversation. He habitually bought her small, thoughtful gifts and her friends and family seemed to be as delighted as she was. They thought it was time she had some happiness in her life after so much tragedy. Except for her grandmother who, when she saw Marlene and Dan's wedding photo said, "There's something wrong with Marlene, she's not happy."

Dan and Marlene were married July 1st, 1988 in Robert Schuller's Crystal Cathedral in Garden Grove, California. A surprise gift from Dan. He'd made all the arrangements without her knowing. He knew she loved reading Schuller's books and watching his Sunday broadcast on cable television. So she thought this surprise orchestration was an act of love. She would learn later that it was another elaborate scheme of manipulation.

Dan had casually mentioned one evening that his contract with the U.A.E. college was signed and he was ready to travel. To expedite things, he'd booked Robert Schuller himself to marry them at the Crystal Cathedral and his step-sister and her husband would be standing as their witnesses. It was done. And her only part was to show up. He made it that easy.

Had she stopped for a moment, she'd have heard the questions rolling around in her head.

What was she getting herself into? Why couldn't he travel alone? She'd just received tuition funding from the Saskatchewan government, which meant she now had the money to enroll in an university transfer program at the college. She wanted her B.A. in psychology and she wanted to stay in Canada. How could she take her son so far away from his grandparents?

In direct contrast to what she wanted, she felt herself being pulled into his dream and into his needs. Another voice was telling her that this was the opportunity of a lifetime. How could she say no? How could she disappoint Dan by ruining the plans he'd made for them? Why couldn't she just be happy that he even wanted a life with her? Wasn't she tired of being the single parent that everyone pitied? Didn't she want a "normal" life and a "real" father for her son? Whatever made her think that she could take care of herself and her son without the support of a man? How was she ever going to buy a house on her own with the little savings she had now? Maybe she could work in the UAE, too. This part of her was relieved to think she wouldn't need to do everything alone; she'd have a man to depend on and she could rest in his care. Yet that still, small voice within her queried: *Is this really what has to be for me now, this leaving?*

Within days, she found herself walking the streets of the city where she and her son had lived since leaving Saskatchewan after Kent's death, searching the shops with her mother, looking for a dress to wear in the Crystal Cathedral. The following weekend, she was on her first commercial flight leaving the country of her birth. The only time she'd flown was with her brother in a small 4-seater plane shortly after he'd gotten his pilot's license. It was a strange sensation for her to be lifted away from the earth. Stranger still was the fact that she expected to *see* the American-Canadian border. When the pilot announced they were entering the United States, she was dumbfounded by her own ignorance. Gazing out the window next to where she sat on the plane, there was no border to look at. No fence. No markings of any kind to indicate that they'd crossed into another country. All she could see for miles was Planet Earth. She was moved to tears by a revelation she sensed directly in her body. A kind of rising and opening. A feeling of deep connection and care. The world was not what she thought it was. *Not at all.*

They arrived at LAX in the late afternoon the day before they were to be married. Dan's brother-in-law met them at the airport and drove them home to meet Dan's step-sister. They enjoyed an evening of food and wine while Marlene watched closely for the dynamics within this family.

The next day was a blur of activity. None of which seemed generated by her. She was a bystander in this episodic adventure. Looking at her from the lens of now, it seems as though she became dissociated with all that was happening around her. She was given a part. She played it well. Smiled on cue. Walking down the aisle in a cathedral that could have housed generations of their families, she remembers feeling desperately alone. She thought about her son, her parents, her brothers and her sister. She missed them yet she didn't want them here for whatever this was. This was for her to do alone. A punishment in the guise of celebration.

A woman sang *Ave Maria*. Somebody video-taped the event. Robert Schuller didn't show so another man in robes officiated. Dan and Marlene exchanged vows. Kissed. And walked the long, long aisle to the back of the church where nobody was waiting. Nothing but dead air there.

Into the car and another surprise. Dan's step-sister and brother-in-law had booked them a table on the Queen Mary for an evening of drinks and dining and the newly married couple would be staying in a cabin reserved just for the two of them. Late into the night, they watched fireworks in the harbour, which seemed out of place. It was Canada Day but they were in the United States. And Independence day wasn't until July 4th. Why were there fireworks? The confusion seemed to echo her loss of place. She'd agreed to be in this world with this man. The ropes of her newly forming life had been cast off, her somewhat settled anchor hoisted up and she was set to sail. The only problem was that she didn't have a clue about where she was going.

On their wedding night, there was no lovemaking. She vaguely recalls resentment in the room with her and her new husband. How could she not have seen what a disaster this marriage would turn out to be? Did she really believe that she'd wake up the next morning feeling like a new woman with a new sense of belonging? The short answer is yes. She'd hoped she'd stumbled on happiness. She'd been motivated by memories of her first marriage and her first love. Those times had been sweet, happy times. She knew what it was to be loved by a good man and she wanted it again. So she'd cobbled together who she thought she had to be from these old structures that were no longer reliable. In fact, they were unreal. This jerry-rigged self was the wrong ship to take her to the far shore of fulfillment. Instead, she would travel on the arm of her new husband, aimless into the Arabian desert, where olive skinned men in white flowing garments, and mysterious women beneath black silk roamed in a surreal landscape.

A few days after Marlene and Dan were married, he was on his way to teach a summer course in an eastern university. Driving across the country, he left her at home in Alberta, the marriage still not consummated. And she felt relieved when he was gone.

He returned less than a month later and together they packed up the household and put their things in storage. It was a month during which a voice inside of her constantly wondered if she could get out of the marriage easily based on the fact that it was not consummated. She thought the thoughts. And she concluded that the marriage would fall apart on its own, that she wouldn't need to do much of anything. Strange comfort, but it held the hope of freedom. Not once did she ask herself why she'd put herself in this predicament. Not once did she listen and act upon that small voice within her. Dan returned to her and with four suitcases in tow, along with her two-year-old son, they embarked on their journey to the Arabian Peninsula. It would be their first and last adventure together. And when it all started to unravel, she'd forgotten that that was exactly what she'd expected would happen.

• • •

It's my first visual of this place and it feels like I'm returning to a place where I have never been. I press my face against the window and feel the pull in my belly as our plane continues its descent. There is both excitement and dread here for me. I want to turn around and go back to the life I've left. I want to face this adventure and become someone new. I'm here now. Can't go back. My son must be near. He's only two years old. But I don't remember him being there as I considered the edge of a new life. My husband. Yes. There he is. Angry with me about something and wanting to fight, again. I just ignore him. I won't be his dumping ground. I already sense there is deep trouble within him and I already know it has nothing to do with me. The first sign of his anxiety showed itself while we were in transit through Toronto's Pearson airport. We were rushed to make our next plane. And we were struggling to get to the next gate with bulky luggage and a cranky toddler. Dan glared at me as though it were all my fault and barked something that shocked me to my core. Thinking about it now, I feel sick. Which is why it's taken me so long to tell this story. I'd rather not revisit this pain. I don't want to be here writing these words on these pages. Yet there is a force guiding me to lay this story down. And because this guidance never leaves me, after all these years, I intuit that I'll not move forward into the woman I'm becoming until I do, in fact, lay this story down.

So, I write. And I tell myself he just needs to settle into this dream of his of living in the Persian Gulf; he just needs to find his work; he just needs to make some money; he just needs to have a place to call home with me; and then he'll come around and be the man I know he can be. Sweet. Attentive. Kind. That's all. He just needs my unconditional support and a little time.

The plane is closing in to the runway and soon we are on the ground, engines reversed, the familiar sound and pull of having arrived some place new. It's August 10th, 1988. Possibility lives here. I take a deep breath. I prepare myself for what I cannot yet imagine. It just is what it is and I unbuckle, stretch, and try to ignore the feeling of anxiety rising from deep inside of me. Dan has no capacity to comfort me now. He's somewhere else. And it doesn't include me. But I am the one he looks to if he has anger to unleash and fear to unburden. Like a pail of shit it gets flung over in my direction and lands on my face, my shoulders, and my hands, everything coloured with the brown of his self-loathing. I pretend I don't know that this man is not for me. I pretend I don't know how I've become the object of his self-hatred. I suppose I think it'll just go away. *It'll just go away.*

With a few things bundled, I pick up my toddler son (I see him now) and I walk towards the exit door of the plane. I'm leaving the safety of this experience, the familiarity of this crew, these seats, and this enclosed world of traveling to get somewhere else. I feel the heat filling the cabin. I feel as though I will melt. I step outside. I step down the stairs and onto the tarmac the sun so bright I feel blinded. My sunglasses have fogged up and it's as though I've placed my head into my mother's oven filled with her bread. *What the hell is this? How can it be so hot?*

We find our way to a bus that takes us from the plane over to the terminal. Inside, a blast of cold air hits our faces. My son is wide-eyed and wondering. Stares fix on us. We walk to another bus after collecting our suitcases. We board. We sit. My baby boy on my lap. I realize how unprepared I am. I've dressed my son in a warm fleece suit and he's sweating like crazy. *Why didn't I know it was going to be this hot?* The bus is air-conditioned but it still feels uncomfortably hot to me. Hard to settle. I just want to get to the hotel. I want a cool shower and I want a big bed. And sleep. Dan offers nothing to me or my son. He is punishing me with his distance again and for what else I do not know. I'll never know. It's always something. I distract myself by watching the strange city pass by me through the windows of the bus. The smell of it all makes me feel nauseous. I try to look ahead and focus on the horizon so I won't get carsick. This is Abu Dhabi. And just when I think this bus ride through hell will never end, I see the Holiday Inn.

Getting out of the bus fogs my glasses again and I can't see. Little do I realize this is the perfect metaphor to embody what I'm now stepping into – a fog that feels like a veil separating all the pieces of me. I am fragmented. Lost to myself. But I haven't been aware of this fragmentation until this moment. There is no strength left in me. I'm not able to contain anything. And nobody is containing me. I want to be held and reassured, but I'm in a freefall. I'm extremely vulnerable in this moment of arrival, but I don't know it. I don't realize how blindsided I am by being here. Shocked out of my senses. Don't know who I've been up to now and I certainly don't know whom I'm becoming. There's nothing from my past to hold onto here and I have no idea about what kind of future I'm creating for myself and my son. My son. He's the only thing that will guide me through this experience. His need for me will keep me sane. I know how to be mother and he will demand this of me. Being a foreigner in this land is the perfect way for me to see over time what I cannot see now: What I want is for all of me to be free and what I'm creating is a situation that will trap me for a very long time.

• • •

He hit me once. Before I married him. Before we were even engaged to be married. When it happened, I reached for the phone and called for help immediately. He fled. Aunt Clare arrived moments later. She stayed with me. We packed his things in a brown paper bag and set them on the front step. We then had the locks changed. It was instantaneous, the knowing what to do. I was clear. I moved swiftly. There was no hesitation. I was supported by my inner knowing and my family.

He was infuriated.

He stalked me. He watched the house from a distance, sitting in his car. I felt haunted. Fear started to find its way into my knowing. Maybe I was wrong. Maybe this was the man for me. Maybe he really loved me.

At what point did I begin to let him back in? Did he just wear me out with his stalking and talking and needing to stay together? What happened to the woman who knew fully what she knew and was willing to act on what she knew? Where did she go?

There is a heaviness as I write this. I want to sleep. It's too much effort to be in this place of telling. Slow, dark mud. *Forget it. It doesn't matter. You've changed. You're not in the same place that you were. Who cares? What's the point? Move on.*

The story-screams are muffled in the deep interior crevice that must be my wound. The story still lives in there. Playing itself over and over ad infinitum. I want the wound to heal. Close it up. But it festers. There's something inside the flesh of the story that needs to be retrieved before the gash will settle down, close itself up and heal without scarring. I cannot die with this story still in me. And when I sit down to write the story, it's still happening. Like I'm living in a loop. The past in the present becoming the future only to be in the past again.

I knew he wasn't good for me. I knew I didn't want to be married to him. I could see through the ways he projected unwanted pieces of himself onto me. When he first started calling me things that no other person has ever called me, it was confusing. Was I really selfish? Uncaring? Cruel? My whole life, people had told me how kind, loving and caring I was. Were they wrong? Did I not know the truth of who I really was? I didn't know it then, but these accusations and constant put-downs were undermining my self-esteem. Confidence was being buried beneath self-doubt. I was being weakened by his insistence that I was a terrible person and I was mistreating him. In a few weeks, he was back in my home. He promised the violence would never happen again. He would take care of us. Time to move on together and be happy. The *we-are-a-family-now* happy. It felt so much better than the extreme discomfort of thinking of myself as a bad woman capable of hurting another human being.

Of course, it was all an illusion. And I wonder what part of the illusion I continue to live today. How do I know when I'm lying to myself? What causes me to lose my internal ground that has me trusting who I am and how I show up in the world? How does that scaffolding collapse and leave me vulnerable to the ideas others have about me? Why would I ever let another person graft onto me their notion of what kind of a person I am, what I'm capable of, and what I need to change?

• • •

Girls learn things about who they are in the world by the responses of the people around them.

When I was about eleven my mother's sister asked me to model for her high school home economics fashion show. She'd sewn a pair of pants and poncho from hot pink fortrel. I was very pleased. It fit me perfectly and I'd never worn anything that felt so original and so *me*. It was fun! And it made me feel free and easy. Putting it on the first time, I begged my mother to let me run up the hill to Grandma and Gramps' house so I could show them.

Loping into my grandmother's kitchen, my cheeks probably matched the hot pinkness of the outfit. It was a sunny spring day and I had energy to burn. I don't remember whether Grandma liked the hot pink pantsuit or not. I don't even remember her seeing me or looking at me. The women in my family never wanted to give me too much attention for fear that it would make my head swell. I can imagine that she might've thought this getup was a bit much, but then again, I'm guessing cause I really don't recall any reaction from her at all.

I do remember asking where Gramps' was. In the shop, I was told. Bolting out the porch door, a few steps later I was standing next to Gramps who was standing next to his work bench. It was a dark shed, more than a shop, with an oily wood and a dirt floor. It stank and I worried that I would get my new outfit dirty. I see my grandfather's piercing blue eyes focus in my direction. But he's not seeing me. His eyes are glazed over with something I don't understand. I'm a little miffed. Can't he see my new outfit? Doesn't he know how special it is?

Somehow he pulls me in. And his hand is reaching inside my hot pink pants. Trusting my grandfather, I stand quietly wondering what the heck he's doing. Then I feel his fingers between my legs and I'm shocked into my senses. Somehow I free myself from his grip and I bolt for the sun-filled doorway. Stepping out into the brightness, I turn around and see Gramps smelling his fingers.

I run past my grandmother's house, along the short driveway, down the long hill, around the corner and into the front yard of my mother's house, through the front door, the porch, the kitchen and into my bedroom. Safe!

My face is flushed. And I'm confused. Adults assume kids know more than they do sometimes. All I knew at the time was that I'd done something wrong. I was too pink and too bright and too happy about myself and it'd made my grandfather act weird.

I stepped out of my clothes. Carefully hung them in the closet. Dressed myself in play clothes and vowed never to wear that pink poncho again. Then I was sad. I loved that poncho. But I didn't like who I was in it: invisible to my grandmother and strangely vulnerable to my grandfather. I suspect that this is the moment I considered that the way men felt around me and the out-of-control things they did in my presence were my fault.

I never told anyone about what had happened. I don't remember thinking I should keep it a secret but it was for many years. It wasn't until I was asked by my first therapist, Doug Emid, whether or not I had any family secrets that it came rising to the surface of my remembering. I talked it out loud to Doug while it rose in my awareness … and I was surprised by it. As though I'd forgotten forever about the girl in the pink poncho. But there she was. Living somewhere in my being without me knowing it. When she found voice to tell her story, there was deep shame in the room with us. I was embarrassed beyond anything I'd ever felt before.

Then something changed.

Doug asked me, *What do you think might have happened had you not run away from your grandfather that day?*

Suddenly the woman in me connected with the girl in me and the possibility of what might've happened had the girl not run away was staring me in the face.

Then Doug suggested that that girl was brave and smart. That she acted to protect herself and her grandfather. That she knew something her grandfather didn't know and she didn't hesitate a moment to act on her knowing. That she was wise and she'd possibly saved herself from being raped.

Wow.

I could feel a sense of pride for that girl. Confidence rising up inside of me as I contemplated this possibility. It changed everything I thought I knew about that girl. It put the glow back into her cheeks. I knew the girl in me was wickedly strong and I loved her.

But then I forgot again.

And she lived through many more strange male moments that caused her to forget her wicked strength.

I think I'm telling my story now in hopes that I'll remember that girl again and resurrect her presence in my life now.

Shame on *you*, Gramps.

• • •

She is transported out of sleep and into the stark reality of being in a foreign land. There is distant wailing she can't distinguish. Not yet ready to face what the day may bring, she pulls the covers over her head hoping it's all a bad dream and she'll find herself tucked back into her life on the Canadian prairie. But she is roused by the droning.

She sits up in bed. Her son is asleep in the second bed. Her husband gone. The room is comfortably cool with the constant hum of air conditioning a buffer against the insistent noise coming from outside.

Throwing back the sheets, her bare feet find the floor. It's dark in the room. A rush of light-headedness almost topples her. She stands up. She walks to the corner of the room. There is a floor-to-ceiling window heavily draped. Light fills the room as she pulls back the curtain. The brightness makes her squint. She realizes she has no idea what time it is. As her eyes adjust to the light, she looks out the window. Her eyes are drawn downward. She must be about fifteen stories up, high enough to fool her mind into thinking she sees a hill of ants. *What the heck?*

Peering closer, she sees one hundred men maybe more.

Men standing, bending, kneeling, prostrating themselves. Up then down then up again. *And there's that sound.*

She tries to focus on the scene below her window. And she is hit by a thought. *I'm in a foreign country.* The thought feels like a line from someone else's movie. For the first time in her life she has a sense of what foreign might mean. She realizes these men she is watching are praying, but she doesn't even know the word mosque yet. Or Islam. And she doesn't know what the call to prayer is, but the sound makes her body feel strangely alive. An old resonance not understood by the mind, it fills her with peace and foreboding at the same time. The echo reverberating through sand and city.

• • •

The romantic state can be one of inspiration, or illusion and deception. I didn't mean to choose illusion, it just happened because I was more invested in who I thought I was supposed to be than who I really am. I assumed if he knew the real me, he would leave.

I always had a way of speaking about things with excitement and conviction when I was a young girl. Talk, talk, talk. I'd know I crossed a line with my father when he'd stop listening and simply walk away. I hated how it made me feel. Too loud. Too much. Too everything. So, after you died, Kent, I attracted a man who was intelligent, creative, articulate – all the qualities I didn't own in myself yet – and he took me to a place where women are generally silenced. Your Marlene Sonder became his Marlene Altea.

He tried to take away my voice by locking me out of our house, by taking my name off our bank account, by forcing me to return to

Canada. Each silencing manoeuvre made me mad. I was scared. But I was more mad. I would eventually become a Women's Studies scholar because of this experience. I didn't understand the power plays and I was naive enough to think these were injustices that I could correct. I would not give up. I would not tell my parents back home what I was facing. How could I? I had talked my way into this mess by talking myself into leaving college, by talking myself into leaving home, by talking myself into leaving family, by talking myself into getting married again, by talking myself into selling every bit of furniture I had, including my beloved piano, and giving all my money to Dan so we could travel toward his dream. I had convinced my parents that these were good things to do and they had quietly acquiesced.

Talk, talk, talk. I sure knew how to talk.

• • •

She stands at the window watching the men pray for a long time. *Now what?* She imagines her new husband standing next to her, wrapping his arms around her, comforting her, reassuring her, whispering in her ear that he loves her. That's what Kent would've done. But Dan isn't Kent. And on day 41 of this marriage, she is hardly prepared to face the terror starting to creep into her heart.

She realizes she is starving. But her boy is sleeping and she cannot go downstairs to the restaurant. She calls room service. Orders toast and coffee. And when it arrives, a sense of order is restored in her world … momentarily. Because when Dan enters the room some hours later, tension enters the room, too. She can't quite put her finger on what the problem might be. She tries. She watches herself move through endless accommodations in hopes of creating some kind of harmony. It's not easy. In fact, it's exhausting.

She learns to look forward to the meals they share as a family in the hotel restaurant. There they meet all the other families here with the Higher Colleges of Technology. They sit together. Eat together. Share stories about what is happening on this adventure together. And in these gatherings, Dan is amiable, even loveable, in his warmth and care for others and at times, for her and her son. He appears to be enjoying his new role as step-dad. Her son draws a lot of attention. He's a gregarious child equipped with abundant energy for new things and new people. Endlessly curious, he keeps his mother moving and maybe it's this constant motion that has her feeling as though she's treading water in a deep pool of dark water. She doesn't get to pause and wonder about who she is being in this new domestic situation unless her son is sleeping and her husband is at the college fulfilling the role for which he was hired. Those times when she is alone and allowed to pause, she takes refuge in the dark hotel room. She can pretend she's safe in the cocoon where her baby sleeps and she doesn't have to face the world outside the hotel's doors.

Dan reports back from the college the things they must do. He gives her instructions about where to go to get passport photos for the endless streams of paperwork that must be completed. He tells her where to take their laundry to avoid the hotel's charges. Some expatriate (that's what she is now) found a shop down the street and like a bunch of sheep, many of the Canadians are carrying their dirty clothes back and forth, day after day. She thinks it's a waste of her time. It is, after all, the women who are doing the traipsing back and forth. The women are the spouses of the teachers the college has hired. Their role is clear. They are here to make home, settle the children in new schools and support their husbands. Being a spouse has given Marlene a new identity in which she wants to feel a part of the community. Wives have certain kinds of conversations with other wives. These women know her as a wife not as a widow. She left that story ten thousand miles behind her. This is a fresh start.

So she does all the things she is instructed to do. They find an apartment in the Garden Tower on the third floor overlooking a spectacular garden that spreads for an entire block. The other side of the building faces the corniche and the blue water of the Arabian Sea. She imagines this will be her haven, a place where she can settle her young son and they'll all be content. They'll be a family. The apartment is lovelier than most of the other expats' places. They were lucky to get into the well-maintained building and it's an ideal location. There must have been happy moments. She did create a home space. She and Dan bought new furniture they liked, including a king-size water bed. Their bedroom had a full wall of built-in closets and a balcony overlooking the garden. She'd carried the negatives of their wedding photos with her from Canada and had a 30 x 48 inch dry-mounted portrait made that hung above their bed. She recalls some months later knowing that Dan had thrown that portrait into an alley dumpster.

• • •

Leaving the safety of the hotel was hard. It had become a familiar place. They'd established ritual mealtimes with the larger community of people. She belonged to something there. A room they'd settled into. A group of Canadians pulling together in a foreign land. A kind of camaraderie that allowed her to sometimes feel less anxious. At this stage of the move Dan was focused on his job more than he was focused on his family – the family he'd claimed to want so badly. He never seemed anxious or disturbed about anything when there were other people around. In fact, he was very sociable. Most people seemed to really like him. He was kind and helpful. Two of the qualities that most likely enticed her parents into thinking he would be a good husband.

So they had fun times. Even though there was the stress of moving and building a home. She wanted to please him. She knew how to be a wife. And while they were staying in the hotel, she loved not having to prepare meals and still have the luxury of shared mealtimes. She liked the adventure of hunting for good places to shop for all the things they'd need because they needed everything. Having sold most of her household to get here, it was exhilarating to think of reconfiguring a life and a style all over again. There was this romantic notion that they'd create a home that reflected the desert environment they lived in. They'd buy beautiful things that they'd eventually be able to take back to Canada. The whole point of being here was to pay off Dan's debt, save some money, and then be in a financial position to return to Canada where they'd be able to purchase their first home together. This was the vision he'd sold her and she'd bought it with what she felt was a full guarantee.

When she'd left the farm after her husband died, she wanted to hold onto everything that gave her evidence of a shared life with him. She wanted to remember. To sense connection to things that held memories. She could then time-travel back to earlier days to help her whenever she was out of sorts. But with all the changes in her life now it was hard to access that time-travel capability. She was quite disconnected from who she'd been and she was desperately trying to redefine who she was now. She just assumed that this new marriage would unfold in the same ways that her first marriage did. That they'd help each other through the changes. She knew enough to not be too hard on herself. She'd taken a big leap leaving her family, her country, her academic career. And she trusted Dan to care for her. She'd worked hard to get to this new place. It took a lot of organizing and planning to clear a household and pack all she'd need for the next two years in two suitcases. It was an admirable feat. One that Dan's sister, Miranda, had remarked on during the weekend they were married. She remembered her surprise and gratitude to have what she was willing to do for this marriage acknowledged by Miranda. At the same time, she felt Dan was unappreciative. But she excused him in her own mind for one or another reason because she was good at excusing the failings of others. Especially the failings of her husbands. She had more expectations of herself than she had of them. It never occurred to her that that might be unbalanced. It seemed the perfect order of things. Isn't that just what women do?

So the day they left the hotel provoked a new anxiety in her. After several weeks of calling the Holiday Inn home, she was now out in the streets of Abu Dhabi as a bona fide resident of the city. It would mean buying groceries, cooking meals, cleaning house, doing laundry and establishing some kind of new normal. Spinnies, the British grocer that the expats raved about, was just across the garden, within walking distance. Dan would need to buy a car and that was the next thing on his agenda. Taxis were cheap enough but he wanted to drive. So, he bought himself a used 1982 blue 4-door Saab complete with sun-roof. He loved it. She thought it the strangest car she'd ever seen.

They opened their first joint bank account together. The college provided housing and furniture allowances as well as an education allowance for children. That meant Dan wanted Marlene to get her son into school so she could find work. Her son wasn't even two and a half years old yet and she was miffed by the idea of having to put him in school. She was looking forward to being able to focus on being with him more now that she wasn't attending classes. She assumed she'd earned herself a bit of a break considering all the changes the three of them were facing and all that she'd been willing to do to support the transition. She served this family well with her time and attention. It'd become her work. She'd understood that her contribution to their finances had been made back in Canada having sold most of her belongings. It was the action that generated the money that had gotten them to where they were now. Yes, Dan had the work permit and contract and yes he would be earning their family income now. But prior to scooping this job, he'd been working as a part-time instructor at the Medicine Hat College in Alberta, making payments on one credit card by borrowing from another credit card. She'd never known anyone to do this. In fact, she'd never known this could be done. But that's how he was meeting his financial obligations. Her experience with money had been a clean one up until this point. The debt she'd had with her first husband had been farm debt; they'd understood that they were building the farm to build their life. She'd been the one earning a wage to pay for all the "other" expenses so she had a direct link to her money and her lifestyle. When Kent died, she received a death benefit from Saskatchewan Government Insurance to the tune of ten thousand dollars. She also received crop insurance monies as Kent's final crop had been hailed out. She took these lump sums of money to pay off supposed farm debt as Kent's family made no effort to help her financially. Actually, that's not entirely true. Kent's mom Faye offered to pay for Kent's funeral expenses because she knew Marlene didn't even possess the funds to cover that. Some months later though, Marlene was able to arrange and purchase a headstone for his grave. On it were written words she wrote as her final parting gift to her husband. Seeing her words in stone made it easier to depart. His place was marked. Their love was testified. So when Marlene entered this marriage with Dan, she paid her own way and then some. She expected the man to fulfill his own part but as time revealed, he had other expectations that he hadn't spoken of to her.

As the discussion between Dan and Marlene about sending her son to play school heated up, she began to wonder just what his debt was all about. She'd never asked. She'd simply merged her assets with his without even knowing what he'd had. Now she remembers another thing Dan's sister had said when they were in California getting married. She'd remarked that their mother (Dan's step-mom) thought it unwise for Dan to get married until he'd cleared up his debt. It hadn't bothered her at the time. They were in love. This was only a question of money. Her first priority had always been love and money came somewhere further down the list. She and Kent had been farmers on family land. She'd supplemented their income by working at the bank. But money was never a thing that they fought about. They just did the best they could … together. It was a mutual effort. And here now was this new husband demanding she put her son in play school and get herself out into a job. She didn't even have a work permit! What was he getting all uptight about anyway?

This argument stirred a deep unrest in her. It forced her to admit she'd wanted this marriage to relieve her of the burden of having to do everything herself. She'd given him everything she had. She'd been eager to follow his dream. She slipped right into playing housewife to provide him with all the support he needed to get on in his new job. She'd made home for their family. She'd worked hard. And this was the way he was thanking her. Telling her to get out and get a job. It didn't sit well with her, not at all.

Yet, she set out to do what he wanted her to do. Despite her willingness to please him, some part of her resisted what was being foisted onto her. She remembers throwing what can rightfully be called temper tantrums. They'd wake up on a Sunday morning and she'd want the day to do what felt good to her. But there he was in her face telling her what he wanted them to do: go to the British Club, meet with friends, be on the beach in the sun, drink from the bar, swim (he was a former Commonwealth athlete having represented his country as a swimmer in the games yet she could count on her one hand the times she saw him actually swim with some skill and gusto) and lay about (his words, not hers). She'd try to find the enthusiasm but something inside her felt inconvenienced. It was work to get to the British Club. And he certainly didn't offer to do any of it. From his perspective, she fussed too much. Worried too much. Made everything into work. She wondered how he'd gotten to be this age without knowing how to meet the basic requirements of living that included managing a household and feeding oneself. He just wanted everything to be where it needed to be when he needed it to be there. Again, she attributed this to him just needing time to settle into this new living arrangement in this new culture. The truth was she didn't really know this man at all.

She'd started dating Dan after being in his business math class. He was charming to say the least. He wooed her with gifts. One particular metal brooch in the shape of an ice cream cone was her favourite. He gave these gifts freely. Took her to dinner. Shared books with her. He was warm and he liked to cuddle. Their first date was to see the movie *Platoon*, which was too violent for her, but they ended up in his parked car necking for an hour afterwards. It was her first real date since being with her now dead husband. It felt wonderful to walk down the street holding hands with a man again. He was sexy and sweet. And being with him allowed her to remember what it felt like to be safe in the world.

They'd been dating for a few weeks. It was now April. And she was to graduate with a certificate in business administration. He'd be her date to the ceremony and celebration even though he was faculty and would need to attend the event regardless. She bought a white silk pantsuit and red camisole to wear with her red snakeskin heels. She had red highlights put in her hair. Dan was a hot dancer and she was ready to dance! And dance they did. She could feel the way they stirred people's attention. And it felt rather good to have that kind of power as a woman again. Widows don't get this kind of attention. People just feel sorry for widows. They pity widows and think they have some sort of magical (read evil) influence. It was a curious situation to be a student sitting at the faculty table partying with her teachers. This was the night they came out boldly as a couple and it felt a bit scandalous.

She remembers the head of the department eyeing her carefully that evening. He knew her backstory and how she'd come to the college as a widow and single mother. He'd advised her on a few occasions about academic and personal issues. He'd been understanding and kind. The first time they were in his office together after the celebratory evening, he cautioned her about being with Dan. And there'd been a moment when she allowed herself to feel the deep care of his concern for her welfare. He suggested she focus more on her academic career and less on being with Dan; that Dan was interested in different things than she was. At the time, she felt a bit defensive. What had she felt she needed to protect? Now she wishes she had listened to his wise counsel. But she'd dismissed it carelessly. And she would pay dearly for the dismissal.

In Abu Dhabi the man was beginning to show his true colours. He'd bark and he'd bellow. He'd laugh in public and scowl behind closed doors. It took her awhile to see the contrast. Curiously, she started feeling safer in his presence while they were with others than if they were home alone.

He seemed patient and sweet with her son. She watched for any signs of distress between them and none surfaced, at least none when she was in the room with them.

They started to invite friends over for cards and drinks, music and conversation. The first few times were easy and fun. Then he'd start to get on her about the bathroom not being clean enough just before friends were to arrive. It dazed her the first time he complained about the soap dish because she was known to be finicky in her housekeeping habits. Who the heck was he to tell her how to clean the bathroom? She was miffed. And she let him know it. And maybe because people were to arrive at any minute, he let her get away with it. But somewhere along the line she lost her ability to be miffed and became just plain scared. Fear replaced her fierceness. And it cost her her confidence, her clarity and the self-contract that keeps one intact.

• • •

Dan won the argument. Marlene found a play school for her son. The British school system starts kids at an earlier age than the Canadian school system so it was easier than she'd expected. Her son's teacher was a Scottish woman. Her name was Morag and her classroom was full of positive energy bursting with creativity. It soon became her son's favourite place to be. He wasn't distressed at all about mama leaving him with Morag and the other children. He had new friends and that made him happy, which was a relief for his mother.

Now his mother needed to find a job.

What happened in-between should have been enough to send Marlene and her son back home to where they belonged. But it didn't. Well, it did and it didn't. And therein lies the mystery she was forced to contemplate over the next several months.

In October (they'd only been in Abu Dhabi for two months) Dan announced that he was unhappy and he demanded that she leave.

Cold shock.

Could hardly breathe.

Who was this man and what was wrong with him?

"I want you to leave. Go back to Canada for three weeks so I can think about it. I'm not happy," he said.

She didn't take him seriously. How could she? After all she'd been willing to do and to give it was inconceivable that he could just turn it all upside down. She refused to believe it.

A week or two passed. Things in the Garden Tower apartment got progressively worse. His behaviour was ever more erratic. She noticed at night, sleeping next to him, he'd sweat profusely. They'd wake up in the morning with their bedsheets soaking wet. Sometimes she wondered if he'd pissed the bed, it was so wet. But he hadn't. Then she started to wonder if he was sick. And if he was, sick with what? They weren't having sex anymore. And if she were honest with herself, as she is forced to be in writing this story, she'd have to conclude that maybe he was fucking other women already at this point in their marriage. But to think that thought then would have caused too much pain; she wasn't up for that. Nor was she up to thinking about the fact that if he *was* fucking other women, she'd be at risk for STDs and HIV. So, she didn't allow herself to go there in her mind. Instead, she became the doting wife making sure the boy and the man had all that they needed because she couldn't live with herself if she'd been a bad mother or a bad wife. And Dan was telling her every day about all the ways she had failed him. That she was selfish and stubborn and unloving. That all she ever thought about was herself and what she alone needed. That she was, he said, "sucking off my tit" and giving nothing back in return. All of these accusations confused her. She'd never been told any such things. And it started to wear her down in the sense that she wasn't sure she could believe who she thought she was and who she thought she'd always been: kind, caring, self-less, compassionate and smart. He had married her because he loved her. That was the assumption she'd made. Now he was treating her like he hated her. Kent had never, ever engaged in such a game. And the contrast knocked her off her feet. She was losing her balance. She did have a couple of friends that she felt she could confide in but there was a risk because they were Dan's colleagues. She was less worried about embarrassing herself and more worried about what Dan would do if he found out she was telling people about their problems. But that was her inclination. To reach out when in need. She didn't want to say anything to her mom and dad back home. They'd be worried sick and want her back in Canada pronto. Who else did she have that she could confide in?

There was one woman who worked closely with Dan. She was also a teacher. And she'd arrived in the United Arab Emirates with her young daughter Kate. Marlene loved the way this mother related to her daughter. Kate was about 12 years old and Marlene imagined having the same kind of closeness with her son when he would be that age. She liked this mother-daughter duo and felt at ease with them. The three of them talked about stories and writing and education and women. She admired the way this mother communicated with her daughter. While they were still back in the hotel, Kate had stayed with her son when Marlene and Dan wanted an evening out. She continued to be their babysitter now that they all had moved out of the hotel. If there was someone here she could talk to it would be Kate's mom, Marilyn. So the next time they were together, she told them she was having difficulty with Dan at home. That things were happening that she couldn't understand. That he wanted her to leave the UAE and return to Canada.

She remembers that Kate was reading Nathaniel Hawthorne's 'The Scarlet Letter' during this time. She also remembers Kate giving her the book as a parting gift, carefully inscribed in her young girl handwriting. Kate's young girl imagination drew some kind of parallel between Hester, the main character of the story, and Marlene's past experience as a young bride, a pregnant widow, a lone mother and now a wife trying to make a respectable family. In a brief and fleeting moment, Marlene glimpsed the larger narrative that was being lived through her personal life story as seen by Kate's wildest imaginings. And in the strangest way, she felt seen by this young girl. And even understood. Kate had the tacit knowledge that Marlene was trying to regain her virtue.

• • •

On December 10th Dan booked flights for Marlene and her son back to Canada. When she asked to see the tickets (back in 1988 airlines tickets were issued with bookings and one couldn't travel without a ticket) Dan's answer was, "If you behave yourself, you'll get the tickets." She was told their departure would be in nine days. She was also told that until she left, she would be sleeping in her son's bed.

Dread rose up from the depths of wherever it usually lives and took residence in her belly. There was nothing in her life that had prepared her for this. She had no way of making sense of what was happening. What she did have was a memory in her body of what it feels like to have your world turned upside down. Of everything you think you stand on slipping out from under your feet. And that memory was activated to the power of a thousand. She didn't have her family near. She was a foreigner in a country she didn't yet understand. She was solely responsible for another human being, her son. She was terrified but afraid to acknowledge just how terrifying all of this was. She put on a brave face. She tried to think through logically what needed to be done. She tried normalizing the situation to protect her young son but that in itself became a kind of dyslexia. The first thing she needed to do was make sure she had money in her wallet in case Dan did something more stupid than what he'd already done. How could he justify spending money to pay for tickets home when he was constantly harping on her about not having enough money? She'd at least need to know she could get food and even a hotel if she had to. Her father had taught her to always carry money in her wallet in the event something unexpected might happen and she could find her way home. She was sure her father had not anticipated this particular predicament she'd gotten herself into.

She lay awake in her son's bed that first night after getting the eviction notice from her husband and she couldn't shut her mind off to sleep. She became obsessed with trying to figure out what had gone wrong and what she was to do to make it right again. The incessant thinking through the night made it hard to get up the next morning. Their bedroom door was closed and she could hear Dan up and getting ready for work. His routine rarely varied, but she noticed he was smoking more; a habit he'd been careful to not indulge in her presence and especially inside their home, but now he didn't seem to care and he seemed to be smoking constantly. If she complained, he was offended and it only made him smoke more. He had a right to do whatever the hell he wanted to and she wasn't gonna stop him from smoking in his own home. It was as though he was trying to smoke her out of his life. She wonders now why she didn't just leave like he wanted her to. Inhaling his cigarette smoke made her physically sick. Why did she feel like she had to fight for something that was so obviously and terribly wrong? Why did she subject herself to the disrespect and the disgust? Hearing him in his frantic rush to get to work, she was careful to not stir and to keep her son quiet until she knew that Dan had left the apartment.

Gone.

She opened their bedroom door and wandered around their apartment. She'd put so much effort into making this space their home and now she was being ousted like an unwanted relative. Her son was just beginning to feel settled again. She'd taken care to create a bright, beautiful room for him with a good bed and a great play space even though he'd had to leave all but a couple of his favourite toys in a storage unit back in Canada. Didn't Dan realize how upsetting this was? How could she just walk away from all the things she had brought with her from Canada? These were precious things that she'd packed carefully hoping to help them make home together. Was she just supposed to turn away from her clothes, her books, the few things she had with her to help make meaning in this adventure? As he ordered her out of the country, he never once reassured her that he'd take care of the things they had brought or that he'd make sure to send them back to her in Canada. There was no logic to his plan. He just wanted her gone. Plain and simple. Be gone, woman.

It's only occurring to her now as she writes this that Dan's vehement rejection made her feel the same way she felt when Kent's mom and dad refused to have anything to do with her because she wouldn't tell them who fathered the child she was carrying in her womb. Her allegiance was to her unborn son and to the man who'd agree to conceive him with her. It was a sacred contract. But in Colin and Faye's eyes, she'd done something so wrong that they could no longer love her. She knew she had the capacity to love unconditionally; it was so deeply ingrained in her that it was unshakeable which made it almost effortless to adapt or tolerate anything. She didn't understand how or why, but it was there. Yet here she was again on the receiving end of having love withdrawn from her because she wasn't living up to somebody else's standards. She could never do to another human being what these people were doing to her. Why were they rejecting her? Why couldn't they see the love and acceptance she was able to give them and in return give her the same? Was there something terribly wrong with her? And if so how was she ever going to see or understand what her deep fault must be? Being pregnant had anchored her in trusting what she felt to be true because she had to care for the life she carried within her. But here in this foreign country, away from all that she ever knew to be true, she was shaken to her core. She didn't know where to anchor herself. She still trusted her mothering instincts and that was a comfort. She knew how to be mom. But her marriage was a farce. And if she didn't know where she was standing then she couldn't see the crude humour of what might have been painfully clear to others – that Daniel Altea was a deeply troubled man and he was acting like a ludicrous buffoon.

She had breakfast with her young son, showered and dressed. She'd need to get him to play school after getting to the bank and she'd need to get to the bank before it was too hot outside. This was the cooler part of the year in this part of the world but she hadn't yet adapted to the heat and still found it intolerable. Getting to the bank meant a taxi ride and she had enough change to do that. Last night Dan had informed her that he was taking the keys to the car away from her. Another punishment for her bad behaviour. She had begged him to reconsider. Their agreement had been she would drive the car to transport her son to play school because it was a long way from where they lived and it was easier for Dan to taxi to work than for them to taxi to school. But he'd decided it was no longer his responsibility to help her get along. She needed to be punished and this was one way for him to do that. If it hadn't been so hurtful, it might've been funny. So she gathered her son into her arms and they headed out of the Garden Tower building, crossed the street and stood waiting in the morning sun for a taxi. She was determined to keep her life together in the most fundamental way. She had family. Her family loved and cared about her. This thought sustained her through the toughest of times. Dan could take away the keys to the car, but that wouldn't stop her from getting to where she needed to go.

And the first place she needed to go was to the bank.

She walked into the building holding her young son's hand. She wanted to make a simple withdrawal of cash. She entered the ladies queue. It would be a short wait. When it was her turn, she approached the teller's window and requested two thousand dirhams (about 650 Canadian dollars) from her joint bank account with Dan. The teller, a young Indian woman wearing bright red lipstick, took her name and account number, turned and walked away.

She remained standing. And waited.

After a long few minutes, a bald Egyptian man with coke bottle lens glasses informed her that she couldn't withdraw any money. Dan had requested the bank not allow her access to their account. She was perplexed by this notion. That a man could ask a bank to not allow his wife access to their family money just because he was inclined to do so. That a man had that kind of unconditional power over his wife and his family was shocking. But here it was. And she was living it. She felt as though she was entering a vortex of unbelievability. She could feel the eyes of people watching her. She must have looked flustered. She certainly felt humiliated. This was her money. She had contributed everything she'd had to merge her life with Dan and now he was clamping down to accomplish what? It was beyond rationalizing. It was the fact that she had her son with her that gave her the strength to breathe deeply and walk out of that place. She could feel people watching her go. They exuded pity for the poor woman who was having problems at home. Yet not one person offered to help. Not one person came forward with a show of kindness. It was as though Dan had everyone's support to do whatever he wanted to her. Total strangers colluding in her humiliation. How could she ever walk back into this place? As she hailed a taxi, she glanced back at her reflection in the windows of the high-rise from the street where she stood with her son who sensed the gravity of the situation, his little hand squeezing hers as though hanging on for dear life. She didn't recognize the woman she was becoming.

The man she'd married was trying to stop her going where she needed to go to be safe and secure. He was setting up road blocks at every turn. Why? This was a question she couldn't answer. Why? Why? Why? Asking made her feel like a crazy lady cause there was no way to rationalize what he was doing and how he was acting. It was crazy-making.

Not being able to make sense of what was happening to her thrust her into a sort of tail-spin. She didn't know which way to turn. She felt like she was a spinning top.

She made a doctor's appointment at the American Hospital because the anxiety rising up in her threatened to overcome her own sense of safety in herself. She couldn't become unglued cause she had a child to take care of. This was probably the one thought that kept her head above the riptide threatening to drown her.

She listened to herself explain to the doctor what was happening in her life. She didn't like the whiny, scared voice that she heard. Who was this in her? This frightened person? This needy woman in crisis? She'd always known herself to be fearless. Hadn't she recovered her life after Kent's tragic death? Hadn't she packed up and moved to start over again while embracing her new responsibility as a mother? Hadn't she welcomed the opportunity to be a wife again and done everything she was able to do to support, encourage and love her new husband? Who was this terrified, anxious woman sitting in this doctor's office? Where'd she come from and what did she need?

Thankfully, the doctor knew she needed to calm down. He prescribed anti-anxiety medication and he offered what protection he could. He knew of a vacant apartment where she could go if she needed. The thought was relieving and distressing at the same time. How did she get to a place in her life where she needed to have a get-away plan?

Strangely, what worried her most was not understanding what was happening to Dan. She knew and accepted that she had to take care of herself and her son, but she spent much of her mental energy trying to figure Dan out. It was exhausting. And she had the idea that if she could only find her way back into his heart then everything else would fall back into place. It's a terrible thing to be so dependent on another human being's state of well-being. To know that if he makes a departure from the way things are supposed to be, then her life comes crashing down all around her. Looking back on it now, there is a profound sense of history repeating itself, but she didn't sense it then. Kent's life had had a direct impact on her life. He died. Then everything she knew to be her life died with him. In the early stages of that dying, all seemed lost. But over time she found her way back into life. And it was this life here in Abu Dhabi with Dan that was to be her new start. However, she found herself in a deep crisis. And not one she could find any humour in. Little did she know that this was only the beginning of it getting really, really bad. Had she been able to see what was waiting around the corner for her, she might have gotten off the road. But she couldn't. And she didn't. She would be hit full force by the weight of a wickedness that lived inside this man she'd married. And it would hurt. Badly.

A few days later, in a state of compounding disbelief, Marlene asked Dan if she could see the tickets. She wanted proof that she needed to be packed and ready to leave.

"If you behave yourself, you'll get the tickets" was all he had to say.

• • •

On December 19th Marlene and her son left Abu Dhabi even though two hours before actually boarding the plane, Dan pleaded with her to stay.

She was tempted by his unexpected behaviour. It felt like he'd come to his senses, at last. But the simple fact was it just felt like too much work to shift directions yet again. She was exhausted. She was afraid about what she might be doing to her son with all of this chaotic bullshit. She had set her sights on getting back to mom and dad on the farm where she knew the land and the people would remind her of who she's always been. She'd come so far away from herself that she didn't know anything other than she needed to get *home.*

The KLM flight taking them to Europe didn't bring her the comfort of feeling like she'd made the right decision. There was a moment on the flight when she thought she'd actually made the wrong decision because surely this plane would never make its arrival in Zurich. Not yet a seasoned traveller, and not yet able to afford the luxury of first class, what she witnessed on this flight scared her badly. A brown-skinned man in a beige suit with a dark bush of hair on his head sat in the seat directly in front of her, and just a couple of hours into the flight was becoming increasingly aggressive. He talked loudly. He staggered up and down the aisle. His raucous behaviour unsettled her and others on the flight. She didn't know if he'd been drinking. She didn't know if he was mentally disturbed. All she knew was that he was in close proximity, she was in danger and there was nowhere for her to go. What she saw next she never again witnessed on any other flight. One of the pilots, along with two members of his crew, one man and one woman, forced this man into a seat near the back of the plane, tied him to it and tied his hands. The disturbed passenger eventually passed out and they did reach Zurich and she did spend the night there in a lovely hotel with friendly people which was almost enough to calm her frazzled nerves. She noticed how relieved she was getting to Switzerland. She didn't know exactly what to attribute her relief to but part of it was making it through the crazy flight, part of it was getting away from Dan's unpredictability, part of it was being around friendly people, part of it was feeling safer in Europe than in the Persian Gulf. All of these elements should have been information for her to pay attention to. Should have allowed her to see she could find places to be and people to be with who made her feel good and welcome and safe. That she didn't need to stay where she was tormented, mistreated and even abused.

They arrived back in Canada on the winter solstice, December 21st.

She allowed herself to settle into home on the farm with her parents and to say they were relieved to have her back would be an understatement. There's a special quality in the way she's been parented. No matter what, she's always known she can go back home to the farm. Wayne and Margaret have held the door open to all of their children unconditionally and still do. It is probably a mixed blessing on some level. On one hand, it gives her a sense of safety and even fearlessness knowing she can return. On the other hand, it gives her a back door out of whatever life she is creating. But that back door feels like a deep pulse in her. She's always feared, even when she wasn't aware of the fear, that she would be trapped.

Coming home to the farm felt like freedom. The contrast with what she'd just come from was stark. When had she become trapped? The story she was telling herself was that she'd remarried to a wonderful man from Trinidad and they were living their dream life in the Persian Gulf. The plot of being trapped was nowhere told in that story. But the experience of coming home to her birth land revealed the trap.

Now there were wide open spaces and deep, quiet prairie. Family. Food. Talk. Play. Life on the farm has always been so simple compared to everything she's had to meet outside of that world. On the farm, you read the weather and that dictates what you are able to do for the day. You feel connected to the land. You talk to your neighbours. Tea time is a daily ritual of sustenance. Conversation is relationship. There's time to play the piano, read a book, bake cookies and watch cartoons with the kids. And after a few days of this it was hard to imagine the nightmare she'd left behind in Abu Dhabi.

Sitting in the rocking chair by the Christmas tree late in the evening after everyone had gone to bed, she'd glimpse their wedding picture in the brass frame by the tv and dream of the good, sweet times when she'd felt loved by Dan. She just couldn't wrap her head around the man he'd become *over there* and she began to imagine that she must've made it out to be worse than it really was. She started to doubt herself and she wondered what was so wrong with her that she'd turned this sweet second chance at happiness into a horror show. She wonders now what she told her parents during that time. Nobody asked questions, really. Nobody interfered. Maybe she didn't invite that kind of conversation. She can't remember. But it seems curious to her now that somebody didn't sit down with her and demand to know what the heck was going on.

Getting through the holidays was easy enough. But when the new year came around, she felt sad about the state of her life and confused about what to do next. Dan was calling frequently and she noticed he didn't seem too concerned about long distance charges anymore. Because while she was there with him, he monitored how many times she called home and how much money was spent on long distance phone calls. She'd taken to writing long letters to her mother and then paying the relatively cheaper rate to have them faxed back home. It was an alternative to calling by phone and it helped her to feel less homesick but it just wasn't the same as picking up the phone. Although at times, talking on the phone just made it evident how far away from her family she really was because the lines were not always clear and there was always the delay in transmission, a pause that if not handled correctly would cut off her mother's voice on the other end of the line.

Cut off.

Away from.

She had wanted distance from her recent past. The past where he died. Turned her world upside down. And she wanted to die, too. So leaving the past behind was the deeper motivation that led her to the United Arab Emirates. She should have known that folks wouldn't just forget and move on. That they'd always and forever have a certain pity for her. What was even worse was the pity they had for her son. Poor boy, they'd say. Poor boy. And she'd been so proud and so pleased with his coming into the world. She had him for her. Nobody else. Because he was all hers. And now she'd have a reason to live. So nix the damn poor attitude please. Let us make a new life. Pack it all up and leave it all behind to start new. And now look at where the hell she was. There must be something wrong with her. Something that other people can see and she cannot.

Marlene called Colleen in Medicine Hat. They'd been friends in college. Colleen's dad was the Dean of the college. She knew Colleen had been seeing a counsellor for some family issues and she was ready to try the same. In mid-January she walked into her first session feeling unsure of what it was going to be about and pretty sure that something was wrong with her, that something needed to be fixed in her.

So the rampage to fix herself began.

Meanwhile Dan continued to call. And fax. He faxed her a card asking her to come home to Abu Dhabi as soon as possible. He wanted her there the first part of February. She suggested she might stay in Canada until March to enable her to continue her counselling. He was not happy. He missed them. He wanted them back home. He resented that she got to have Christmas and the holidays with her family while he was stuck there in the desert working. When she reminded him that it was his decision that she leave in the first place, he denied it completely saying that he was in an impossible position because she had problems and she needed to solve them.

Phone conversations continued between the two of them as well as fax transmissions. She wasn't ready to go back. She knew that. But she didn't yet face just how badly she *never* wanted to go back. She wanted to stay home in Canada. Period. And when she dared to imagine that possibility, a voice in her head would tell her she was a coward. She should be brave. She should create a new kind of life. She should break free of everything expected of her and just dare to be different. She should travel. And explore. Have adventures. Now all of that might have been true. But what wasn't evident to her was the fact that she was putting herself in harm's way even though her intentions were to simply break free of everything she'd been taught about what her life should be. She was actually stepping into the lion's den thinking she was somehow protected by her good intentions. Innocence may be sweet. And naiveté sometimes dangerous. But the only way through ignorance is education. And she was embarking on a journey that would inform and shape the rest of her life.

Two of Dan's friends from Medicine Hat called her while she was on the farm with her parents and invited her to dinner one evening. They knew she was back because they'd been speaking with Dan. She was happy to connect and curious to see if they could tell her something about Dan that would help her understand what was happening in her life. She didn't know these people very well. She knew that Dan considered them among his best friends. She wasn't even sure if they were a couple. She knew they were both nurses, they both worked at the hospital and they didn't live together. His name was Mike and her name Susan. What stands out most in her memory now was how neither of them were alarmed or even surprised by what she had to tell them about her experience with Dan overseas. They both shrugged their shoulders when they announced that they'd always thought Dan was manic depressive. Didn't she know that?

Jesus, Mother Mary and God! How could these people not have spoken to her before she married the man? They'd had plenty of opportunity to talk to her before she'd uprooted her life here in Medicine Hat and followed this crazy dude into the desert. She immediately felt betrayed by these so-called friends. She better understood why they'd invited her to dinner this evening. It was to appease their guilt. They wrapped their arms around her, empathized with what she must be going through and offered their support. It was a little too much and a little too late. She was sick to think that maybe she didn't know Dan at all. That there'd been things kept from her purposely. She felt like the last one to know something that everyone else had always known. It was the same feeling she'd get when her mother, her aunt and her grandmother would talk about things she wasn't supposed to hear or know about. They always had their secrets from her and she was always trying to find a way to hear what was really going on around her. Maybe it was this kind of secret-keeping that prevented any of these women from sitting her down and asking her about what was really happening in her life. Her translation of this was that nobody really cared. They all had their own lives to deal with and didn't want to be bothered with what might be bothering her.

Soon enough it was February and she wasn't in any hurry to return to the desert. In her phone conversations with Dan she sensed something had changed in him. And based on what she'd learned from his friends, she became suspicious about a few things. She confronted him about many things and for whatever reason, she had the impulse to ask him if he'd been seeing another woman while she was here in Canada. To her complete horror, he replied that, in fact, he had.

Frozen.

Stupid.

For a moment in time she allowed herself to feel just how stupid she was. And how stupid this marriage was. But it was only for a brief moment.

Now you'd think this would've been the perfect moment to get out of this marriage. He'd committed adultery. She was back in Canada, safe with her son. They'd only been married for seven months and it had been a terrifying experience so far. But what came next in her mind was something that she has come to understand as her social conditioning. A well-trained voice in her head telling her what she should do. The voice so loud that she couldn't hear her own wisdom speaking not only in her head, but in the rest of her body, too. She felt sick to her stomach. Weak in her knees. A heavy weight bearing down on her shoulders. Her heartbeat raced even as her world came to a spinning halt. What she thought about and did next is incredible to the woman now writing this story. The proof of her thinking in response to Dan's infidelity lives not in memory because the woman telling you this story would prefer to forget this part. And she conveniently has. Until now. The proof is in the diary Marlene wrote when a lawyer, some weeks later, wanted her to keep a record of events. Marlene actually booked flights back to Abu Dhabi thinking that *regardless of what had happened while she was apart from Dan, this marriage deserved a fair chance.*

Really?

A fair chance?

Completely duped.

Innocence, naiveté and ignorance turned stupid.

In her final session with her counsellor before departing to return to Abu Dhabi, he said: "Marlene, have you ever considered that maybe you're not the problem?"

• • •

On March 13th, 1989, Dan phoned Marlene placing conditions on her arrival in Abu Dhabi. The agreement was that if things didn't work out this time then they would work on a fair separation. She reassured Dan that she'd be willing to move out of the Garden Tower apartment, make it on her own in Abu Dhabi or move back home to Canada. They agreed that they didn't want to repeat the same mistake again because of the pain it caused for all of them. And if the marriage wasn't going to work a second time then they promised to take care of each other. Dan stated that he was not in love with anyone else even though he had been seeing other women while she was away.

Women.

On March 14th she and her son began the long trek back into the desert.

They arrived in Abu Dhabi to be met at the airport by a friend of Dan's who was instructed to take them to "Dan's apartment." It felt like the deepest betrayal to not have him there to welcome them back and take them home.

That first night, she discovered in speaking with Dan that he had not only been *seeing* other women while she was away but he had, in fact, been *sleeping* with other women.

Stupid fuck. (That's the voice of the woman telling you this story, not the voice of the young woman facing the truth of her second marriage.)

On March 30th, the day before her 27th birthday, she and Dan went out to the British Club to a UB40 concert with new friends that Dan had made while she was away. He introduced her to the woman he'd been fucking as "Clyde." Picking up on the collusion between these two, she asked Dan what Clyde's real name was. His reply was that Clyde had requested she, Marlene, not know her real name. About a week later, Marlene learned that another woman who'd been partying with them at the UB40 concert had enjoyed a night of raucous sex with her husband on New Year's Eve. Her name was Kumar.

The next few weeks had Marlene feeling on edge. How could she trust this man after all she'd learned? She watched and listened and asked more questions. And it became evident that Dan hadn't just been seeing two women during the time she was way. He'd been out frequently with different women. When she asked him to clarify just how many women he'd been going out with, he replied: "What do you want me to do, go through the yellow pages?"

She also learned that Dan had actually seen a therapist twice while she was gone. She felt more hopeful hearing this and suggested they go for marriage counselling. He agreed.

• • •

Marlene still needed to find paid work.

So she did the only thing she knew how to do. She went to the English daily newspaper, *The Gulf News*, and started looking in the classifieds. She built her resume with Dan's help. It didn't look bad. She had her newly acquired business diploma. She had some work experience that supported her desire to work in an administrative position. She found two job possibilities. One with Reuters and one with a company called Star Energy. Both offices were located in a building that was only a block away from their Garden Tower apartment.

She dropped off her resumes, one to each company.

And within the week she had two job interviews. Dan helped her prepare.

Out came her navy blue suit and freshly pressed white blouse, heels and hose. The desert heat in September was not conducive to this kind of attire but everyone she saw working in offices conformed to this western dress code. Only the Nationals, or "locals" as they were referred to, wore clothing that looked loose and cool. The men, that is. In their attractive white dishdashas and ghutra. The poor women were clad in black from head to toe. This she didn't understand but they still looked more elegant than she felt in sweat soaked nylons, lined suit jackets and skirts. At the time, it was stated the population of the United Arab Emirates was comprised of 85% expatriates from around the world and only 15% were locals, the people whose family generations originated in the Arabian Peninsula. Marlene noticed she was deeply curious about these traditional families as they held such a contrast to all the expats around them. She wanted to know more. She wanted to know them. Hearing Arabic spoken all around her had a strange affect on her. It felt like a memory she couldn't quite put her finger on. But she wouldn't be aware of this desire until much later. Right now, all she wanted was home, job and family in some kind of pattern that would feel good and true. She longed to feel safe. She wanted to belong. And for some reason, she believed this all hinged on the man she'd married a little more than seven months ago.

Both job interviews produced job offers. She could hardly believe it. Dan was obviously pleased and insisted she take the job that paid more. Fortunate for her, the job that paid more was also the job she was most intrigued by. She knew nothing of the news industry nor did she know anything of the international oil trading industry, but the latter held sway for a number of reasons. It was owned by a local. The woman who interviewed her and who would be working alongside her was an affable Texan from Houston; they immediately hit it off. Mona assured her that she'd known the owner of the company for several years and "he's a good man." Unlike the reputations of many locals, this man was known for being a happily married man ... happily married to *one* American woman. He was western educated and well-travelled. He was respectful to everyone who worked for him. And there seemed to be an air of feeling protected in his presence. Everyone knew they could ask "Boss" for help and he'd help.

Marlene was called in to meet Boss. Mona wanted her. But Mona needed Boss to want her, too. Although it became obvious that Boss depended on his executive assistant to make such decisions. And she was expected to make it look like it was he who'd made the decision.

She remembers meeting him that first time as if it'd happened only yesterday.

He was soft. Quiet. Thoughtful. It was probably to her advantage that she never felt the need to fill silence. Because there was a lot of silence in the room with them. He wasn't exactly handsome but there was something captivating about him. She felt drawn in and held. She didn't know how to be with him or what was expected of her but she noticed that she felt exceptionally calm. It might have been her unworldliness that caused her to give him her unearned trust. She wanted to work for him. But the truth was she felt ill-prepared for this executive admin position. She didn't let it show though. And she took comfort in the fact that Mona was taking her under her wing and giving her insider tips not only about the job, but also about the culture. The thing she had most going for her seemed to be the fact that she was Canadian. People weren't hesitant here about who they thought Canadians were and what they thought Canadians valued. Then they automatically grafted onto her those expectations and values. It was the first time in her life that she experienced being identified as a Canadian in such a distinct way. If you never leave your home country then you really don't know what it means to be out in the world as a citizen of that country. Or at least, she didn't. Not until now.

The meeting didn't last long. Maybe 15 minutes. And the sparkle in Mona's eye shortly afterward was enough to let her know that Boss approved. In fact, she wanted Marlene to begin that afternoon! It was a Tuesday, she remembers it clearly, May 2nd 1989. The second of May has been an interesting day throughout history: Anne Boelyn was arrested on charges of adultery, incest and treason and imprisoned in the Tower of London; Leonardo DaVinci died on this day in 1519. Looking back on her second of May, and the course her life took based on this one decision, has her wonder what the trajectory of her life might have been had she not taken the job.

So on the second of May, 1989, it was just before lunch, which would make it around 1 o'clock. The office would close for lunch and staff would be back to work at 5pm. It was what they called a split shift and it was the way this part of the world accommodated doing business with the "western" world because the time difference could be as much as twelve hours.

Boss insisted that she not start work that day; she got the sense he thought it rude that they ask her to. Mona was disappointed. Marlene would begin tomorrow morning 8 o'clock sharp.

• • •

She cannot recall why, but on July 7th they packed up their Garden Tower apartment and moved to a villa in the Bateen area. A white villa with a garden enclosed by a five-foot tall concrete wall, also white, and draped with bright pink bougainvillaea. It was dreamy beautiful so there must have been hope. There must have been a rebuilding of trust. There must have been positive possibility. She really can't recall. Because what happened in the villa overshadows any of the quieter moments that may have also lived there. Her heart breaks now to remember what she might have subjected her young son to without even realizing it.

Dan began to engage the same behaviour that had briefly shown up prior to her leaving for Canada back in December. He'd ask her to leave their bedroom and sleep with her son. He'd then proceed to take his personal papers and passport into their bedroom, bolt the door with a chair and crawl back into bed. She would lay next to her son and try to imagine what was going through Dan's head. By morning, he'd be up with them getting ready for work. The villa was big enough that they could avoid contact as they moved around with their morning chores. She'd take her son to school on her way to work; she'd bought a car from Mona, a white two-door Mazda five-speed manual with sunroof that was fun to drive; she also hired a nanny/housekeeper, Yolly, who'd worked for Mona for many years. She no longer needed to depend on Dan to get them where they needed to go and thanks to Mona, she felt completely supported in her new job with her new car and Yolly's help. She was feeling the thrill of building a life that would support all three of them. By evening, Dan would return to the villa from work and act as though nothing had happened the previous night. It was like living with two different men and at times, in the way he'd look at her, she'd get a glimpse of the turmoil inside of him. It was the part of him that she didn't understand and it frightened her.

This was their rhythm of life for about six weeks. Marlene was adapting to Dan's peculiar behaviour. She had come to the conclusion that if he had mental health issues that she hadn't seen in Canada then it was probably some kind of culture shock that was bringing them to surface now. She hoped that over time he'd feel more secure and settled. Meanwhile, she and her son were managing quite well. She felt proud of the way she'd been able to pull it all together and create a new rhythm to life. But this was a thin veneer over sinister forces that were gaining momentum in Dan.

By September, it was getting more challenging to live with him. Whenever they were out socializing with friends, everything would seem to be okay. Returning home in the evening, Yolly would need to be taken home by car or an Al Gazelle taxi called for her. Dan refused to allow Marlene to drive her. He felt it wasn't safe so late at night. And he thought it was too expensive to call an Al Gazelle taxi. So he'd take Yolly home, all sweet and nice to her, and then return to the villa full of resentment. Late one evening, he stood over their bed and raged at Marlene as she lay there stunned: "I am sick of accommodating you and your son. You are an inconvenience to me and do nothing but cost me a lot of time and money." This on a Wednesday night when she needed to get up Thursday for work in the morning and take her son to school. Dan, on the other hand, enjoyed a two-day weekend – weekends being Thursday, Friday – and he had the next day to enjoy as he pleased. She remembers being confused. How could he purposefully jeopardize her ability to do the very things that he was demanding of her? It didn't make sense.

During this time, things became more intense again. Marlene and Dan continued marriage counselling until they reached a dead-lock. The counsellor suggested that preparation for a separation begin. Dan refused to follow-up on the counsellor's guidance and support. He wouldn't honour his prior agreement with Marlene that they take care of each other. He was in fight or flight mode. He needed to protect himself. From what, was a mystery. And he needed to control Marlene in every aspect of her life.

Ironically, she was doing pretty well through all of the chaos with Dan. In addition to her job at Star Energy, she'd applied and been hired by Abu Dhabi National Television as their first English-speaking program announcer and they were training her in the news department. Even though she'd been hired along with a British woman, she was the one chosen first to broadcast live. Why a second job? Because Dan wanted her to make more money. This opportunity was exciting to her. All the years of public speaking seemed to have opened this door for her; her hard work and experience counted for something. Dan seemed pleased. He'd purchased a small tv and set it up in the living room so that Marlene's son could watch his mama on tv; he and Yolly were thrilled! There was even a half-page spread in the Arabic newspaper about the visionary changes in the television network, along with pictures of the women and stories about how they were being groomed to meet the needs of the English-speaking expat community. But this second job meant that Marlene was rarely at home and she depended fully on Yolly to manage her son and her household. It was liberating and exhausting. She watched herself become less patient with her son and he seemed to be acting out more; more anger, more misbehaving, more aggression. In fact, one day she received a call from Morag at her son's school because he'd bitten another child and his behaviour was becoming uncontrollable.

Marlene was deeply disturbed by the change in her son. She made a point to get home for lunch every day because he was also at home during that time. But stress was shifting their relationship. He'd fight for any kind of attention and she was too tired to give him what he needed most times. Dan stayed out of the way, as far as she could tell, when they were all together. But she wonders now what might have been going on at home while she wasn't there. She formed a trusted alliance with Yolly who would report to her anything distressing. Yolly protected and cared for Marlene's son as though he were her own. If Yolly left, Marlene's world would've come crashing down around her. But Yolly stayed. As though she were a guardian angel to watch over this episode in their lives.

The internal pressure to meet the demands of the life she'd created increased daily. She rarely had a day off from work. And she mostly didn't have to be in the same room with Dan. But she remembers him standing in the corner of the dining room while talking on the phone to his brother. Marlene stood next to him after having cleared the table of their dinner dishes. He inadvertently put his arm around her shoulders for a moment and she felt herself melt with affection. It'd been so long since he'd shown her any kindness or care that the contrast almost dropped her to her knees. She was hopeful that tonight might be a good night. But it wasn't. The minute he was off the phone, all hell broke loose. She can't even remember what it was about. It was just the same shit spewing out of his mouth and her concerted efforts to protect her son from Dan's raging.

It wasn't long before she began to make the connections between Dan raging and her son's aggression. One was modelling for the other. With this awareness, she felt compelled to make changes but she didn't know how. All she knew was that this little boy of hers was a reflective mirror for the life they were living. He was simply acting out what he was being exposed to in his daily life. She could understand the forces at play in her son's development. Partly because of her college education in psychology. Thinking about the courses she'd taken, she suddenly remembered one of her teachers and a dialogue the two of them had had in a college office. Marlene had gone to talk to this teacher about her confusion around the time Dan had hit her in the jaw. They spoke about how Marlene had instinctively called in her family for support, packed up his belongings, left bags of his things on the front step, and changed the locks on the door. The way she'd felt badly for taking those actions because Dan was constantly calling, dropping off gifts for her and even sitting outside her house in his car watching her. Marlene wanted to get advice from this teacher whom she admired and sensed might understand what was going on better than her family had. This teacher did not hesitate to warn her: "Don't pick up the phone. Don't let him back into your house. Be done with him. I tell you. Be done with him." How was it that despite this clear warning after the guy had fractured her jaw, he'd actually made his way back into her life shortly thereafter? Thinking about this now frightened her. How could she have made such a grave mistake? Why hadn't she taken her teacher's wise counsel?

Marlene couldn't linger long in these thoughts of the recent past. She had to deal with what was facing her now. She talked to her son's teacher, Morag, who offered unconditional support when Marlene confided in her about what was going on at home. She talked to Mona who helped to orchestrate playtimes for Marlene's son with her daughter Laura at their house; this made Yolly very happy because Yolly had practically raised Laura and she loved having the two children together. All of this resulted in Marlene and her son not getting much time at home together. It was a pace hard to keep up. But keep up they did. Because their lives depended on it.

Until it all came crashing down around them.

One November 25th Marlene walked into the Star Energy office and faced the mound of work on her desk. It was going to be a long day. She was tired. Dan had kept her up late last night and she hadn't gotten enough sleep. Her son was tired, too, and he demanded more attention from her this morning than usual. But she'd kept it all together, as she always does, and arrived to work on time and ready to meet the day.

Directly across from Marlene's desk was the office of Mr. Kapur, the company's financial manager. There were 16 staff in this office, mostly British, Indian and American. The dynamic in this work place had been an education for her. What she found hardest to reconcile was the way the Indians treated one another. In particular, the way Mr. Kapur would verbally abuse (in her opinion) the "lower status" Indians, the guys who worked as telex operators, drivers and tea boys. On this day, Mr. Kapur was ranting in his usual manner and she was finding it difficult to concentrate. What she was about to witness would change the course of her life. She couldn't look away. She couldn't pretend she didn't notice. And she certainly couldn't collude in the behaviour.

Mr. Kapur at least had the decency to close his door before he yelled for an interminable time at one of the guys. She looked up from her desk to see the rage in his face and the poor, sullen soul who was the brunt of his fit. She could feel her own body tense up. Her heart beating faster. The stone in the pit of her stomach. When the door finally opened, Mr. Kapur emerged as though nothing had happened and it was back to business as usual. A few minutes later, he requested something from her in a tone of voice that made her cringe. Without a moment's hesitation, she threw her gaze in his direction and said, "Why don't you go fuck yourself."

She might've been mistaken but she could've sworn he gasped. She then ignored his request and carried on with her own work.

A few minutes later, Mr. Kapur called her into his office. Reluctantly, she complied. He fired her on the spot. She laughed. She didn't believe for a moment that Boss or Mona would allow this almighty man to dismiss her in this manner and neither of them were in the office until later today. Mr. Kapur insisted she leave immediately. She did.

That afternoon she learned that, in fact, what was done was done. Mona explained to her how Boss would never undermine Mr. Kapur's authority or put him in a position to lose face. She was to come into the office and gather her things first thing next morning. She did. In a state of shock.

Three days later, Marlene approached Dan about how he'd feel about her attending a Higher Colleges of Technology (HCT) National Day celebration at the Cultural Centre for the female teachers and students. She'd been invited and she wanted to go. The trauma caused from losing her job had her fighting to keep her confidence intact. She felt it would be a good opportunity to be with friends and feel the support of a familiar group of people. Dan didn't want her to go. He felt *he* couldn't take the pressure of what people were going to say to *him* and he simply didn't need to deal with that now. He showed no concern for Marlene or for how she might be feeling. If she was feeling insecure then he didn't care. He physically pushed her away.

Late that night, Dan demanded that Marlene pack her bags, take her money from Star Energy and go home to Canada for Christmas. Marlene insisted that this was now her home and she wasn't going to run away to Canada again. He replied: "This is not your home. This is my home, my house, and these are my things and you are not welcome here anymore. None of this is yours." He further shouted: "You're not going to suck on the gravy train any longer!" He then demanded that she get out of his bed, sleep with her son, and once again the paranoid behaviour of gathering his personal belongings and locking himself in the bedroom until morning repeated itself.

During this time, it was a deep concern for Marlene that whenever she disciplined her son, he would in turn mimic Dan's behaviour. He would lock himself in a room by putting his little plastic chair against the door and in a very angry voice insist on being left alone.

Four days after she'd been fired, she decided to attend the HCT function. On her way out the door, the phone rang. It was Dan calling from his college office to wish her a good time. Holding the receiver next to her ear, she thought this strange behaviour on his part. He was totally disregarding the fact that he'd asked her not to go the previous night. She wondered if maybe he was purposefully talking loud enough to let any of his colleagues who might be near him overhear. Because she certainly couldn't believe at this point that he was truly sincere in his wishes.

On November 30th, Marlene suggested the two of them sit down, face to face, and discuss Dan's desire to send her back home to Canada. They both agreed that neither of them was happy. And in a moment of clarity, Marlene decided she was no longer going to resist this man. She agreed to go back to Canada. Immediately. Less than an hour later, Dan suggested that she stay in Abu Dhabi until the following June, get another full-time job to supplement her tv work, work towards paying "their" debts (they were in truth Dan's debts, the debts he came into the marriage with) and then, depending on whether or not Dan was happy by then, decide on the next plan of action in June. She agreed *again*. And she stated that her happiness should also be taken into consideration when they plan their next step.

Moving into the National Day long weekend, they decided the three of them would get away. They felt that they could afford such a luxury because Marlene was staying in Abu Dhabi and would be working again soon. They wanted the weekend to relax and reconnect. They felt a change of scenery might do the trick. So they invited their good friends Wolfgang and Mabel along with their young son Heinz. But driving to the red sands of Ras Al Khaimah turned out to be an emotionally draining excursion. The tension between them was palpable and reflected back to them through their friends and their children. The sweetest moments were when the two women and their sons could get away from the men and enjoy the wide vistas of desert and ocean. They walked. They talked. They played with their boys. They shared stories of trouble in their marriages. The coastal landscape, the edge of all things named and unnamed, expanded their friendship and by the time they left the region, Marlene felt more connected to herself and supported by her female comrade. She was renewed. Until Dan yelled at her again. This time, she yelled back which only escalated things.

On December 4th the two families returned to their villas in Abu Dhabi. That evening, Dan and Marlene sat at their dining room table with the intention to draw up a family budget for the months to come. The peace of their good intentions lasted about 15 minutes. Something set Dan off and the rants began again. Marlene calmly suggested that they'd made some progress and perhaps it was best to continue working on the budget the following evening considering it was almost 11 o'clock and they were both tired. Dan became extremely upset. "You are a selfish, self-centred woman," was his familiar refrain.

Marlene excused herself from the table and went upstairs to bed.

He met her in the hallway as she was coming out of the bathroom. Again, she was told to sleep with her son. She collected the clothes she'd need for the morning from their bedroom closet. She grabbed the wine coloured leather bound Bible with her name gold-embossed on the front. She settled into bed beside her son, trying not to disturb him. Outside the bedroom door she could hear Dan going through his ritual of locking himself away. She placed the Bible on her chest and prayed for protection and understanding. When she woke up the next morning, she was in exactly the same position with her Bible on her heart.

• • •

Dan was getting more aggressive with each passing day. Marlene repeatedly asked him to not curse her the way that he did in front of her young son. But he ignored her. And her pleas seemed to make it even worse. He swore at her loudly, and called her a stupid woman so many times that her son was beginning to do the same. And coming home one afternoon from a job interview, she noticed the glass on their living room coffee table had been smashed. Both Yolly and her son reported that "Daddy" had gotten very mad and put his fist through it.

On December 5th Marlene suggested to Dan that they continue working on the budget. He replied that he was going out to bowl with friends (he didn't invite her) and that maybe they would when he got home. The budget didn't get completed. She waited up late and when he didn't return, she went to bed with her son.

The next day, Dan informed her that he'd asked their counsellor to come and see them in their home. The counselling session was scheduled for the following evening.

On December 7th, with their counsellor present, Dan announced that he was not happy and he wanted a separation. Marlene didn't resist. She agreed to the separation and stated she would not pursue the marriage any longer. The counsellor suggested that because the two of them had to live in the same house, they not provoke each other by keeping their distance from one another. She also suggested they each put on paper what they felt would be a fair settlement. She agreed to visit them on the following Saturday and to intervene as negotiator for the both of them. Marlene expressed her concern about living in the same house with Dan because of the intensity of his emotion. He reassured her that he'd consider leaving the house, but not at this time. And with their counsellor as witness, he promised to leave Marlene alone. Because she felt she had no choice, Marlene accepted this plan. But she was afraid. Very afraid.

In the days that followed, Marlene took seriously the counsellor's advice and stayed out of Dan's way. It was difficult because he continued to badger her. She was deeply worried about her son caught in this situation with her. And she did everything in her power to keep peace.

In addition to keeping the peace, Marlene continued looking for a new job. She also wrote her version of a fair separation on paper as advised by their counsellor. She would stay in Abu Dhabi until June at which time the situation could be reassessed. She would get another job. Her son would continue in school in the hopes that the consistency would help him through the emotional upheaval and give him a better chance of recovering. She wanted Dan to move out of the villa, as he suggested he was willing to do, because it would be easier for him, as a single man, to find temporary accommodation than for her and her son to. She felt it best to allow her son to stay where he had a familiar routine in their home, with his things, and with Yolly's continuing support. She stated she'd be willing to give Dan visitation rights to her son even though Dan had said in their last counselling session that if they were to separate then he wasn't sure he'd want to see him. She asked for 3,000 dirhams a month (less than $1,000) to help cover expenses and enable her to save for a ticket home to Canada in the summer; she was expecting to find another job that would pay her a salary of at least 4,000 dirhams. And she suggested she'd be willing to continue counselling with Dan to help them all through this challenging time.

On December 9th, Marlene learned that Dan hadn't given any thought to his part of the separation agreement. She called their counsellor. The counsellor called Dan and reminded him that the three of them had made an agreement and he should follow through on his word. Later in the day, Dan and Marlene met with her to negotiate the terms of their separation. Dan's terms were simple and non-negotiable: he was sending Marlene home to Canada whether she was ready to go or not and that was his final decision. The meeting ended. They'd all meet again on Thursday, December 14th.

The next few days were hell. Marlene didn't know how she'd get through the days until their next meeting with the counsellor. Whenever she could, she'd send her son and Yolly out to be with friends to distract them from the emotional conflict rising in their home. But it got so bad that she let Mona take her son for a couple of nights. She felt such shame for not being able to provide a peaceful home for her son. Deep, deep shame.

She needed things to change.

She called their counsellor who suggested that Marlene ask Dan to meet her in a public place where they might discuss their separation and come to some kind of agreement before they were to meet with the counsellor again. So, she asked Dan to dinner at one of their favourite restaurants. He agreed to meet with her. There, she tried to negotiate but her efforts were hopeless. Dan was determined that she had no right to make any decisions on her own. Only he knew what was best for her and her son and he insisted that they return to Canada. He did hint to the fact that if she were to "ask nicely" then they might be able to stay, but it would depend on what he would be willing to give up by having her there. He glared into her eyes and stated loudly enough for others to here: "You, Marlene, are a poor excuse for a human being, a cold-hearted man in a woman's body." Publicly degraded and feeling humiliated, she got up from the table and left the restaurant.

She couldn't bear the thought of sleeping in the villa with Dan, albeit in separate beds. She feared being alone with him, especially at night. It always seemed to get worse at night. So she made arrangements to have her son stay with Mona. And she called friends that knew both she and Dan; she wanted their support and possible insight into how to move forward. After hearing what was happening, they kindly offered her a bed for the night insisting that she should stay away from her husband.

The next day, December 13th, Marlene returned to the villa to get ready for a job interview when she knew Dan had gone to work. Yolly was in the kitchen when she arrived. In the bedroom, she was getting undressed to shower when Dan walked in unannounced and demanded her car keys. At the time, they owned two cars. A blue Saab, which was paid for and in Dan's name. And a white Mazda that had a loan against it and in Marlene's name. She was driving the Saab at the time. But they each had keys to both cars.

She agreed to give Dan the second set of keys to his car in exchange for getting the second set of keys back to her car so they'd both be assured of having a car regardless of what the other was doing. Dan became furious. He disagreed. And he left the villa in a rage. A bit shaken, she mustered the determination she'd need to continue preparing for her interview. She was getting dressed again when Yolly yelled to her from downstairs: "Come quick, madam … come quick!"

The two women reached the villa gate in time to see Dan get in the Mazda and drive away, a plume of dust rising. They didn't know whether to laugh or cry. When Marlene was in the shower, Dan had driven the Saab somewhere to hide it, flagged a taxi back to the villa in time to drive the Mazda away, too.

Marlene would need to leave within 15 minutes to make her appointment on time. Both cars were gone. Making sure Yolly and her son were good to get him to school on time, she left the villa in search of one of the cars. No luck. So she flagged a taxi and was on her way to her job interview. Trying to breathe deeply to calm herself was the most she could do in the back seat of the cab. How could this be happening to her? As she gained distance from the villa she realized that she shouldn't leave Yolly and her son at home. The realization hit her like a ton of bricks. They might not be safe.

Arriving to the interview on time, she asked the front receptionist if she could use the phone before meeting with the general manager. She called Mona and then she called Yolly, instructed her to pack a few things for her son, get out of the house immediately and go to Mona's house; Mona would get them to school but she needed to call the school first and give strict directions to not allow anyone but Yolly to pick her son up at the end of the day. Dan was to have no contact with her son. All the precautions in place, she turned toward meeting the man that might hire her for a job that she really couldn't focus on now with all the chaos unfolding around her. Still, she pulled herself together and walked into the room where the general manager was sitting behind his desk waiting for her. She imagines now that everyone in that office that day must have sensed the terror in her. She remembers them being kind. She also remembers feeling like she would burst into tears at any moment.

Getting through the interview, she went straight to Mona's place. Being a fierce friend and wise woman, Mona decided they should set out to find the car. She tried to take the fear out of the situation and soon had Marlene laughing about the absurdity of it all.

So off they went in Mona's car on a mission to find the Saab. Mona had a reputation of being a wickedly smart sleuth. When Boss had needed to dig for anything, it was Mona that he turned to.

She knew how to locate everything from carpets to oil trading information. If not for her friendship, Marlene wonders what might have happened to her during this time.

Mona took Marlene down streets, alleys and hidden driveways. And within an hour they pulled up alongside the Saab cleverly hidden in a remote part of the Bateen district. The women wailed with joy, jumped out of the car and danced in the sand! Without wasting a minute, Marlene pulled out her car keys, unlocked the car and jumped into the driver's seat. Mona led her out of the maze and back to her house where they hid the car within walking distance of Mona's place.

Back in the refuge of Mona's home, the women celebrated their successful mission. But underneath the hard-won victory was a dread that spread throughout Marlene's entire body. What might be next?

• • •

Dan cancelled their next appointment with the counsellor.

Marlene decided to get on with her own plan to survive the untenable situation. She took her son to the Christmas party hosted by the Higher Colleges of Technology so she could connect with friends and somehow get back the feeling of normal (Really? What *was* she thinking?!). Upon their arrival, it was apparent that Dan was not there. However, shortly after, he appeared. And he approached the two of them. He asked Marlene if she had the Saab. She replied that she did. Then he presented her with the itinerary of the flights and hotels that he'd booked; she and her son would be departing Abu Dhabi on December 21st, only seven days from now. Marlene stated that she chose not to return to Canada at this time because it would be making the same mistake all over again. She refused to take the itinerary. Keenly aware of the people around him, Dan toned it down and left the party without saying goodbye to her son who had been listening to the entire conversation. Moments after Dan left, her son asked; "Mama, why did Daddy come to the party?" He was confused. And so was she. But she did her best to reassure him and together they turned toward their friends and the party.

One of her friends was a social worker from Calgary, Alberta. Diana had come to the UAE with her husband Ron and his son. In her wisdom, Diana had sensed something going on and had asked Marlene about it. She started to confide in her. That night, Diana suggested she and Ron take the Saab in exchange for letting Marlene take their car because both women feared that Dan would take the car away again. Marlene agreed. And she continued to try and normalize the situation for her young son who was increasingly anxious about what was happening around him.

On December 16th, Dan agreed to meet with Diana and Marlene in the villa. Diana insisted that Marlene not be alone with Dan and she extended herself as a mutual friend in an attempt to defuse Dan's tendency to rage. The women were on a mission to get a separation agreement that would allow both Dan and Marlene to move forward. The meeting turned out to be just more irrational nonsense with Dan insisting he was sending Marlene home to Canada. "If you go to Canada," he said, "I'll send you 3,000 dirhams a month for one year. If you stay here in Abu Dhabi, I'll cut you off—no house, no money, no car. I don't care what it takes to get you out of this country. I'll lose my job if I have to. I'll just cancel your sponsorship and you'll be out."

Marlene got up from her chair across the table from Dan, taking with her a piece of paper that Dan had referred to as their agreement; it was the agreement they'd made over the phone before she'd returned to Abu Dhabi. She ripped the paper in half. Dan sprang to his feet and grabbed her. Diana intervened, forcing Dan to let go of Marlene and telling Marlene to go upstairs and pack a few personal things because she'd be coming home with her.

Dan helped the women carry Marlene's luggage out to the car.

• • •

She tries desperately to keep her head clear through all of the turmoil and upset. She knows that she must for her son's life depends on it. Hers, too. They are staying with Diana and Ron. Marlene has a single bed. Her son sleeps on the floor next to her. They feel safe and protected by their friends. But strangely removed from what they have come to know to be their life. Her parents have called from Saskatchewan. They are extremely worried. They say this is a repeat of what happened last year. Dan calls them. Tells them he is sending their daughter and grandson home. They are hopeful. This is what they want. (It isn't until much later that she learns Dan has told her parents that she is running a "prostitution" ring in Abu Dhabi.) But Marlene insists that she needs to resolve this before returning to Canada. She is not about to walk away from what she was building; she has a right to recover something from this marriage so she can start over yet again for herself and her son. She reassures her mom and dad. She tells them Diana and Ron are good friends and they'll help her work through this situation. But she knows her parents are disturbed by the things Dan tells them. He makes Marlene out to be irrational and difficult. So her mom and dad are left wondering if she is, in fact, losing her way. They feel helpless. Their daughter has suffered enough. They just want her home where they can see to it that she'll be okay.

But Marlene will stay in Abu Dhabi. She is sick with worry, too, but she thinks this is the way to come back to herself. She cannot make sense of the power games that Dan seems to want to play with her. She needs to understand how this is happening. And she needs her reputation back — the reputation she has of being kind, capable and loving.

What she doesn't know is that it's about to get worse than anything she could imagine. Much worse. Fast forward many years later and she is left wondering why she couldn't sense the danger she was opening herself to.

• • •

It is Christmas even though they are living in a Muslim country. The expats pull together for parties and support each other knowing how hard it is for all of them to be away from family back in Canada. Marlene tries hard to catch the spirit. For her son's sake more than her own. She knows she cannot get through this alone. So she reaches out to friends who are quickly becoming her family.

On December 23rd, Dan called Marlene and insisted they meet in their villa right away. She was hesitant. He was persistent and urgent. She allowed herself to be coaxed into the situation. Some part of her felt she owed their marriage this meeting.

Of course, it would turn out to be a mistake.

As soon as she entered the house, Dan was physically touching her, telling her that he loved her, insisting that she come home to him. She pulled away. She tried to keep distance between them. She wanted to talk. But Dan wasn't interested in talking. She made sure the front door remained open in case she needed to get away quickly. Twice, Dan tried to close the door. She felt extremely uncomfortable with this absurd dance she was enticed into with her husband. Nausea crept in. She felt sick to her stomach.

One hour. She put up with this dance for a full hour. And then her better self took hold and she walked out the front door. This would be nothing but trouble. Dan followed her out the front gate and to her car. He begged her to come back in. She continued to explain to him that they needed to live apart for awhile, needed to have a living arrangement of some sort to give them each time to work some things out. He ignored her. He pleaded for her to come home immediately. She drove away when she finally accepted the fact that he wasn't the least bit interested in what she was saying.

Later on in the day, Dan appeared at their neighbour's house where Marlene was having coffee. Obviously, he was following her. He apologized for what he had done and begged for her to move back home for Christmas. She sensed he felt he was losing control of the situation and would do anything to regain that control. He told her that the woman he'd been seeing before Marlene had returned to Abu Dhabi was calling him again. He pointed out the fact that he could have this woman and if Marlene didn't return home then she was forcing him into the other woman's arms.

She resisted his ploy. And with her friend's help, convinced him to leave.

Back at Diana and Ron's house, Dan dropped off an envelope for Marlene. The envelope continued 1,000 dirhams and a list of names that he wanted her to buy Christmas gifts for.

The next day, Christmas Eve, Dan dropped off Christmas presents for Marlene and her son while they were out.

Christmas day was shared with Diana, Ron and their son. Late in the morning, the phone rang. It was Dan. In a sarcastic voice.

"How is your Christmas, Marlene? Hope you are having a good time, Marlene. You are so self-centred and selfish Marlene that you think of no one but yourself, Marlene."

The angry conversation with Dan continued. He insisted on coming over to see her son. She insisted that he was welcome to come over but not in his current frame of mind. That he'd need to put his anger aside because the last thing her son needed was Dan transferring all of his ill feeling onto him on a day that should be peaceful. She told him to cool off and call back in an hour. Dan was bitter. He hung up the phone. And never called back.

The next day was a reprieve. No phone calls. No harassment.

The next few days had Dan calling sporadically to badger her. She continued to ask for a separation agreement, but he simply ignored her and her request. She begged for understanding. Didn't he realize that she had no home, no money and that she lived in fear that he would take her car from her? His only response was to insist that if she moved back into the villa with him then she'd "have it all."

It was insane to believe that if she remained in Abu Dhabi living separately from Dan that he'd give her no support, but if she were to move back to the villa into the disastrous situation, she'd "have everything." This was Dan's logic. So why did she feel like *she* was the one losing her mind?

She'd remind him that he was the one who asked for the separation and she was only complying with his wishes. That they could not go back to living in the same situation without changing something otherwise they'd be right back where they started from. She insisted that she and her son needed stability in their lives. If they were causing him so much unhappiness then why on earth would he want to have them back in the villa? She begged for a separation agreement, a living arrangement that would allow some emotional mending. Then they'd be in a position to get back to counselling and better understand what forces were at play to bring them to this impasse in the first place. She never wanted this repeated in her life again. But Dan simply turned a deaf ear.

• • •

Early on the morning of December 28th, Dan came banging on the door of Diana and Ron's home unannounced. Everyone was still in bed. But Dan wasn't concerned with that. He demanded to know if Marlene had done something in the last week that he should know about. She answered no. And she had nothing to prepare her for what was to come next.

He accused her of sleeping with another man.

It was a ridiculous thought.

He then informed her that the registration on the Saab was overdue and asked her to renew it. But she knew that he would need to do it because the car was registered in his name. So she suggested that they exchange cars. He agreed. She asked him to give her his keys to her car and she would give him the keys she had to his car so they'd have autonomy over their own vehicles. He reassured her that it wasn't necessary, he would not take the car away from her. She didn't believe him, but she didn't say that out loud. She let it go, happy to have her Mazda back to drive.

The harassing phone calls and games continued. She was driving her own car now, not Diana and Ron's, because she'd figured out how to disconnect the starter every time she parked the car.

Dan stopped asking about her son. And never not once offered her any money even though he knew she had none.

The next day, Dan called to ask if he could drop off a letter he was writing for Marlene. He'd come by the house between 2-3:00 p.m. She said okay. And asked if he could bring her academic certificates over at the same time because she had a job interview Saturday morning and she required copies of them. He said he would.

He called at 3 o'clock saying he would be another hour.

She said she might not be around then. Her son was cranky from being in the house all day. She'd purposely rearranged her day based on Dan's plans. Now she knew she needed to take her son out for some exercise and playtime. Dan was angry. He hung up.

While she was out with her son, Dan had, in fact, been to the house because he spoke with Diana. But he refused to leave the letter and he hadn't brought Marlene's certificates. Diana also noticed that he had a woman waiting in his car.

Marlene wanted to stay as far away from Dan as possible. She went to her job interview without her certificates. It wasn't enough that this man she'd married was terrorizing her home. He was now interfering with her job search and any chances she had of rebuilding her work life. Had she signed a contract with the devil? What kind of a marriage was this?

• • •

Marlene managed to stay out of Dan's way until January 6th when she received a phone call from him at 7:30 in the evening. He wanted to exchange cars with her again as he was driving to Dubai in the morning and felt it better if he took the Mazda. She said that'd be fine. He'd be over to pick it up in a few minutes.

Dan arrived at Ron and Diana's door when expected. Marlene immediately noticed that he didn't look well. He seemed to be in a hurry. She asked him in as Diana and Ron were at home, but he declined saying he'd forgotten a letter which had come in the mail for her from Canada. He'd run over to his office at the College to get it and bring it back to her if she would still be around in twenty minutes. Yes, she would. She wasn't going anywhere. Before he left, Marlene asked if he'd renewed the registration on the Saab and Dan replied that he had. The booklet was in the car. And off he went in a hurry.

After he was gone, Ron, Diana and Marlene went out to the Saab as they suspected something was wrong. They checked the registration. It had, in fact, not been renewed. Dan had lied. Then it became clear to all three of them that Dan was up to his antics again. He'd come to take the Mazda, hide it, and return in a taxi … but to do what? Leave Marlene with a car that she couldn't drive?

Before Dan's return, Ron and Diana left in hopes of finding Marlene's car for her.

Dan came back to the house. Marlene invited him inside. They sat in the living room and tried talking. He appeared extremely nervous. She asked him about the letter he went to get for her. He replied that he'd left it in the car. He asked when Ron and Diana would be back. He wanted to speak to Ron. It was important. She answered, "Any time now." Meanwhile, Ron and Diana were back at Dan and Marlene's villa where they discovered that all the locks had been changed.

The minute Ron and Diana returned, Marlene asked Dan again about renewing the Saab insurance. And again he reassured her that he had. She revealed to him that she knew he was lying and asked him why. He wondered how she knew. She explained that it was as simple as having checked the registration booklet that was in the car. He made no attempt to cover up what was so obviously another lying game.

The energy in the room darkened.

Dan presented first to Ron and Diana, then to Marlene, an order to appear in Shariah court on the morning of January 8th. In a state of fury, he said: "You will cry bitter tears, woman, for you have thrown away a good love!" Turned away. Walked out the front door.

The three of them stood in stunned silence.

• • •

Marlene spent the next day calling embassies, friends and lawyers to learn what rights she had and get a sense about what she was coming up against. Late into the day, and feeling deeply frustrated, she finally got through to a Mr. Hussein Samahoni who kindly advised her to do the following: seek an adjournment from the court on the grounds that she needed time to execute a power of attorney for her lawyer who would be representing her in court; and request a copy of the statement of claim because Dan had not given her one.

She was momentarily relieved. But extremely anxious about the mess Dan had gotten her into.

He called.

He wanted to meet.

So she invited him to meet her at Ron and Diana's, making sure that Diana knew Dan was coming over (Ron was at work).

She pleaded with him that this was a crazy thing to do, go to a Shariah court. She feared for both of their lives.

He laughed.

And he gave her an ultimatum: move back into the villa immediately or be in court tomorrow morning.

She braced herself for court.

. . .

The next morning, January 8th, 1990, Dan appeared at Ron and Diana's front door, again unannounced. This time to beg for forgiveness. It was 7:30 a.m. He wanted to see if he could cancel the court hearing. When asked why, he said that he'd been told by a legal translator that he better be careful in the wording of his statement as he could cause Marlene to be jailed. He assured her that he didn't want her to go to prison. And he presented the idea as if he were giving her a gift.

She was sickened by the sight of him. She wanted nothing to do with him. She wanted out of this mess he was creating. She wanted to rewind her life back to the day when she met him and replay the whole event so that they simply passed one another in the hall. No connection. No conversation. No colluding. Prevent this twisted fate from playing itself out. This was not her destiny, she was sure of it. But how was she gonna extricate herself from the web he was weaving?

At this point in the game, she had to show up in court. Or the trouble would get bigger. They agreed to meet there.

Entering the Shariah Court was like having yet another veil of horror revealed to her. There were clerics at tables with mounds of paper handwriting reports and providing judgments and signatures as individuals stood or sat before them telling their stories. Tea boys rushed in and out providing for the clerics. Halls lined with people waiting their turn. Lots of shuffling. Muffled voices. It was a mysterious labyrinth populated by locals. She was acutely aware of her white skin and blonde hair. Quizzical looks aimed in her direction. What was *she* doing here? Every woman was accompanied by at least one man and here she was alone. She must have seemed unprotected to those staring at her. Or maybe worse. Probably worse.

Dan appeared in the hall.

They didn't speak. She was trembling with fear. Afraid like never before. Keenly aware of losing power over her own life.

Dan seemed to know his way around. He approached a clerk of the court in one of the rooms off the hall. She stood in the doorway. She could overhear Dan saying that his wife had moved back in with him and everything was back to normal. The men shook hands. Dan met with her in the hall.

"Have you told the clerk I've moved back in with you?"

"I don't recall using those words," he said.

She was called into the room with the court clerk. And it was made clear to her that she must not enter without her husband. Dan joined her. They approached the desk with the man sitting behind it. Once in the room, she could see there were a few men present along the walls. And they were all wishing Dan "Mabrouk, mabrouk" which translates to "congratulations!" The clerk reassured her that the court hearing was cancelled. "Mabrouk, madam, mabrouk." Terror struck her inside. Was she lying to this court? Wouldn't that be an offence? Did it matter? She was silent as she signed the court summons that had "reconciliation" written on it. She was lying. And she knew her life depended on it.

Outside the courthouse, Dan pathetically begged forgiveness and claimed he loved her very much. She wanted to vomit. But she kept herself calm and clear enough to ask him for money considering the fact that she had none. To her surprise, he handed her a 500 dirham bill.

She thanked him.

She walked away.

She found her car and drove out of the parking lot. She knew with every fibre of her being that she needed to get out of this marriage. She could see that Dan was a tormented man and his emotional instability had nothing to do with her and her son. She was prepared to walk away with nothing because that's exactly what she had now. Nothing. And if she had to start from scratch *again* to provide a home and a decent life for her son then that's what she'd do. What she wouldn't do is subject her son or herself to this fucking crazy man anymore. She was done. Done. Done. Done.

• • •

The games continued on the very next day.

She learned to take the phone off the hook at night so nobody in the house would be awakened before they were ready to get up in the morning. On this day the phone rang almost immediately after she replaced the handset in the cradle. Of course it was Dan. And he wanted her to see a priest from one of the churches. Now he was appealing to her sense of religion and godliness. Would she please speak with Father Mathew and then meet with Dan after doing so? She agreed. But then he decided she needed to meet with him, Dan, that night, and when she said that she wouldn't because she'd be seeing Father Mathew first, Dan got angry and hung up.

Two days later Dan showed up at the door at 2 o'clock. He handed her an envelope. On the front he had written: *Marlene Altea (please open now)*.

He said, "Please take some time now and read this and later make some special time for us. Maybe I can come to The Club later and we can take a walk on the beach." He knew that the Higher Colleges of Technology were throwing a party at the British club and he knew she had purchased a ticket to attend.

"What for?" she asked.

"I can only try so much."

"Maybe I don't want to try anymore."

"Fine. You always think of yourself. You are a self-centred person. You don't think of me being at the party, what people will think as we sit on opposite sides of the room. No. Not you. Only think of yourself." He grabbed the envelope from her hand. "Forget it!" he yelled. And proceeded to rip the letter into shreds and storm out of the house.

She closed the door.

She was no longer unsettled by his craziness. She attended the party. And noted that Dan was not there.

On January 13th, Marlene called the Canadian Embassy in Kuwait as there was no embassy for Canadians yet in the UAE. She spoke with Louise. She explained her situation. Louise said someone who could advise Marlene would be calling her back.

A little later in the day, while she was out, Ronald Waugh called from the Canadian Embassy and spoke with Diana. He advised that Marlene should speak with a Canadian lawyer; that if things continued to escalate and she was forced to jail he would send someone to step in and try to help; he suggested that if her permanent address was the UAE that she could, in fact, get a divorce there and that Canada would likely honour it. Hearing this counsel, Marlene felt somewhat relieved by the fact that she'd be able to notify somebody about what was happening to her. But she took little comfort in facing what might lay ahead for her. There'd be no easy way out of all this.

It'd been so damned easy to marry the man.

What a mistake!

At 9 the next morning the phone rang. It was Dan. He wanted to see her. She said she was busy and it wouldn't be possible. At 12:30 that afternoon he called again. Would she please see Reverend Wood with him? According to the reverend they didn't need clinical help. What they needed was to talk to someone about the love and hope in their marriage. After relaying this less than helpful insight from a man she'd never even met, Dan hung up abruptly. His secretary called her back a few minutes later to say that Dan had been called into a meeting and he'd be calling her again in one hour.

At 2 o'clock Dan called again asking to see her. "I've been trying to see you for two weeks."

"About what?" she asked.

"About finances you need."

"Dan, this is the first time you've called about money and you know it. Does this mean you'll give me a separation agreement?"

"Don't you understand that I love you?"

"No. Dan, don't you see the priorities you've forced on me? I have nothing. No home. No money. You've taken it all. You don't care at all. That much is obvious to me now."

"What is it that you want? Do you think this is the end?"

"I think we need to stop. And that means talking to end it all. I am busy this afternoon but let me call you tonight. What's a good time?"

"Well, I'll have to come home for your call."

"I don't want to make you do that so you tell me what's a good time."

"Look, I've been invited out to dinner."

"Okay, shall I call at 9 o'clock?"

"I'll have to come home."

"Dan, I don't want you to come home for my call. Please tell me when to call you."

"I want to see you. Can I see you tonight?"

"Let me tell you when I call. I'll have to see how my day goes. I will call you at 10 o'clock."

"Never mind," he said angrily. "You're playing games with me, girl. You're playing games with a full grown man!"

She knew what was coming next so she hung up.

But 15 minutes later he called back. She picked up the receiver to hear him say: "Marlene, I won't be home at 10 o'clock. When you want to see me, I'll put you off as long as I can and when you're really desperate, I'll see you at my convenience! Goodbye Marlene."

On January 15th, Marlene met with Hussein Samahoni, who turned out to be a lawyer in Abu Dhabi for more than twenty years, ten of those years sitting as a Judge in the Labour Court. Mr. Samahoni advised her that Dan had called him as well but after they'd spoken for a few moments, Samahoni realized who Dan was and immediately informed Dan that he couldn't speak further as he had, in fact, given counsel to Marlene. Before ending their conversation, the two men agreed that Samahoni would inform Marlene of their dialogue, ask her to consider reconciliation and call Dan back. But as soon as the lawyer heard her side of the story he realized that the couple were beyond reconciliation. And he advised Marlene to change her sponsorship as soon as possible as Dan was using the fact that he'd sponsored her into the country to threaten her with the power he had to send her back to Canada. Mr Samahoni suggested Marlene continue to live with her friends or find her own place so that if Dan tried again to take her to jail on the grounds of desertion, he'd not get away with it. After speaking with Marlene, Samahoni said he'd be calling Dan to advise that he settle with her outside of the court system and not get involved with lawyers. He reassured Marlene that if she ever needed his assistance with anything, she was to call him.

It was an unlikely coincidence that Marlene and Dan had contacted the same lawyer. Marlene's former boss' right hand man,

Ibrahim, had put her in touch with Hussein Samahoni. Dan had been referred by the Undersecretary of the Ministry of Labour, Mr. Al Oteiba. It caused her to wonder just what forces were at play in her life.

Many weeks later she would come to realize the extent to which Mona, her former boss and Ibrahim had been orchestrating to help her. It was as though a silent web of support was weaving itself into a net to catch her if she fell.

And she did fall. But not into what she thought might be waiting for her. It turned out much worse and much better than she could ever have dreamed up herself. How many years would it take for her to learn precisely how she'd set these wheels in motion?

On January 15th at 7 o'clock in the evening, Marlene met with Mr. Sabah Mahoud for the second time; a meeting arranged by Ibrahim with a lawyer who could represent her in court. Mr. Mahoud advised her to go to the Higher Colleges of Technology and let them know that she wanted an amicable divorce from Daniel Altea. He was hoping that the college would take an interest in the case and put some pressure on Dan to agree to the divorce.

The next day, Marlene called Bruce Hill, the Abu Dhabi Women's College director, Dan's boss. She informed him of her personal problem, asked for his confidence and a time to meet with him. He wanted to know more. So she told him that she wanted an amicable divorce. He gave her his regrets and reassured her that the call never happened. He suggested she continue to try and talk with Dan. But if she was unsuccessful then the college would get involved to help, all she needed to do was call and inform him.

Feeling relieved by the offer of support, Marlene called Mr. Mahmoud to update him. He advised her to keep a record of events, put everything on paper. He wanted her to arrange a meeting with Dan on Saturday evening, with witnesses present, and ask for an amicable divorce. He also told her to not expect Dan to agree. And to be prepared to go to court Sunday morning. "The worst thing the court can do," he said, "is document that you must move back into your husband's house."

Two days later, Marlene received a phone call from Ibrahim Durbas, a friend of Dan's. Mr. Durbas claimed that he'd met with

Dan, heard his story, and wanted to help. He said that he'd told Dan he wasn't interested in the details of the story, as Dan would recount it, and would rather have both Dan and Marlene meet with both him and his wife, Amne, in their home. He said that he believed Dan loved her and regretted all that he'd done to cause her to leave. Marlene was careful in her response. She didn't know this man and she was a bit alarmed by his involvement. She responded saying she'd call back Saturday evening being careful to not tell Ibrahim Durbas of her decision to file for divorce.

Later that night, Dan called pleading that it was "critically important that I see you now, only for fifteen minutes." He claimed there'd been an event three or four months ago that may be the reason for what was happening to them and "something else that may have had an affect."

She was silent. What on earth was he going on about now?

"I love you," he said. "Please for us make one extra effort. I'm supposed to be seeing friends tonight but I'll change my plans for you. Don't take anyone else's advice. Do this for us. My heart is breaking and I don't know how much more I can take."

Again, she said nothing.

"Use your sympathy and understanding," he pleaded.

She started to speak, but he was quick to interrupt her.

"Never mind, I ask too much. I make myself too vulnerable. I just want to talk to my wife, the woman that I love. I shouldn't have called."

Her measure of patience with this man never ceased to amaze her. It was as though she could see his soul, which was beautiful, but his personality was all fucked up and kept diverting her attention. Yet she persisted. Why? Why? Why? She sincerely wanted to know why and her tenacity would be the death of her unless she woke up and dealt with the truth of her situation. But here she was yet again reassuring him that it was okay to call. And she asked him to call again tomorrow so they could arrange a time and a place to talk.

He showed up on her doorstep in the early morning hours of the next day, January 19th. He insisted they talk. And he wanted her to come home immediately.

He also had a plan.

He wanted them to go to England within the next four days to visit Peter and Jules, his brother and sister-in-law. He would sleep at his niece Laura's house so that Marlene and her son could be alone at his brother's house. Upon returning from England, if they'd decided that they couldn't live together again (well, d-uh) then he'd give her the villa to live in as well as a separation agreement. He insisted there were two things that Marlene should know about, things she should seriously consider when thinking about how things had unfolded: 1) Ibrahim Durbas confronted Dan yesterday and claimed he feels Dan has been seeing another woman since Marlene returned from Abu Dhabi but Dan assured Marlene that that simply isn't true; 2) and Cathy Martin, their counsellor, suggested to Dan three months ago that he should take Clyde up on her proposition, that maybe that's exactly what Dan needs right now. Dan pointed out that these two points explain his hesitation to continue seeing Cathy as a counsellor.

In her mind, at this time, she just knew something was misfiring in Dan's reasoning capacity. None of this made any sense to her at all.

Dan then promised Marlene that if she'd come home today he'd give her, in writing, certain things to provide her with a sense of security in their marriage. There would be a monthly amount of money deposited to her personal bank account so if anything like this happened again, she'd know she wasn't completely dependent on him for funds. He would also sell the Mazda, keep the Saab and have it transferred into Marlene's name. He mentioned that he was glad she never saw the Catholic priest. As it turned out, Father Mathew gave Dan the cold shoulder when he discovered that Dan was a divorced and remarried Catholic. Dan said the priest was "hung up" on that fact and therefore couldn't really help us.

Then he professed his love for her again, and again. He apologized for the mistakes he made. And stated how terribly lonely he was. By this time, her young son had come to the door and stood by her, hanging onto her leg, listening. Dan reached down to say a prayer with the little boy. But her son wasn't interested. Dan pleaded with God that they forgive him for what he'd done. That they understand how much Daddy misses them and that he wants God to bring them all back together as a family.

Before leaving, Dan handed her a package to read and asked her to call him later in the evening.

But he didn't wait for her call. Instead, the phone rang around 9 o'clock and it was Dan. He insisted on seeing her. Marlene said she simply wasn't up for it. She invited him over the following night for a talk with Diana and Ron present. He agreed.

So, on January 20th Marlene confronted Dan with Ron and Diana present. She asked for an amicable divorce. And of course, he wouldn't hear of it. He pleaded for their marriage. He talked them into circles until they were all exhausted. But they didn't give in to his pleas. And finally, he did verbally agree to give Marlene a divorce. Marlene stated what she wanted. He showed disbelief at how little she was asking for. Wanting to leave the dialogue while things were good, she excused herself and went to bed. Ron and Diana stayed with Dan, trying to keep the situation neutralized. They all agreed that they'd meet tomorrow evening to talk terms of the divorce.

The next day, Marlene called her lawyer to give him an update. He suggested to her that she not provoke Dan in any way and get the agreement in writing. He much preferred that they agree to divorce than having her file to the court alone. He felt there was a bit of a risk by waiting, but wanted her to be patient, give Dan one day and work on the settlement in the evening as planned.

Dan and Marlene met as planned, Diana and Ron were also present. The agreement was drawn up. Although Dan was saying he would give her the divorce, in his next breath he was going to prove to her that their marriage could work. He was obviously still trying to manipulate her, but she wasn't playing his game any longer. They would meet with her lawyer in the morning and go to court together.

Early the next morning, the phone rang again. It was Dan. He wanted another day to do a cash flow report as he wanted to give her a lump sum payment up front and then monthly payments until June. Marlene agreed that they could wait one more day; they would go to court the next morning. She would call in the evening to check in with him and see how he made out with the report.

That night, she called. Several times. Dan didn't pick up. She went ahead and made the arrangements with her lawyer to meet at Shariah court the next morning at 9:30 to proceed with the amicable divorce. Mr. Mahmoud advised that the court procedure would be very simple. They'd appear before the court. Fill out specific forms. And have the judge sanction the divorce. If the judge decided to refer them to a marriage counsellor then Mr. Mahmoud would try to bypass that decision by informing the judge that that route had already been taken, unsuccessfully. He wanted her to take her passport to the court as well as the Arabic translation of her marriage certificate, which she didn't have but could only hope Dan would bring with him. *If* he showed up. (He refused to give her a copy of their marriage certificate.) She would also need to bring the separation agreement even though Mr. Mahmoud thought it was unlikely that the court would require it.

The phone rang at 1:30 a.m.

It was Dan. She could hardly hear his voice for all the noise in the background.

"I love you. Our marriage can be good. I won't be seeing you at the court in the morning. I need a week to think about this. It's too much too fast. I'll give you some money this week. But right now, I have to go. Goodbye."

She was able to get back to sleep by not allowing herself to think about what Dan might be up to. But the moment she opened her eyes in the morning light, she knew.

She just knew.

He'd left the country.

At 3:25 that afternoon, Dan called and left a message with Diana to tell Marlene to be waiting for his call at 9 o'clock that evening. Diana thought it sounded long distance.

At 9:45 that night, Dan did call and he confirmed he was in England. He wanted Marlene and her son to join him there. He had booked flights for them on Turkish Airlines leaving in 24 hours. He instructed her to follow up on the details with his travel agent and banker.

Was there no end to this man's impulsive tactics?

She assured him that she would not be joining him in England. She said she was happy he was with family and told him he should just enjoy having the time away from work and from Abu Dhabi.

This only inflamed him. He was seriously pissed off. And she was getting clearer everyday about the fact that Dan was beyond her scope of understanding. She just wanted her life back. And she felt relieved that he was out of the country. Maybe she could find some breathing room now. Settle back into her own wisdom so she could figure out what best to do next rather than being in a constant state of high alert.

He gave her Jules and Peter's phone number in case she should change her mind.

Not a chance, crazy man!

He called again on January 24th, this time handing the phone to his sister-in-law. Jules wanted Marlene to know that they'd like her to visit any time, that she was welcome. She said she understood what it was Marlene was going through and that Marlene shouldn't forget that Jules was married to an "Altea boy, too."

Marlene decided to be bold with Jules. She asked her direct questions about Dan. She wanted to know why nobody in the family had spoken to her about Dan's "problems" prior to her marrying the man. Why hadn't anyone been transparent with her about the insider knowledge they obviously had about this man she now called husband? Jules spoke for a long time about Dan's "situation." She reassured Marlene that she wasn't losing her mind and that if she, Jules, were in the same position she'd respond exactly the same way Marlene was. Jules advised Marlene to "stand firm" and know that Dan does love her and her son, but "he just has a lot of problems and it is up to him to decide if he wants to go on living like this or he wants to change a few things."

Love? He loves us? Really? This family has a twisted definition of love!

Jules concluded her conversation by saying: "If you need to get away, home to England is closer than home to Canada and you are welcome any time."

Marlene had mixed feelings. It was good for her to connect with Jules and feel that this woman saw her and understood the mess she was in. But it was also disturbing to realize she'd married into systemic problems that existed long before she showed up. How could she have gotten herself into this predicament? How did she take such a wrong turn?

Two days later, Dan's sister Miranda called. "You are doing the right thing," she said. "Marshall and I understand that Dan has got a lot of problems, we hear them on the phone when he calls us."

Miranda went on to say they were very concerned and more than worried about Dan and his "extreme behaviour, irrationality and distorted perception."

"Keep a clear head, Marlene," she said. "Do what is best for you and your son because Dan is not capable of seeing any sense of reality in his present state."

Jesus. Where were these women before we got married? Why didn't they take me aside and talk to me then as they are talking to me now? What exactly were they hoping for from me?

That night, in her journal, Marlene wrote: *I understand now that Dan must walk this road alone and only he can decide if he even wants to walk it at all. Therefore, I must do what is best for all three of us — keep my sanity, my son's sanity and allow Dan room to choose what he wants to do with his life. It is my responsibility to stand tall through this and not let myself or my son become all consumed by the emotional turmoil, as Dan has let it consume his life and it is controlling him. God give me strength to do what I must do and guide me along the path I must walk.*

She was strengthened from talking with Jules and Miranda. These women brought her relief. And relief was allowing her confidence to rise once again. She knew what she must do. And she still trusted life to show her how it was going to play out. Which is, in hindsight, a fucking miracle.

• • •

In high school my favourite classes were English and Composition. I could hardly wait to arrive in grade 11 because that was the first year of taking these courses. But it wasn't just the anticipation of the course content. It was the excitement of being in Archie Eichorn's classes. He was unlike any man I'd ever known. Funny, soft, generously spirited, dramatic and creative. All the cowboy guys I hung around with thought Mr. Eichorn was "fruity." I didn't know exactly what they were referring to but I knew it wasn't a compliment. He was the second teacher to acknowledge that I was not only a skilled writer – the first was Mrs. Hester in grade 9 – but I was also a thinker who engaged my deepest thinking while I was writing. The comments Mr. Eichorn wrote on my essays left me feeling I had something of value to develop. It excited me. And inspired me. In the context of high school classroom boredom, this was a big deal. In grade ten, I'd been introduced to Shakespeare by Mr. Coulter, another English teacher. Mr. Coulter's idea of teaching Shakespeare was to have us listen to him pace back and forth at the head of the classroom while he droned on for fifty minutes reading directly from the text every class period until he completed an entire play. He never raised his voice nor varied his intonation. It was monotonous and put most of us to sleep. Dreadful! Mr. Eichorn, on the other hand, made Shakespeare come alive by illuminating nuggets of wisdom found in the text and teaching us to self-reflect on the ideas and how they might apply to our own lives and our dreams. It was challenging and invigorating! Shakespeare became imminently useful.

Archie Eichorn also helped me find voice as an actor, giving me the courage I needed to be on stage for our school's drama production that year. I wasn't any good, but the voice I discovered also showed up in my essays as I learned I had something to say and I knew how I wanted to say it. The following year, in grade 12, he was the guiding force as I wrote and spoke the valedictory speech.

Mr. Eichorn was known for his other-worldly skills, too. He could read palms and intuit the future. He did it as fun, but we, his students, all sensed there was something running deep and profound in our beloved teacher. When he spoke, some of us really listened as we expected some great hidden secrets to be revealed. This was how he introduced me to the impending drama of my lived experience — the way life would teach me how it was going to play out.

One day during lunch break, a few of us girls convinced Mr. Eichorn to read our palms. We were all intensely curious. We gathered around him as he indulged our pleas. It started out as playful amusement. I hung back a bit and listened while he read the fortunes of my friends. Finally, he asked if I wanted to let him see my palms. I did. And I offered up my hands. He tuned in. He could see that I'd have a long life. Two children. Maybe three. No, most likely two. He talked about things I don't remember now. What I do recall though is how the energy shifted in the room from promising to fateful.

"You'll have a marriage proposal. Yes. The love of your life. You haven't met him yet. You'll meet him soon. If you don't marry him this time, you'll get another chance later on. Another proposal. Some hardship, yes. It's not easy. There's travel. Far away. You will marry. What you don't sort out the first time, you'll get right the third time," he said.

Then I got the sense that he saw something ... something that caused him to get serious and withdraw a bit. Up until this moment, it'd all been good fun. But it wasn't fun anymore and I could see that he was making a decision about how much to tell me. And I was making a decision to not press him because I wasn't sure I wanted to know what he could see etched in the palm of my hand.

While holding my right hand in his left hand, he put the palm of his right hand in the palm of mine. He looked me straight in the eye and a depthy silence passed between us. It felt like reassurance and acknowledgement. You'll be okay, his presence told me, and I'll not tell you more.

Even though there were other girls who wanted their palms read, Mr. Eichorn waved them away as he breezed out of the room.

My friends seemed oblivious to the communication that had just happened in the room. They didn't tune into the same place that Mr. Eichorn and I had. They were somehow outside of this experience that left me with a sense of foreboding. I knew it had also shaken my beloved teacher. He was completely transparent to me. Whatever it was that he'd glimpsed about my life path, it was cause enough for him to want to wave away the other requests from my friends and quickly leave the room. He made it look breezy but he wasn't feeling breezy at all. I could see that. And he knew it. Some change in the weather had taken the air out of his carefree sails. There was a storm on the horizon. And that storm was going to be my life experience.

Fate would have its way with me as the thread of destiny seeded in my soul would call me forward to the tempest.

I'd always thought I was special. That I would live into some great destiny. The greatness having to do with something in me that I had yet to discover. I was eager to meet it all. I never wondered if anyone else ever felt this; I assumed it was all about me. I also never wondered what I would need to do or be to make it all happen. I just expected it to all show up on time and I expected that it'd be easy and relaxed. It never once occurred to me that life might have some disappointment in store. Some hard learning. Some tremors, quakes and terrors. Some hell.

• • •

Telling this story is changing something inside me.

This morning I awoke from thick, heavy dream.

I stand before your mother and father. My knees buckle. I feel a deep sensation of grief rise up from my bowels, flow through my intestinal tract into my belly, through my heart, and out my throat as I fall to the ground. My eyes are closed and I hear the wail of my own pain. My face contorts. My jaw aches. Another part of me watches as Colin and Faye kneel next to me, smiling at one another. Finally, they understand that I really did love you. My grief real enough for them to accept me into their hearts where they hold you dear.

They see me.

They hear me.

They hold me.

They acknowledge our love.

I awaken from this dream feeling that some thing has been released from my body. A deeply held desire has been met. Twenty-seven years later and I'm still processing grief.

Time heals nothing.

Facing and feeling the pain is what heals. Sharing the pain is what heals. Belonging in family and community is what heals.

The miracle of the human soul is that it pursues us at the same time as we reach for it. And what others fail to do for us we learn to do for ourselves.

Even in our dreams.

• • •

When I was a small girl, I had a doll named Drowsy. She was pink flannel with white polka dots. She didn't wear the flannel; she *was* flannel. I never liked polka dots but I loved this doll. None of my friends had anything like her. Her eyes would open and close depending on whether she wanted to be awake or not. She was a talking doll. I would pull the string with a white plastic ring attached to the end and one of six messages would sound from her body. I could tell there was a little recording device in her belly because it distorted her shape. I wondered if every Drowsy had such a strangely shaped belly or if mine was a damaged doll. It didn't bother me. In fact, the thought made me love her more as I imagined her uniqueness and how it belonged to me because I knew I was unique, too. In her high baby sing-songy voice she would say simple sentences. *Dad-dy loves ba-by? I love you, Mom-my.* She laughed and she cried with the same five syllables except when she said goodnight. *Go-ing to sleep now, night-night* was the longest sentence Drowsy said.

I could say Drowsy has been one of the themes of my life. There have been many times I must have chosen *Go-ing to sleep now, night-night.* How else did I shut down the voice within me? The voice telling me I was about to make a wrong choice. Some part of me believed difficult was good and right and necessary. Yet when there was trouble, I always expected things to get better. The resonance of being drowsy seems appropriate when I remember the times I *knew* something was wrong but I stepped into the fray anyway. As if having my eyes closed to prevent me from seeing the truth would somehow keep me from the harm on the path I'd chosen. If I couldn't see it then how could it be so bad?

I remember thinking fearlessly that things could never get worse because I'd been through the worst thing possible losing you in that car accident. I also remember my big brother, Brent, correcting me. He said, "That's not true sister, things can always get worse."

I wonder how he knew that.

• • •

I found out when I was a little girl that if you're crying uncontrollably and want to stop, the thing is to do something useful with your tears – water a plant, say. They'll dry up of themselves. The same happens when you try to make sentences out of painful material: the material lightens as it is put to work.[10]

• • •

By stumbling along not knowing what I should be writing, I write nothing at all. A process of self sabotage. However, telling this story is teaching me that the writing is *for me* and it's as necessary as breathing. I need this written dialogue with you for my mental and emotional health. It's the thing that makes me feel most alive. In the past it has felt selfish to spend time putting words down, making myself feel connected to something larger than all the mundane things that I've been trained are mine to do. Somewhere in me is the belief that telling my story is self indulgent. Yet I long to write these sentences that take me places within myself. There is a contrasting belief to the one of self-indulgence: *This is the way I heal myself,* it says.

Why have I been telling this story to myself since you died? And why have I been waiting for years to be good enough, clear enough, smart enough to write? It's probably less about writing and more about telling; less about readers and more about you and me. But who really knows? These pages I create are the container for our life together now. This is what we have. Together we meet in this space and I tell you my life. Without your hugs and encouragement, yes. Without your Danish blue eyes telling me true, yes. Yet, you're still here. You never leave. And you still love me.

---

[10] excerpt from the memoir *Almost There: The Onward Journey of a Dublin Woman* Nuala O'Faolain, page 37

I made you my compass when I was eighteen years old. Strange for me to think of that fact now. Where was my own compass? How does one know what inner guidance feels like until you've had the opportunity to make trouble in your own life? There is no fairy that tells us we've made a right choice or a wrong choice. But there is some thing that shows up to let us know whether or not we're on course. As a twenty-something, I had no idea what it meant to be inner directed except to let someone lasso me around my heart and pull. My reaction, and this is the key word – reaction – was to feel the pull and let it take me to another place. If I was moving then I must be growing and to keep growing, I felt I must never linger. This probably explains my restlessness in our early months of marriage. The sense that I should be somewhere else. Looking for something else to pull me and yet it was different then because I loved you and you loved me. I felt connected to you and the life you envisioned for us. You never made me feel obligated to you. You possessed a freedom that I am now only beginning to taste in my forties and fifties and you were in your early twenties! I wonder how you came to have such wisdom at that age. Whenever I would try to pull away from this thing called our marriage, a thing that seemed to threaten me by choking me even though I had no desire to pull away from you, you would simply let go. You would be still. You would listen. And you would allow me to go through whatever motions I needed to go through. I, standing at the door with my suitcases packed, and you calmly suggesting I rest and see how I feel in the morning. You never made it about you. You saw me. You saw my struggle. And you were strong enough to hold me in that struggle so that I might glimpse myself. I love that you were able to love me this way. But I became a deaf-mute in the two marriages that followed ours.

THREE

Crossroads 1990
BENEVOLENT CAGE

We now see that the hijab *can express a spatial dimension, marking a threshold between two distinct areas, and that it can hide something from view, as in the case of the* hijab al-amir *(the* hijab *of the prince). But it can also express the opposite idea, as in the case of the Sufi* hijab, *which blocks knowledge of the divine. In this latter example, it is the limited individual who is veiled. So although the* hijab *that separates you from the prince is to be respected, the one that separates you from God should be destroyed.*[11]

---

[11] excerpt from Fatima Mernissi's *The Veil and The Male Elite* p.95

Mona tells you that Boss wants to meet you for lunch at the marina tomorrow and you must not say no. You wonder what he wants. You assume he feels badly for not challenging Mr. Kapur over your firing. You somehow thought that when Boss returned from his overseas trip to learn that you'd been fired, he would intervene and invite you back. He seemed to like you. So maybe this was going to be that invitation.

• • •

You arrive at the marina on the hour for the 1 o'clock meeting. It is lunch time but you are more nervous than hungry. Underlying trepidation threatens to overtake your calm demeanour.

He is there. Standing at the entrance to the restaurant in his white dishdasha and ghuttra. You hesitate. He hasn't seen you yet. You consider turning around and walking away before he knows you are there. What are you afraid of? What do you sense? You talk yourself into being brave because at this stage you have absolutely nothing to lose. Or so you think. The only way to get your life back from Daniel Altea is to demand that your life is yours again and live it free from him. And this feels like a first step towards doing that.

You recall the visit to Boss' home to meet his wife and his daughter. His wife then expecting their second child. You'd been newly hired and invited to their home in Dubai. You felt proud to tell Dan that you had a new job, and that your new boss was a local man educated in the United States and married to an American woman. Finally, you felt as though you were finding your own way in this country and Dan would surely be pleased.

The three of you drove from Abu Dhabi in the blue Saab and arrived mid-afternoon at the family residence. Your small son delighted to have a playmate and you were just as delighted to be building relationships to make your stay in this country more meaningful.

You were served tea. You sat in the marble-floored majlis with the family. The children played quietly in the corner with toys while watching Sesame Street on a big screen tv. Boss offered to video tape you with your husband and your son. He wanted you to send something back to your family in Canada. You sensed that he knew you missed them terribly and you needed them. He didn't say much, his wife doing most of the talking. He sat still. His gaze soft. You got the distinct feeling that he sees more than most people.

Now, you will sit across the table from him and talk about what?

Despite the weakness in your knees, you walk purposefully toward the restaurant entrance. He greets you. You follow him inside. People know him. He keeps his boat moored here. You sit at a table, face to face. And you feel as though he reads every part of you.

"How are you?"

"Oh, I'm good."

"I hear you're in some difficulty?"

"Yeah, a bit."

"Tell me what's going on."

And you do. You tell this man all about the trouble you're in. It's embarrassing. You feel awkward. But you sense his concern is genuine. He wants to help. At this point, you're really not sure how he might be able to help, but you know this is his country, his language, his culture and he no doubt has access to things that could make your life easier. So, you tell your story. Even though it doesn't sound at all like it can be your story.

This must be happening to someone else, not you. You were the one everyone envied back home in Canada. The one who met the handsome lover who asked you to marry him, then carried you off to California for a wedding in the Crystal Cathedral, and then off to the Persian Gulf to make a dream come true. This story that you're telling Boss surely doesn't fit the narrative in your mind of the story you were stepping into when Daniel Altea became your husband. There is a serious disconnect here. Something doesn't quite add up. When Boss asks you if you have any money, you confess that you've learned from Yolly, your nanny, that you can donate blood at a clinic out in Bateen. The UAE government pays you 200 dirhams and stamps the booklet they've given you each time you do so. It's enough to buy groceries for more than a week. It's the way you learned your blood type, "B positive," a kind of funny irony.

Only Boss isn't laughing.

"I have advice for you," he says. "I like to fish. Sometimes out in the boat when I am fishing, the lines get all tangled up. It's a mess. What do you think I do when the fishing line gets all tangled up?"

I shrug my shoulders, not sure where this is leading.

He holds up his right hand and makes a scissor with his index and second fingers. "I cut the line," he says, demonstrating with his scissor fingers how exactly that happens. "Just cut the line."

He looks directly into your eyes as if to measure whether or not you are listening.

"So, you're saying I need to cut the line between Dan and me?"

He is quiet.

"Oh, if only it could be that simple. He's taken everything. I gave him everything I had so we could start a life together."

"What did you have?" he asks.

"Well, I had everything left from my life with my first husband. I had money. I had furniture and things to make a home. I was in school, studying. I had plans about how to provide for my son. I sold what I could, even my piano, and put the money in this marriage with Dan so we could get here. And now he takes it all and gives me nothing. It's not fair. He blocked me from our bank account. Every now and then he'd give me a little money, just enough to try and manipulate me into doing what he wanted. But I can't even talk to him now. If I want something from him it'll mean him having some kind of control over me. And I can't trust him anymore. For anything."

"Do you want me to help?"

"What do you mean, help?"

"If you want to cut the line, then I can help."

You feel a flutter of hope in your chest. Is it possible that you've found a way out of this mess? And right on the heels of this thought comes the unbidden worry about what this is going to cost you. What will you need to give in exchange for this help?

You ask Boss, "What can I do?"

And he says, "You do nothing. Leave it up to me. I'll take care of everything."

Everything inside of you believes him. He's real enough and he seems to possess a kind of power that puts your fears at ease. You notice your whole being softens a bit. As though he has delivered the only ease that might be possible now. Give it over to him, you tell yourself. He has a reputation for being the go-to guy when people have problems. You've watched how people are in his presence. He seems to have earned deep respect from all those around him. Let him do for you what he has done for others – let him solve your problems and make them all go away.

• • •

Driving away from the boat club you realize that not a single word was mentioned about you coming back to work. The meeting hadn't been about that, at all.

You phone Mona the minute you get home to tell her about Boss wanting to help you. "Well, that's a relief," she says.

"Really, Mona? I mean, what might I be getting myself into?"

"What d'ya mean, getting yourself into? You can trust Boss. He helps people all the time. He's not like some of the other locals. You know that." Mona was alluding to the widespread knowledge in the expat community about many affluent locals, mostly married men with families, who take western women as mistresses providing them with accommodation, jobs, travel and a lifestyle that only money can buy.

"Do I? I mean, Mona, am I to just put myself in this man's hands because he says he can help? I don't know what his help is gonna mean."

"Well, what did he say?"

"He just said he'd be in touch. So, I guess I wait."

"Then you just wait. I tell ya, Marlene, if Boss says he can help then he can help. Things work differently in this part of the world. What else are you going to do?"

"Good question. I don't know what else to do. All I know is that I cannot go home in this state. If I do, I'll never want to take another risk in all my life. I've got nothing to go back to. No home. No money. No place to start. I've got to at least grow another foundation and it feels like there might be opportunity for me to do that here. I need to be able to earn some money and that's more possible here than back in Canada. I think. Maybe I can even earn enough to return home and go back to school. That'd be something I could hope for."

The conversation with Mona put your mind at ease. You trusted her. She'd done everything in her power to support you. In fact, it became apparent that she'd been the one who actually told Boss about your situation otherwise he'd never have called. All he knew was that you were fired by Mr. Kapur and he wasn't going to interfere with the decision that'd been made to let you go. It was Mona who had told him your story and asked him to help you. It was Mona who was looking out for you in so many ways. So, if she was sure you could trust Boss to help then the least you could do would be to trust her enough to trust him, too. You had nothing to lose. Because Dan had taken everything you'd given him and more. It was time to smarten up. You had a child to raise and a family back home who loved you. That would be enough to rebuild a life worth living. One thing was certain. Daniel Altea was nothing but trouble. And even though a big part of you was resisting letting go of your marriage, you knew that you had to. It was painful. A pain you hadn't experienced before. And something in you said you just needed time and space to get back to yourself. You felt like a fool. You'd been so open and available to a man who was willing to hurt you. Yet you still wanted to believe in the goodness of people. And in the possibility of love. After all that he'd put you through, how was it that you still felt you loved Dan? Where did that come from?

Over the next few days, you learned to let him go. It helped that you had no contact with him and he was miles away. There was a moment of pure insight when you realized you could let him go and still love him. That the love you had for this man that you'd been too quick to marry was a force inside of you even though it wasn't inside the marriage. It didn't matter what he did or didn't do. You loved him. And nothing changed that. He'd never take it away from you. Knowing this eased the way out of your marriage. You learned that the fear of letting go was actually the fear of letting the love go, which, it turned out, you didn't have to do. Inside the love, holding it together like a kind of crazy glue, was something that felt pure and right and good. And in the years to come, you'd learn to stay connected to the purity and rightness and goodness regardless of the looming potential for skepticism because it was actually the only reliable guide.

• • •

It's Boss' chief right-hand man who calls you a few days after your meeting at the marina. Ibrahim has been charged with finding you a place to live.

Over the next few weeks, a plan emerges. You seem to follow in the wake of Boss and Ibrahim as though they are your brothers. You find ease in their presence. You sense an immediate trust that seems to lift you above your anxiety. When you find yourself talking to Boss about the things that trouble you, he simply replies, "That's not a problem," and you are somehow assured that it is, in fact, not a problem at all.

You find a one-bedroom flat in a building along the Corniche that suits you and your son fine. You shop for furniture: two single beds for the bedroom, a round dining-room table with four chairs, a sofa-bed for the living room, a wall unit for books, television and stereo and some kitchen basics. Everything brand new in colours and styles that you like. With Ibrahim's help, you move yourself and your son from Ron and Diana's house into your new flat with the assurance that Boss is taking care of everything. You tell him you will pay him back for everything he is spending on you as soon as you establish a new job with a good income. You tell him you've never not been able to take care of yourself and how much you appreciate his kindness. He says the most important thing at this stage is regaining your independence so you can make the right decisions for yourself and your son. It is upsetting to him that you are a widow and Dan has failed you so terribly. In his culture, he says, widows are always taken care of. Widows are not to be left alone and their children must be provided for; it is a responsibility that must be shared by family and community when a woman loses her husband. You are so enchanted by the things he tells you about his culture and his people that you start reading Qur'an and asking him more questions. You want to learn as much as you can because his open generosity touches you deeply. He makes you feel special in a way that people back home in Canada refused to do. They wouldn't acknowledge your loss and your suffering. Nor would they imagine the ways you were trying to help yourself through your own pain. There was only shame and judgement, as though you'd done something wrong. The yoke of widowhood was too oppressive for you to bear so you took the first opportunity you had to run away from it all because you thought you could leave it all behind. Boss seems to understand this about you. He can see your need. And more than that, he wants to do the right thing by you and fulfill your need in a respectful way. His honouring you as widow makes you feel dignified and worthy of being cared for. You want protection. And stability. A place to belong. For both you and your son.

Early one evening, you make tea for him in your new kitchen. You ask him why he is helping you.

"Because you are the kindest person I've ever met," is his reply.

You smile at him. It feels so good that he sees this about you. You need not convince him that you are a good, true woman. He already knows it. Knowing that he knows it makes this new life that you are building feel more and more like home. You hope that this is your chance to start all over again. You want to create a life your son will be proud of living with you.

You can now spend whatever free time you have reading and thinking, but you mostly focus on your son and his needs. You decide the part-time work at Abu Dhabi National Television isn't really what you want. There are dynamics at the job that make you feel uncomfortable. You watch the way the men treat the women and realize you were probably hired more for your looks and personality than for any real skill or talent that could be developed. So, you quit that job. Your son goes to play-school. Your life carries on in spite of Dan, his threats and his world. You don't even know if he's back in the country or what he's up to. You try not to think about it even though it seems to constantly haunt you. You realize your unease when the phone rings or someone knocks on your door because you nearly jump out of your skin! When you're out in public, you are watching over your own shoulder and keeping close tabs on your son as though disaster is lurking around every corner. It's nice to imagine you'll have some peace in your life again. But the thought is short-lived. Because Dan finds you. He shows up at your door one afternoon. He knocks. And you jump

You are frightened by the sound. Only Ron, Diana and Mona know where you live now and you're not expecting them to visit. You are startled. You have the good sense to not rush to the door and open it. Instead, you sit quietly and wait. Thank goodness your son is at school. Then you hear Dan's voice. He calls for you. "I know you're in there," he says. You freeze. In your mind, you silently will him to go away. Eventually he does, but not until he's said disturbing and mean things. Once again, he threatens you in the only way he knows how – by saying he's gonna send you back to Canada. You feel sick with worry. What if he is watching you? Sees you coming and going from the building? How will you stay safe?

The next time there is a knock on the door, Boss is having tea with you in the dining-room. You jump at the sound and you can see the worry on his face. His expression mirrors the fear that has moved into your life and refuses to leave. It turns out to only be the doorman from downstairs with a message for Boss. You are shaken. And relieved. But Boss takes note.

That night, you decide to call Dan's sister, Miranda. You tell her where you are and how you're managing. You ask her to convince her brother to leave you alone. She feels badly for what you are having to live through. She promises to do whatever she can for you and she insists that you focus on taking care of yourself and your son. But you don't need her to tell you that. Everything in your body is repulsed by Dan and his erratic behaviour.

"I'm trying my best," you say. "But your brother has some serious issues."

"I know he does," she says. "And I'm sorry you're all caught up in this. I'm really sorry."

And because you are breaking silences and talking about the truth of your life with people who are able to acknowledge your experience, you start to feel a bit normal again. The normality pulls you out of Dan's twisted reality. Hope springs back into your life.

But there is still fear about how this is all going to play out. You can't quite imagine that Dan will leave you alone altogether. And you can't quite imagine what it will take to make you safe again. There's a constant sense of being watched and the real possibility of being attacked in some way. You fear that he'll try to pick up your son from play-school so the teachers there have been alerted. This is no way to live, you think. And you just want your freedom back. It's a complicated freedom though. A freedom that includes your reputation. Your integrity. Your belief in your own ability to make good choices. In a candid conversation with Boss, you try to make sense of all the terrible things Dan has said about you to you, to your son, to your parents and to other people. "Don't think about that," Boss says. "Men construe according to their own fancy."

You later realize he was quoting Shakespeare.

• • •

Boss travels frequently. And he starts bringing you gifts from abroad. Mostly books for you and toys for your son. The first book he brings to you is M. Scott Peck's *The Road Less Traveled*. You are immediately drawn into the text. Peck defines love as a choice, an effort, an act of will and the idea causes you to question Dan's ability to love you. You know you love him because despite all he has done to you, you can still locate a feeling of care, compassion and understanding for him. You want to invest in his well-being and his growth. You want what is best for him. You realize that what is wrong in Dan's life was wrong long before he met you. You had been rushed into this marriage on purpose by him as though some part of him didn't want the luxury of time because that would have caused you both to really know each other. You can begin to sense he may have had a deliberate agenda that may or may not have been conscious. It had been your mistake to not pay closer attention to the early signs of distress in him. You had seen and felt those signs, but you didn't trust yourself enough to heed them. Was Dan intentional about hiding his inner turmoil from you? You don't know. And you'll never know. But if love is a choice, an effort, an act of will then Dan has chosen to not love you because nothing in his actions reveal an intention to love. You realize in your quiet moments of reading that Dan has attached himself to you as though he were a child. Peck writes that another misconception about love is that it is dependency. And you recall all the ways that Dan tells you that you are responsible for the way he feels, that you don't love him enough, that you don't care about him enough. He's so busy pointing out all the ways that you fail to love and care for him that he has no thought at all about the fact that he is acting in the most uncaring and unloving ways toward not only you, but your son also. You wonder if all those small gifts and big surprises that he bestowed on you during your courtship were, in his mind, a way of cementing your attachment to assure his own future care. Because the moment you married him, he seemed to slip into a place of wanting to receive effortless love. And you just couldn't fill his void no matter what you tried to do. He became a bottomless pit interested only in receiving and he decided he had nothing more to give to you.

When you read about Peck's notion of self sacrifice, you slowly recognize what must *not* be your role in relationship to Dan. For months you've been trying to figure out how to change to please him. What to do differently to make him happy. For a while you even believe that there is something distinctly wrong with you and that is why he keeps sending you away. You spent months in therapy only to have your counsellor suggest to you that you might not be the one with the problem. What if this is true? What if you only need to acknowledge that the more you try to give to him, the more he demands of you and in this way you do become part of the problem? You begin to think he was probably attracted to you in the first place because he could sense you had a quality of self-love he wanted to usurp for himself. Every time you twist yourself around his demands, you are feeding the monster that threatens him from within himself. You can see you must not dance to this music the two of you create together any longer. Boss is right. Cut the line. The sooner the better. But the decision doesn't answer the question that will haunt you for years to come: *Why on earth did I ignore those early tremors of trouble and say yes to his proposal?*

Then something hits you.

Did I say yes because I dared myself to risk the pain of life in order to expand it? There's been a willingness in you, even before Kent's death, to move towards life and people and possibilities. You've never been afraid to extend yourself. After Kent died, you were worried that life would leave you behind; you also entertained the notion that his death was a gift for you ... a way to get back on track with your own dream rather than the Sonder Family Farm dream which was never yours in the first place. The real trouble was that you hadn't realized you wanted to explore the dream seeded in your own destiny before you met your first husband. You married Kent and attached yourself to his dream. When he died, you didn't know who you were without him. There'd been no space in your togetherness. So when Dan showed up, he became the missing piece. You erroneously believed that it would take a man and his dream to lift you out of whatever life you didn't want. Having been taught that being needed by a man was the reason you were a woman made you vulnerable to follow whatever came your way.

But none of it was true.

How did you know?

You looked at the mess you were in.

It became your mission to learn the lies you'd been taught. Everything you'd ever expected for your life was collapsing before it could even materialize. The world wasn't what you thought it should be. You could hear Mr. Eichorn quoting Shakespeare in your head: *Things aren't always what they seem.* A man could tell you he loved you and then set out to hurt you. Kindness could be deceptive; people could have ulterior motives. Just because you acted generously didn't mean others would do the same. Money could be used against you. It was shocking to you. And the experience dismantled some fundamental identity structure that had built you. *Who am I if these things are true? And who can I be in a world like this?*

Now there was this lovely Arab man.

He was kind and generous. But so had Dan been in the beginning. The difference seemed to be that the lovely Arab man saw these very same qualities in you – kindness, generosity – whereas Dan cursed you, believed you to be selfish and conniving.

The contrast between these two men was so stark that it felt like they were from different planets. The thing they had in common was that each would help you find the deeper currents running in your own story. It would be a genuine education. The way for you to discover that you have all the resources you need for your life within you, and your soul is the narrative force keeping your story alive. But your soul would demand you wake-up at every critical junction. You'd be called to make hard life decisions. Something seeded in you wanted to sprout and grow. Peck's claim that the road to holiness lies in questioning *everything* provoked you to cast aspersions on all the beliefs, attitudes and assumptions driving your life. You were now in a different culture from the one you were raised in. You were surrounded by different beliefs, languages and world views that you felt hungry for. Nothing was working for you where you came from making you feel like a foreigner in everything you'd grown up with. At least here, in the UAE, you really were a foreigner, an expat, and that truth alone made you feel more comfortable. It was like living a bit closer to the truth. This is ultimately what seduced you into staying. There needed to be hope. Hope for change. Hope for a better life. Hope for belonging and believing you were worthy.

On your twenty-eighth birthday, you start reading the Qur'an. When the lovely Arab man discovers your interest, he brings you the English translation by Abdullah Yusuf Ali. You don't remember exactly how the idea comes to you, but soon you are memorizing the Shahada in Arabic; the Muslim statement of faith in one God, and only one God, acknowledging Muhammad as being God's most recent prophet. All that is required for a person to become a Muslim is the single, honest recitation of the Shahada in Arabic. So even though you tell yourself and you tell the lovely Arab man that you truly believe and therefore are willing and capable of going to Shariah Court to become a Muslim, it is this idea that ultimately frees you from your marriage to Dan. You promise yourself that divorcing Dan is not the reason you become a Muslim, it's just one of the bonuses. Because you are keenly attracted to the teachings of Islam and you commit yourself to learning as much as you can.

A court date is set.

You are advised to dress like a local woman not to prove anything to God, but to convince the men at the courthouse of your true intentions. You buy your first abaya and hijab. You practice dressing in front of the mirror. The transformation feels complete when you hear yourself saying out loud with confidence: *Ash-hadu an laa ilaaha il-la-l-laah wa ash-hadu anna Muhammadan rasulul-laah.*

Ibrahim arrives to take you to court. You feel safe in his care and you know that the lovely Arab man is ultimately the one providing for you at this juncture. The thought gives you dignity. You walk a little taller than the last time you were in Shariah court. There is an element of respect around you. You like this feeling. People treat you differently when you dress in abaya and hijab.

You follow Ibrahim's cues. You're led into a room. There is a man sitting behind the desk. He is dressed in local garb – dishdasha and guttra. He motions for you to sit in one of the chairs in front of the desk. Ibrahim sits in the other chair. The two men talk in Arabic. You listen and wait. There's a sense that you are the centre of the meeting but you remain invisible at the same time. Central and invisible. You wonder if these men would continue to talk if you were to leave the room. Would they even notice? It's a curious sensation. You're here and you're not here.

Ibrahim turns to you. "Please," he says, "make your Shahada." He motions for you to speak to the man behind the desk.

You do as instructed.

"Ash-hadu an laa ilaaha il-la-l-laah wa ash-hadu anna Muhammadan rasulul-laah."

And it is done. You are declared a faithful Muslim.

The men sign papers. They shake hands. And Ibrahim escorts you out of the building and into the car.

The next time you return to this courthouse you are dressed as a Muslim woman in local garb. Men usher you here and there. You've achieved a new status among them. Again, you sit across from a man behind a desk while Ibrahim speaks on your behalf. Your husband, Daniel Altea, is scheduled to meet you here. You wait. He doesn't show up. You fret. This man you married cannot even give you the slightest sliver of respect or acknowledgement. Lost in regret, you fail to see what is going on around you. The men are laughing. And they are saying, "Mabrouk, Madame ... mabrouk!"

You turn your attention back to the room. *What is happening?* Ibrahim is smiling. Papers are being signed and stamped.

"What's going on?" you ask Ibrahim.

"The judge has granted you your divorce," he says. "Mabrouk!"

You can hardly take this in. You are baffled and relieved at the same time. You feel as though you're lifted into a new zone of awareness as something falls away. These men in this room have granted you your freedom.

You learn later that Ibrahim met with Dan prior to the court date. He talked with him and suggested what might happen if Dan didn't cooperate and grant the divorce. Was Dan threatened? You'll never know. That is privileged information that lives in the male realm of which you are not a part. What you do know is that Ibrahim and the lovely Arab man used their *wasta* [influence] to liberate you from a dangerous marriage. You also learn that Dan fled the country the day before the court date. And even though you live with the constant feeling of being watched by him for several years following your divorce, you never see or hear from him again. Ever.

It is a sweet victory.

Yet you wonder at times what impact your decisions had on Dan. And a part of you aches for him. What life experiences seeded such confusion and violence in him? How did he come to be the way he is? Your heart hurts to imagine what he might've lived through himself. And even though you live in fear for years to come, fear that was seeded in you through your marriage to him, you are still capable of being loving in your thoughts toward him. But it's for his soul, not for his personality and there is a tremendous gap between the two. You see the beauty and goodness of his soul but you still need to learn that some people are not in alignment with the aspects that you are able to see. Their conditioned personality is a social construct that requires awareness and healing. Dan was such a human being. Lost to himself through god only knows what experiences (obviously someone had hurt him), he was capable of generating a lot of pain. And you were one of his victims.

There is a moment in a shopping mall in Canada several months later when you swear you see him sitting and watching you. Your blood runs cold. Your knees buckle. The fear in you is triggered immediately. You run out to the car and drive home as fast as you can, making sure he isn't following you. You don't know if it is real or a figment of your imagination. There is never another trace of the man. But he haunts you. You spend years looking over your shoulder, expecting him to be tracking you down.

• • •

The "I" is heavily burdened with the weight of this story. It is May 22, 2012 and I've been writing this story since you died. I sit in the hills of Tuscany with the intention to reveal myself to myself by telling this story on these pages. On this day, the 27th anniversary of your death, it rises unbidden once again. *What is it?*

A gray feeling.

So gray it shuts out the light, the birdsong, the technicolour green that I am sitting in. Yesterday, there was joy. A true sense of well-being and connection. The night next to my lover perfect. Sweet dreams. Deep sleep. Yet I rise this morning and the gray feeling has found me once again. I cannot escape it.

So, I turn toward it. And I ask: *What do you want with me?*

Will there ever be a May 22nd when I forget about you? Why must I carry this memory after having been through so much? It should be easier now. Some part of me knows this struggle is unnecessary. Yet the burden is in my body.

"I" becomes "she" to witness the pain and the distance I feel from myself.

"She" becomes "You" as yet another layer of the journey unfolds and I limp along. Widow etched in the lines on my face. A sadness that will not go away despite my efforts to live. A heaviness that will not dissipate although I move through the motions of my life.

I really don't miss you anymore. I can't even really remember you. The girl that I was with you has grown into a woman without you.

I ask again: *What do you want with me?*

I listen for the answer.

Silence.

Nothing.

Where are the words inside the words that I can usually hear in my deep listening?

What do you want with me? I ask louder this time.

I really have no more to give. To you. To anyone asking anything of me. To the world. I am done, done, done. I long to claim my life and live it fully. That is why I am sitting in the hills of Tuscany writing this story. To free myself from the tyranny of having it live inside of me.

I never asked for any of this. Truly, I didn't. What I did do was accommodate those along the way who have refused to do their own inner work. They pull on me. And you, even at the young age of 26 years, pulled on me, too. You pulled me into your family problems. A cruel father whose approval you were seeking. A mother aware of her son's pain yet unwilling to do anything to change the circumstances causing the pain. You were lost in ways that I didn't understand. You came home drunk some nights, passing out in the porch where I'd find you and bring you to bed. I would never do such a thing. So, what in me tolerated such behaviour?

Your death was a gift. I'm better off now than I would've been had you lived. Maybe this is the burden I carry. Widow lines etched in my face false testimony to the gift of getting my life back. Of being able to leave your family farm. Of becoming mother on my own terms. Of breaking free from the tyranny of being a wife.

Maybe this gift was too much for me to bear. So, I said yes to a second marriage because the pressure of not having the life that I really wanted was what I was trained to. How could I be happy? How could I dream again? How could I move freely in the world unencumbered by the demands of being a wife? This was something I wanted yet didn't dare allow myself to know the desire of wanting it. That would've threatened all I'd been allowed to believe would make my life worth living.

Even as I write this, I do not understand what I am writing.

I hope that when I go back to reading what I've written here, it will make some kind of sense.

I married again to punish myself in the way the world wanted me punished.

Women are to belong to men. Women who do not belong to a man are a threat and an uncommon nuisance to the order of things.

My second marriage beat me up badly. And I stayed until the lovely Arab man put a halt to the self-denial, self-abuse and self-perpetuating masochism. There was something in me that wanted to be punished the way that the world wanted me punished. People will read this and say, "Oh no, that isn't true!" But I tell you this is truer than we want it to be.

On the surface of things, people said they wanted me to be happy after you died. Yet there were a thousand ways that they demonstrated to me the lies they were living by.

I had my son for me ... that I might have something to live for. And for this I was shunned. Nothing in my life tells me he came for any other reason than to be a gift to everyone whose life he touches. So, how is it that people felt righteous in their judgement of me? Who the hell is anyone to judge anyone? Or to ask forgiveness of anyone? I did claim a life for myself after you died. My choices caused a backlash of flogging. The pain inflicted on me relentless. Not one person owned their part in the ever-deepening circle of agony. "Poor widow," they called me. "Poor baby," they called my son. *What the fuck?*

My son brought life to all of us. And for this we owe him a lifetime of gratitude. The we I refer to is anyone whose life he has touched. He was and remains a light in all the darkness. He restored our hope to live and to love again. He was real and alive. A bundle of unconditional love.

Could it be true that I've had to live as though you're still here and that is why I cannot seem to complete the telling of this story?

This story is the space where you live with me. Is it the only space?

If I give this story to the world, where will you be?

I've never wanted to say goodbye. Maybe that's my problem. You died. And I've spent all these years saying you shouldn't have.

If a story is a pool of reflection then I've just glimpsed what might be my path moving forward.

Let go.

· · ·

You are lovers now. The lovely Arab man has become the lover. He invited you and your son to Dubai for the weekend. Had his driver pick you up and take you to the Hilton along the Corniche. He met you there. Watched while you skated with your son in the indoor rink which at the time was a real novelty. Skating in the desert! You weren't sure why you were there in Dubai other than he seemed to want to entertain you. So, you were entertained. Because it never occurred to you to say *no, thank you.* You followed wherever he led. You enjoyed his company. He was funny. Kind. Sweet. There were long moments of silence between you. Not uncomfortable silences. Just a kind of space. And ease. You enjoyed a long dinner together. He checked you into a room that evening. You settled your son in his bed while the lovely Arab man made phone calls on his mobile. When you thought it was time for him to leave, he paused to kiss you on the forehead. Then your cheeks. Your nose. Making his way to your lips. You were dumbfounded. *Why is he kissing me?* You felt awkward and flushed. You pulled away from him. Confused. Yet not wanting to offend him. You ask him why he kissed you. He tells you he has never wanted to kiss anyone as much as he wants to kiss you. You remind him that he is married. He says it doesn't matter. That he and his wife are not lovers now. That she gives him permission to be with another woman. And this doesn't seem strange to you at all. You know that Arab men sometimes have more than one wife. You know that this is normal in this culture. So it is easy to believe him because there is something about him that you trust so completely. You're right there, in the moment with him, starting to feel the heat of your own desire. And he makes it easy for you. He is gentle. Slow. Lovingly present. You find your way to the second bed while your son sleeps peacefully across the room. You lie down together. He caresses you softly. You notice his legs are quivering. He tells you he is nervous and the vulnerability of it opens you emotionally to receive him. He slips underneath you while you lie on your back, and he's inside you with such ease that you are released into the pleasure effortlessly. He holds you there. A strength you've never felt before. Your body yields to his motion. A rhythm in your union demands you both succumb. Your lovemaking so tender it makes you weep.

Later, he leaves you and your sleeping son to go home to his wife and daughters.

In the morning, you awake to the smiling face of your boy. He wants to go skating again. So, you take him downstairs to the restaurant for breakfast and then to the rink where you rent another pair of blue skates for each of you. While your son makes his way around the rink by holding onto the boards, you break free for a few moments and glide fearlessly on the ice. You can still feel the lovely Arab man on your skin. There is a definite tingling sensation throughout your body and around your space that feels light and beautiful. The world looks different to you today. And you can't reach where you were yesterday. Everything has changed.

The driver arrives after lunch to take you back to Abu Dhabi. You wonder, when he sees you, if he knows. Can he sense how you've been changed? You feel as though you are in a pleasure-filled dream state and the truth is, you are. And it's a state so intoxicating that it doesn't leave you or let you go for the next six years. The lovely Arab man has captured you.

• • •

Your reunion a few days later is passionate and sweet. A rhythm of meeting and making love establishes itself. He comes to your apartment. He takes you and your son for long drives in the desert, teaching you the history of the place and the people. He's a charming storyteller and both you and your son are enchanted by his presence. He's funny, too. Makes you laugh. It's a relief to feel happy again. He reassures you that you are safe. He will protect you. He thinks you have an uncommon sophistication and he likes it very much. He explains his feeling in a story about a man finding a beautiful, polished stone. And how this man immediately knows to not let anything rub up against this stone. He never wants it scratched or scarred. "You," he says, "are that stone." He's soft and quietly tender. There is a magnetic force field building in strength as it binds you one to the other. You've never felt this alive. Or loved. You've never been adored. When he is near, all in your world is at peace and in balance. When he is away, your mind starts to question what you're up to. Even though he is married and even though he tells you his wife approves of him being with you, you can't shut down the internal judge who condemns you. The judge has a western voice. He doesn't understand the Arab culture or the Muslim way of life. He beats you into feeling ashamed in public and has you worried that someone you know might see you with the lovely Arab man.

You are sitting with him in the restaurant at the tennis club. He is busily doing business by phone while you and your son sit in silence around him. A young man and two women walk by on their way out of the club. You recognize the red-haired man. He works with the Canadian Embassy in Kuwait from his office here in Dubai. You feel the heat rising from your belly into your face. You are surprised by the force of your reaction. You will die if he sees you here with this lovely Arab man. What will he think? You know the reputation some western women have of being mistresses to Arab men in this country. A part of you wanting instead to be with this young man and his friends because they are your age and laughing and talking the way you'd like to be. Suddenly you see the lovely Arab man as being too old for you. And too different. You don't want to be caught up in his web. You have the urge to excuse you and your son from the table, get up and walk out the door straight onto the next plane home to Canada. You don't belong here. This is not your life. And you don't want anyone from the world in which you belong to see you here like this.

But you don't leave.

You sit with the lovely Arab man politely even though you can't really understand why he is here with you when he obviously has business to do. When he's not on the phone, he is making calculations on pieces of paper, deep in concentration. As though you are not even sitting across the table from him.

Your mother would think this rude of him.

He is teaching you to be obedient and you don't even realize it.

One afternoon you are driving between Abu Dhabi and Dubai with him in his white Mercedes car and he hands you a small box. It is a gift. You hesitate. He smiles and encourages you. Opening the box you find a long 22kt gold chain with an exquisite gold heart on the end of it.

"I want you to remember your beautiful heart, always, and the day you became a Muslim," he says.

You wear the gold heart. You love it. It lays cool on your skin in the desert warmth. He admires it on you. He loves what he sees when he looks at you. You can tell. And it fills you up in places that are parched and empty. You don't see from this place where you are sitting next to him that some twenty-one years later you'll be forced to sell the heart to a gold exchange so you can pay your property taxes during a time when he's relinquished all financial obligation to you. Because right now, from where you are sitting, the world is gloriously bright and you are warmed by his love and attention.

• • •

You are startled the first time he shows up late at night with his own key. He lets himself in the front door. You are in the bathtub, soaking. He strides in the bathroom and sits on the toilet seat, watching you. You feel shy. He seems bold in his action to claim you and your space as his own. You're unsettled by this. After a few minutes, you ask him to leave the bathroom. You like your privacy. You feel intruded upon but you don't say anything about that to him.

He politely acquiesces.

You never know when he'll show up or when he'll call. You seem willing to comply with his wishes. You are incurably open to receive, all the time. You start missing him when he is away. And you start wondering about this arrangement he has with you. He gives you a card. His written words tell you he loves you, that he will prove his love to you over time by his actions, and that you deserve to be showered with a rain of pleasure.

You relax into his love.

You talk to him about his wife and his daughters. You are reassured that he needs you, he wants you, and you can trust him to manage the details of your life together so everyone remains content. You have three months of bliss. Then he asks you if you want to go home to Canada to see your family while his American wife takes their daughters home to see her family. He will spend some time with them, and some time with you while managing his international business affairs from his office in New York.

Your life becomes more expansive. You step into it effortlessly. It all feels right and good. You assure the lovely Arab man that when you are able to work again and earn your own money again that you will pay him back. You tell him you've never been in this position before of having a man pay for everything. You've always made your own way. Had your own money. And even supported your husbands financially more than they supported you. He reassures you that all you need to do is allow him to show his love for you. He wants you to have a good life. He wants your family back in Canada to see that you are taken care of and there is nothing for them to worry about. He provides a monthly allowance for you. He pays all your travel expenses. It is such a contrast to the way that Dan treated you that you have moments of feeling overwhelmed by his generosity.

You fly home to see your family. There are arrangements made to have you join the lovely Arab man in New York. Then the two of you come back to the prairie and he meets your family. You feel jubilant. And you feel odd. It is a clash of cultures and you are the bridge between them. He doesn't stay long with you there. He has family and business to get back to. But before he leaves, he tells your parents that you are a good daughter and he feels badly for what you faced in his country. He is here to correct that now. You will be well taken care of. He assures them that he is a man of integrity and no harm will come to you or your son on his watch.

He doesn't stay on the farm with your family. He insists on staying in a hotel some eighty-five miles away. You drive with him and show him the countryside of your youth. He has an idea. He wants to explore the west coast of Canada. Fly to Vancouver. He books flights for the two of you; your son delighted to be staying on the farm with his grandparents. So even though this is the land of your upbringing, it is the lovely Arab man who takes you on an adventure in your own country.

When you arrive in Vancouver a few days later, it is late in the evening. He wants to take the ferry to Vancouver Island. You are lucky to make the last ferry and a couple of hours later, you arrive on the island not knowing where you'll spend the night. You read a rack card advertising a bed and breakfast in Brentwood Bay. You make a call. The hostess will be pleased to receive you as guests.

You drive in the blackness of night on island roads that wind their way into the wilderness and you don't know where you're going. But you get there. And you are welcomed into a home.

At dawn the next morning you are awakened by unfamiliarity. Birds you've not heard before. Light you've not seen in this lifetime. Air so gentle and sweet you wonder if you are dreaming. You feel all the tension in your body slipping away, something deeply harmonizing in your being. You breathe different here. Everything is softer. Something tells you that you'll never leave this place, if ever, for long. Home is here. It is a knowing so deep in your soul that it's unquestionable. Of course, you don't see what will come in the future. But you can see, from where you are standing now, that this island will nourish and protect you in the years to come. Some part of you belongs here.

• • •

You haven't learned your own needs yet. But this island and the lovely Arab man are teaching you.

You say goodbye to your island host and find your way into the city of Victoria meandering through woods and along ocean roads. It's so beautiful here that it makes you feel beautiful. You're remembering how to move elegantly in your body because your breath is different now. The sun is warm on your body, not hot like the prairie sun, not searing like the desert sun. The wind softly caresses your face and for the first time in your life, you want to grow your hair long.

When you walk along the inner harbour there is new magic between you and the lovely Arab man. He's more affectionate in public here. Not so self-conscious about showing you how much he loves you. This island suits him, too. He's a soft-spoken man who chooses his English words carefully. You love to hear him speak in his mother tongue. Somehow when he is expressing himself in Arabic he becomes more animated in a deeply masculine way. He's all man in Arabic. And it melts you like butter. When he is making love to you, you ask him to speak his heart language to you in Arabic and the heightened passion awakens the lover in you whom you didn't know existed except with him. It's like listening to Frances Cabrel sing in French, of which you don't understand anything, and yet you hear the love song in your body and without knowing the words he is singing, you understand the song. Making love in Arabic is the sweetest thing you've ever known. And it bonds you to the lovely Arab man as though you are under a spell.

He books a suite for the two of you in a hotel along the inner harbour. It'll be your home for the next week because he wants to look at properties. You begin to see he might have an agenda (or perhaps that's the woman writing this ... *she* can see *now* he had an agenda, but then ... I'm not so sure the lovely Arab man's lover could fully comprehend what he might be up to). You're not sure how it all happened, but your eldest brother is now your lover's right hand guy. There's talk about buying a plane (your brother is a pilot) and there are several properties to consider purchasing. There are maps spread out on the dining room table in your hotel suite and lots of meetings over the phone until finally there is a lawyer involved, (who, incidentally, gets to live on one of the properties) and a real estate agent and talk of bringing your lovely Arab man's wife and children to the island next summer. There will be renovations and shopping and planning and general fuss about making life here on the island. You eventually get back to the prairies to get your son and then return to spend the fall and winter months in the Arabian desert. In December, the lovely Arab man buys you the condo you fell in love with on the island. A condo perched on a cliff overlooking Cordova Bay where, in the years to come, you'll watch whales swimming by while you bake banana bread in your kitchen. The place is so extraordinarily beautiful that when the lovely Arab man suggests that you stay in Victoria to continue your studies at the University, everything you've ever dreamt might be possible for your life gushes forth from an invisible well of wishes within you.

Could that be possible?

He smiles the smile of a man so in love with you and so delighted in making you happy that you are filled with glorious anticipation. But the next thought is this: *If he loves me so much, why doesn't he want me to be living with him?*

The excitement of going back to school and getting your degree quickly supersedes that thought. You didn't realize how much you longed to get back to the dream of your life and you're not exactly sure what the heck you've been doing in the desert for the past several months other than learning to love this man, his land and the vision he has for a life with you. With the lovely Arab man, anything seems to be possible. There's no shortage of money. Beautiful things abound. Conversations are about ideas not people. Ideas that can change the world and make it a better place. And you are in the throes of being constantly and continually intoxicated by his love. His touch brings you such peace that you forget about all else in your life. When there's a problem, any problem, you take it to him and he takes care of it. Like he has a magic wand and can make every bad thing go away. You feel like there's an invisible force field of protection around you. And you've been able to spend your time focused on your son, his needs, traveling, enjoying the best of the best of everything in the UAE. It's a surreal kind of existence. Curiously, though, you've adapted and you thrive.

The next spring, in April, you move into your new condo. All you have with you are the two suitcases you packed for you and your son. Walking into Seascape #16 you can hardly believe that you will be living here. The beach is your front yard. The view from almost every room is ocean and the Juan de Fuca islands. Your son is delirious with joy because his favourite place to ever be is on the beach playing.

So, it begins. Another new start.

You and the lovely Arab man spend a weekend in Seattle buying everything from rocking chairs to kitchen cutlery. Your brother is back on the island renovating other properties and arranging details for shipments and containers and purchases. You seem to float between all the things that need to be done and this delicious love affair. Soon, the lovely Arab man's wife and daughters arrive on the island, too. And when they do, it all suddenly feels a bit strange. His freedom to come and go with you is curtailed and you watch him play the husband and father roles while you sit on the sidelines in your beautiful new home. You try hard to not let it bother you. You remember one occasion when you show up at the property that is being renovated, there he is, the lovely Arab man, driving out the yard with his wife and daughters in the car with him and he hardly acknowledges you. Your brother is standing there in the yard and is witness to the sudden onset of pain that you feel in your heart. It almost knocks you down. But he catches your gaze, tilts his head in a way that says, *Sister, it'll all work out and I can see this is hard for you.* Part of you feels the heat of shame. And you wonder now exactly what your brother was thinking and you wish you would've walked over to him and asked. He probably saw so much more than you were willing to look at and when he eventually gets fed up with working for the lovely Arab man, and leaves the island to do some flying up north, you can't really understand why he is leaving and why he seems to be so angry with you.

The part of you that felt the momentary heat of shame is quickly shut down but not before you gasp with shortness of breath and feel the sting of your own tears. How is it that you were able to shut down what your body knew to be true?

• • •

You make home for you and your son, again.

This time it feels easier because you are back in Canada and on this exquisitely beautiful island where things generally operate in familiar ways for you. Your parents are relieved. And the truth is, so are you. But you're not always willing to admit it to yourself because if you are happy to be back in Canada then what does that say about your relationship with the lovely Arab man? You are somewhat confused. But then you tell yourself you've expanded to a new way of living. You are a world traveller now. Your lover is from a different culture and has a different worldview than you. And because you no longer fit in the world from which you came, it makes sense that you must find a new way to move forward and make life. So you are open to any and all possibilities. The lovely Arab man has plenty of ideas and seems masterful at creating those possibilities.

He leads.

You follow.

Soon you are in university. The courses you completed in college before leaving the country prove to be your ticket into a full and rich palette of academic work. You begin in the creative writing program. For a year you immerse yourself in the reading and writing of fiction, screenplays and poetry. You find the hub of writers in Victoria and avail yourself of writerly workshops and writing groups. Your social outings are to literary readings, live theatre, ballet, opera and musical gigs. This city is alive! And you are finding the pulse of your own desire for the first time since you were a young girl. The young girl in you revelled in stories and music. She'd sit on the edge of her bed at the green foldable card table and type on her mom's old manual typewriter. When she needed a change, she'd slip out her bedroom door and into the larger basement area where her dad's guitars were poised in the corner ready for playing and her mom's mahogany upright piano was the centrepiece of the room. She'd play all her favourite songs on that piano and when she got through her usual repertoire, she'd make up her own songs, testing each musical phrase repeatedly and writing lyrics she could sing out loud. Then she'd go back to her typewriter or she'd go outside and walk along the old stone fence around the front yard, singing and chanting and sometimes even praying. That girl was content.

It's curious how being on Vancouver Island connects you to that girl again. A new vision for your life is unfolding beneath the thinly veiled social construction of who you're supposed to be. Your young son begins to blossom in his own creativity. His room is a laboratory of fun and discovery. How you enjoy building it all for him! And for yourself, you hire a craftsman to construct a suite of bedroom furniture that includes a writing desk and a library for your books and your music. It is an oasis of pleasure for you. You enrol your son in a Montessori school close to the university. Your days soon find a rhythm and routine that supports this new life you are building. Every few weeks the lovely Arab man visits for a few days. Then you miss him when he leaves again and you protect yourself from realizing that his time with you is always a bit disappointing. But you quickly slip back into the life you are creating. In the second year of your studies you wander over to the psychology department and soon find yourself in graduate level courses for counselling psychology. But you become disenchanted and the women studies department becomes your academic refuge as it cracks your world open with ideas that light you up from the inside out. It is a rich and robust time of discovering how much you love to think and write. When courses are completed and you have a break in-between semesters, you take your son to the farm to be with his grandparents and you meet the lovely Arab man in some exotic part of the world. Together you explore Europe by train. You walk through Arab Street in Singapore to buy rich fabrics for the lovely Arab man's sisters and mother back in the UAE (or maybe it's for his wife ... how will you ever know?). You bask on your own island in the Maldives, line-fishing by hand in the moonlight on a silent donnie which eventually takes you back to your island where you have a cook prepare your fresh catch. You are served the savoury meal while sitting at a table on the beach. You can still feel the sand between your toes in that moment when you look in your lover's deep brown eyes and see yourself reflected back. You are dressed in white, flowing linen. There is a soft, warm breeze. The water is calmer than you've ever known. A sweetness in the salty air. And there is such a deep peace in you that you wonder how you let this dream into your life.

In that moment, you also miss your son. You wonder what it would be like to have him here with you. He doesn't really fit into this picture. You long to have him near but you realize that you are on an island in the middle of the Indian ocean miles away from any kind of medical support should it be needed. It's a strange thought and you wonder why you are thinking it. How could one have a toddler in such a remote place? If there were an accident or if he were to get ill, what would you do? Thinking about this makes you sad because you sense how removed you are from what really matters to you. And you can't even call home to see how he is because there is no phone service where you are. In a flash, you feel deeply alone and disconnected. You want to be back on land and among life with your family and your studies. But you will remain here for a few days because who wouldn't enjoy this privilege of adventure with the lovely Arab man? You'd have to be crazy to turn away from such experience. Maybe you'll write about it one day.

And with that thought you indulge yourself in the dream.

Until you catch yourself thinking a thought that threatens to awaken you to a different way to view the life you are agreeing to indulge.

You are sitting on a wooden bench in a donnie across from the lovely Arab man. Two local Maldivian men are taking you out for more fishing. It is the clearest of days. The *putt-utt-putt* of the donnie soft and soothing on the still water. You see your lover looking past you as he gazes into the far horizon. You wonder what he is thinking. What magic does he have that allows you to be in this place at this time doing this thing alongside him? Never in your wildest dreams had you imagined this life. Or him. How did you get here? You look closely at him. He is wearing a cap which looks rather silly. The flat beak. The cap pulled down too far so his ears are slightly folded over. He looks less like himself, or who you think he is, in western clothes. As though he doesn't quite fit into his own skin. Or he's forgotten where his skin actually is. You glance at his crotch. You notice his balls falling out of his shorts. You try to get his attention without embarrassing him with the other men on the boat. But when you do, you realize he's not even slightly bothered and you are the one who is embarrassed. For a brief moment, he appears to you as a little old man. Someone you don't even know. Who speaks a language you cannot understand. And lives a lifestyle that you haven't even read about in any of your books. *Who is this guy? And why are you here with him?* He's too old for you. He doesn't know your people or your land. You have nothing of shared value except the peace you bring to each other in times of closeness. And maybe that's a chemical bath of hormones that is keeping you distracted from what you really want. Or maybe you just don't allow yourself to imagine what you might really want. What you do know for sure in this moment is that you definitely prefer him in his dishdasha and guttra. You like to be with the lovely Arab man not the Arab man trying to adjust himself to fit a different code of dress or behaviour because then he becomes something else and it muddles the story that you're telling yourself in your own head about who you might be to him.

• • •

Coming back to Canada always makes you feel a bit larger than when you left. There are mixed feelings. On the one hand, you are relieved to be "home" because with that comes the relaxation of knowing who you are and where you belong. The moment you land at the Victoria airport and walk off the plane you find yourself wanting to kiss the ground because the air here makes it so easy for you to breathe. You feel yourself taking deeper breaths and being back in your own body. It is this sensation that defines homecoming to you. And you begin to notice that it only happens on Vancouver Island. Landing on the prairies isn't the same at all. In fact, when you arrive in the Medicine Hat airport there is a dread that descends upon you. *You are here again,* a voice in your head declares. *Back here again.* And with that rises memory and loss and dark moments of feeling outside of everything you step into. It is so obvious to you that you don't belong here anymore that you begin to take pleasure in making the statement as boldly as you can. Like the time you arrived back in Medicine Hat wearing hijab quite deliberately to mark the distinction between you and your mother. It upset her and you could see that it upset her. But you felt proud of the fact that you were donning the dress of a Muslim woman. *I am different from you. I am living differently than you. I will make different decisions than you. Can't you see by the way I am dressed that I have been to foreign places and I am different now?*

You don't realize then the pain you must have caused her. Or maybe you did and you simply don't care. It does occur to you as you write this part of your story that you yourself as a mother might do well to remember this stage of your life, and what you were experiencing, when your own son, now the age you were then, seems to do things deliberately to hurt you. It might help to not let it hurt so much.

You wonder if your mother remembers that time. Would she admit to feeling anything in response to your defiance? Or would she blithely deny the emotional agitation that you sensed existed between the two of you then. More than anything you wished that she'd take an interest in where you'd been and what you'd seen but there was never any curiosity about any of it. The only common ground you seem to share with your mother is your son. He is the bridge you travel to connect with her. Deeply steeped in her role as mother it seems to be the only identity she is able to relate to you. Now that you are both mothers it gives you something to talk about. Yet you remember talking with your mother when you were a teenager and speaking proudly to your friends about being able to talk to your mom about anything. Even though there was never a discussion about menstruation or birth control. And you noted its absence to yourself. Now in your mid-twenties you want to show her how worldly you are and how exciting it is to explore life beyond the farm but she simply isn't interested. Her world is exactly the same as when you left it except how can that be true? She lost a son-in-law in a terrible car accident. She is being forced to learn to live a great distance away from her eldest daughter and her only grandson. But if this grieves her, she never shows it. Nor does she ask her daughter what her life is like now, what her dreams are, what she is hoping for. Margaret is deeply entrenched in her own world. And not interested in anything beyond it. At least that's how it feels to you at this stage.

So you continue to want to prove something to yourself. What is it exactly? That when Kent died, you lived? That you're still able to build a dream without him? That life can be trusted and the world is full of interesting people and beautiful places which can make the leaving of your old life less painful? All of it seems plausible enough. When you arrive back in Victoria to your home on Cordova Bay with its breathtaking views your everyday normal, you feel hopeful that life has, in fact, found you again. Seascape at 4771 Cordova Bay Road is your refuge, the place where you and your son learn to drink in the possibilities for your life together. Your mother even agrees to visit. First with your father, and they enjoy a brief visit with the lovely Arab man while he is there, too. And then your Mom brings your granny and your sister with her and you bask in having your female family in the arms of your beloved Seascape. Granny makes coffee in the morning in your kitchen. Your sister braids your hair while you sit in front of the bathroom mirror. You've not had long hair since you were four years old. Now you've agreed to grow it because the lovely Arab man wants you to. You are surprised at how quickly it grows and in a couple of years it reaches past the middle of your back. You love the freedom of long hair. You wash it and leave it to dry on its own. You wear it up on days you don't want to wash it. Your sister has taught you how to braid it. These all feel like girlie things you never allowed yourself. Having long hair makes you feel more feminine and sexy. Or maybe it is the reflection you see when you look in the lovely Arab man's deep brown eyes. There is simply a sexiness in you that has not existed until now. You seem to ooze sensuality and you are softer than you've ever been. Things don't rile you up like they once did. All your needs seem to be taken care of. You love to walk and when you're on campus at UVic you walk for miles. The physical strength in your body that comes from walking makes you feel confident. The thinking you are engaging with your mind also makes you feel confident. You completely trust the lovely Arab man to provide for you – he owns your condo and he makes sure you have money in your bank account. You imagine he is your patron as you develop your academic career and build your writing life. You promise yourself that he will benefit from his investment in you. And you imagine that your ability to allow his help into your life is your way of learning to receive because you've given so much of yourself to others and continue to do so.

There are times when the money isn't in the bank when he says it will be and seeds of doubt begin to sprout. When you ask for details, he withholds information under the guise of not wanting you to worry. You tell yourself that he is just protecting you but some part of you knows that is not true either. The deeper truth is that he doesn't think you have any right to ask about such things. He is the arbiter of your money and your home. There are terrifying moments when you glimpse this truth but you quickly distract yourself away from what might be the ultimate ramifications of living this way.

Sometimes you talk to him about the doubts. You suggest to him that maybe the two of you are on different trajectories. You want a husband and a home and a shared life. You want to complete your academic career and develop a writing life. You want stability. You don't like only seeing him once every few weeks. And you notice that when he is with you, he is usually jet lagged because he doesn't stay long enough to adjust to your time zone. So there's never a sense of being in alignment with one another. Sure, you might have heated sex in the middle of the night that elevates you into places you never knew existed but when the morning comes, you still feel alone in your life even though he is in your bed. Because *you* get out of bed and you live in the life you are building with your son. *He* stays in bed, sleeps off his jet lag, eats breakfast when you want dinner, doesn't have much time for you or your son because while he is up, there are business calls to attend to and you are both living in two different worlds. You can see all this now. You didn't see it so clearly then. Although your nanny, Rhonda, did make a comment once that threatened to wake you up. She suggested that you and your son deserved better. She noticed when the lovely Arab man was visiting that he really didn't have that much time or energy for you.

It was an observation that became a hair-line crack in your heart.

If this is true, then what is this man up to?

You fish a little. You ask him questions. You cuddle with him after lovemaking and suggest that perhaps you are his mistress. He is incensed with the idea. And he tells you that you don't understand. That your culture is too narrow-minded to fully appreciate the decency of allowing a man to build another life with another woman when his first life isn't fulfilling to anyone involved. He assures you that his American wife wants him to find a second wife, to be happy in love and to create a second home. She, according to him, is no longer interested in sharing his bed. She only wants to share their daughters and live in peace. If that means the lovely Arab man needs another woman in his life then she is all for it.

You listen to this story over and over and over again. Because you keep asking him for assurance and he seems happy to give it. It's as though you need to be told the story repeatedly so that you might believe it. When your friends and family want to know what the status of your unconventional relationship is, you repeat his assurances to them. You comfort yourself with the acknowledgment that your friends and family know nothing of the Arab culture or about Islam and they have no desire to learn about it either. You find such blatant ignorance hard to accept. They're not like you. You don't know why, but they just aren't. You seek new experiences and insights. You read books. You travel. You are curious and open. And from this moral high ground you convince yourself that you're okay with the way you are living. It's even liberating at times. You haven't lived any kind of "normal" since Kent died so why would you start now? You don't need to live with your lover full time. You can write and focus on your studies. You don't have any influences interfering with the parenting of your son and you like this. He is yours, after all. And you want to protect him from any male domination that might stunt his growth. This boy is the light of your life. He's so full of goodness and loves you so much that it keeps you tethered to all things good and loving. He's the reason you're pulling your life together. You want him to have all that he needs to thrive. You understand it is a privilege to be his mother. You don't know how to be the best mother all the time but you do know this: it is your job to protect your son from any interference that might keep him from knowing how good and true and beautiful he is. You believe your son came into this world perfect. And you only want to allow him the time and the space to grow into himself without being harmed by others. To this end, it works to have the lovely Arab man as a kept-at-a-distance male protector. After the nightmare of your second marriage, it is a relief to have time and space to yourself and not to live with the constant fear of being overpowered by an unpredictable man.

So the contract is silently written between you and the lovely Arab man. You are colluding in whatever dance this is and your intention comes from the purest part of your heart. And in the face of all the disapproval that comes your way, you learn to stand tall and firm in your conviction that this is the life that you want for yourself and your son. Even when you're criticized by some of your sister students in the women's studies classes you're enrolled in, you don't succumb to their judgement about why you wear skirts rather than pants, and why you argue for the right to wear hijab if you choose, and why you allow the lovely Arab man to treat you like a mistress. You learn how to defend yourself. You also learn how to criticize the dominant western woman's stance about other women's lives in other parts of the world. You become quite vocal in the classroom. You write letters to newspapers and magazines about women's rights. You meet a woman who becomes your best friend. Sandy is married to a Muslim. She is also a scholar of Islamic art and history. Together, you head the Muslim Student's Association at the university. In fact, you are elected the Vice President of that association. You spend many days and nights talking and thinking and trying to change the world's perception of Islam. When the lovely Arab man visits, he is curious about your engagement with such issues. He encourages you. He bets that you can't learn by memory the first sura of the Qu'ran. He wagers that if you can then he'll buy you a prayer rug. When next he visits, you impress him with your Arabic recitation. He is deeply moved. And soon enough he brings you an exquisite silk Persian rug that you cherish for years to come.

A part of you is intensely happy with this situation. You have your own home. You are financially supported by the lovely Arab man. All you need to be is student and mother. You live by the ocean. Your son enjoys playing on the beach day after day after day. You explore the rugged coast under your house with him. Seascape is a home perched on a rock cliff overlooking Cordova Bay. You sit on rocks and read while he runs and plays and discovers whatever delights him. There is peace here. And possibility for turning your life back into what you always dreamed it would be. You are alone, yes. But you relish in the presence of yourself. How you hated the dark cloud of your second husband always following you wherever you went. Now, you are free. You feel full and alive. You enjoy long phone conversations with the lovely Arab man. And you are always planning your next rendezvous. This is the internal experience from one aspect of yourself.

There is another though.

The other part of you feels sad that you don't have a normal life. You feel people's judgement of you and your son when you go back home to the farm. You know you'll never again fit into that lifestyle and something has been lost to you. Eventually you give up trying to be anything other than who you are becoming. But it is painful at times. Because you long to live the life you thought you were promised. A husband and children. The safety of a home. The stability of a life shared. You have none of these things now. And you have the enduring stigma of being widow. The lovely Arab man is doing his best to erase that stigma for you. If you belong to him then your life was been righted. He has claimed you for his own and that somehow makes you legitimate again. You sense he can't quite figure out why your family hasn't taken care of you. How can they just leave you alone and expect you to rebuild your life with a child? Where is their support and guidance? He feels they should have protected you and provided for you. In his culture, a daughter who has lost her husband would never be left to fend for herself. His interest in your well-being has sealed your attachment to him. You'll do whatever you can to support him through the changes in his own life because he has been unwavering in his support for you. This will be the contract you live by until the pain becomes so great that you simply cannot bear it any longer.

• • •

Now fully immersed in your studies about women's history, psychology and spirituality you wonder how the desire to write books will fit into this freshly discovered love of thinking and producing scholarly work. It seems the two are disconnected. It feels as though you're moving away from what you learned in the first year of creative writing but it somehow feels more useful. You don't yet trust the trajectory of your instincts to guide you. You don't realize that for you, writing *is* thinking and you really don't know what you think unless you've written it first. These are the early days of learning to see yourself as a thinker. And learning to value your capacity to draw connections between ideas, synthesize information and make meaningful relationships to build your life forward. You really don't yet appreciate the contribution that you offer and the skills you possess. And because you don't appreciate these things, you don't take yourself seriously enough to own your own path in life. Here you are with everything you need to live the writerly life you dream of. Yet, you allow yourself to be distracted by the need to figure out just what the lovely Arab man wants from you. Something doesn't quite add up. He is thousands of miles away from you. And still you feel a bond so powerful that you are constantly distracted by thoughts of him. You feel him on your skin. You sense him in your dreams. It's as though his loving connection with you has awakened something you didn't know you had. It's a power surge of confidence and sensuality. You love your body. You love being in your body. You practice yoga religiously. And shiatsu. You also love to think hard about hard things. You feel fearless in your academic life. You produce good work and you surprise yourself with the intensity of your conviction about certain ideas and theories that help you make sense of the world. It's a heady time. You can hardly believe your luck sometimes when you look around you and see all that you have access to. You've won your freedom back. And this boy you birthed is a miracle in himself. He is smart. And artful. A light in the room. His energy demands that you keep up with him and his needs. Rhonda helps you maintain a balance in your life. When you can't be with him, she can. Also a UVic student, she becomes a friend to you, too. You are really a family of three. She introduces your son to all the things he innately loves: painting, beading, drawing, building. An art history student, Rhonda enriches his and your life with her creative talent and knowledge. You are so deeply engaged in this life you are building that it worries you.

Shouldn't I be with the man I love?

Don't I need to be taking care of him, too?
If I'm not his wife, then who am I to him?

When these conditioned thoughts take over your head space then it's difficult to stay present for the work of your academic life, your writing life and your family life. You don't like the sense that the lovely Arab man is a distant piece of whatever it is you're building and rather than just picking up momentum and moving forward, you keep stopping the train, stepping away from the engine, and walking backwards down the tracks to make sure everything is running okay.

It's a peculiar pattern. Go. Stop. Go. Stop. Go. Stop. It's like trying to drive forward when you're constantly looking back.

So, you try to compose a story you can live in. Maybe you can complete your academic studies, become a licensed psychologist, move back to the UAE and with the lovely Arab man's help, build a transition house for all the women who find themselves in the same situation that you found yourself in. You will have the knowledge and the power that is required to make a safe place for women. There is much work to be done in support of empowering women. And you've learned first hand what it takes. You're still not entirely sure how you were lucky enough to attract the help of the lovely Arab man. And you wonder how women find their way back home to themselves without such support. Our societies are flawed both here in the western world and there in the middle eastern world. You see that you can be a bridge. You understand now that there are many expat women living in the UAE who are feeling trapped. They have children. And they know that if they go home to their own families in other parts of the world they will be forced to leave their children behind because they are married to Emirati men who have powerful access to all the forces that would make that so. You know this from stories you've heard from other women while you were living there. And you know this because the lovely Arab man has also told you of the stories only from the perspective of the Emirati father. He has friends who are dealing with this very issue and he shakes his head in dismay. You sense it breaks his heart a little and that he might be worried for himself. If his wife, the American woman, decides that she doesn't want he and you to be married then he will be in this predicament himself. You don't doubt his love for you. But you do wonder about his ability to manage this first wife in a way that will keep his life intact and the doors of possibility open for the two of you to grow your own life together. It seems to be a precarious situation. You watch closely. And listen intensely. It is what allows you to be patient. This is all he really asks of you. To be patient and wait because one day, he assures you, the two of you will live openly as a married couple.

As you write this now, today, you wonder why you couldn't see then that you were still at risk with the lovely Arab man. You trusted him so completely because he'd saved your life from that second marriage that turned out to be a nightmare. You transferred the trust you once had in Dan directly into your relationship with the lovely Arab man. As though naively trusting every man who said he wanted you and loved you was your default setting. It never, not once, occurred to you to say *thanks, but no thanks ... I have other plans for my life. I have a dream I want to create.*

Or did you?

Was that response in you? And if it was then what got in the way of you hearing your own preferences?

What was it in you that kept you open to saying yes?

The lovely Arab man made you feel safe. He gave you your own home in your own country. He didn't interfere in the rearing of your son. You wouldn't admit it then, but having a lover who was a married man provided a kind of safety net, too. It was a double-edged sword. On the one side you resisted the notion of being a man's mistress and on the other side you contemplated using the fact to keep your freedom.

If you could've been brutally honest with yourself, you'd have acknowledged that maybe you didn't feel so free. There were moments in your relationship with the lovely Arab man when he withheld things from you. There were questions he wouldn't answer. Things he wouldn't share. All in the name of protecting you and not troubling you. He assumed a position of power over you that irritated your sensibility of freedom. You began to ponder what it'd be like to move back to the UAE where you could see for yourself exactly what he was living and exactly where you fit in that living scheme. Part of you thought that maybe you were to blame for this arrangement. If you could just give yourself over to him completely and show him that you were willing to take on his family and his culture then you were sure he'd be more transparent with you.

It is this line of thinking that eventually has you consider leaving university before completing your degree.

He needs me, you tell yourself. You know he is weak with worry about the possibility of losing his daughters. He lost a little sister to illness when he was young and the emotional resonance lives in him as fear. He will not lose any more little girls. Yet he is in a precarious position. His American wife does not sleep with him anymore (or so he tells you). He loves and adores you. He wants to marry you. He knows it will take time to integrate you into his life in a respectable way. His family has accepted his American wife and he fears they may not be so open to you. It's not that they don't want him to have a second wife. They do. They just prefer that he marry a local woman this time. Because a local wife will understand his needs better and take better care of him is their reasoning. He is sometimes frustrated by the cultural road blocks in his way but he is sometimes flattered by them, too. You can see that part of him likes to be taken care of in the way that these traditional women in his family take care of their men. Yet another part of him wants to break free from cultural restraints. Choosing an American wife and then a Canadian mistress is his way of resisting his socially constructed identity. He is a world traveler. He is well-educated by western standards. He's a visionary. He builds companies. He puts forth big ideas to people who have the power to enact big changes in his country. His reputation for integrity and innovation supersede his traditional ties to ways of thinking and ways of being that feel outdated to him. It's a tension that lives in him and you can sense it. You remember how surprising it was to discover the lovely Arab man has a different persona that only emerges when he is with you in Europe or North America. It is liberating for you as a couple. You can walk in public together, holding hands. You can steal a kiss or a cuddle. There is always self-restraint but less when dressed in western clothes. It is a mysterious luxury. Always at the core of this luxury is the way the lovely Arab man holds you in the highest regard and somehow bestows on you noblesse.

Your orientation to life is shifting. Again. And it has something to do with the state you are in when you're with the lovely Arab man. Your goals and values are changing. Everything you once believed in is now open for negotiation. You are willing to question it all. And the thing that holds you constant is the love you feel in his presence. There is electricity in his touch. Voltage that up-levels your life experience.

It is your son who grounds you.

You begin to see that you need support in helping your son process the experience he lived through with you in the Persian Gulf. It'll be years before you fully understand the wheels of energy that were set in motion through that demonic second marriage.

You find a family counsellor. Doug Emid is the man who helps you put all the pieces back together again for both you and your son. In play therapy you discover how your son understands what he's been through and it informs your own perception of what is now part of your life story. It is natural for you to see that your son is a mirror for you. Doug remarks that it isn't common knowledge. That most parents he works with don't get that their children are reflecting back to them pieces of themselves. He's curious about how you have this knowing.

You're curious, too. But you really don't know. It just seems true.

Doug invites you to tell your story to a group of counsellors who are in training. He will interview you in one room. It'll be recorded on video while at the same time fed live to another room where there are a circle of people witnessing the conversation.

You accept his invitation.

And the experience changes you.

For the first time in your life you story for an audience of listeners the death of your husband and the birth of your son as it lives in you. You have no idea how the story will be received. But Doug makes you feel safe and protected. You reveal all.

When the interview is over, Doug invites the other counsellors into the room to meet with you in person. They become a reflecting team who give you back your dignity. A dignity that you hadn't even realized you'd lost. They do this by accepting the lens of your understanding. They don't try to make the story something that it is not. They accept your internal experience and they do not judge you. You can hardly let all this acceptance in. It is the most liberating moment of your life. This group of people sitting around you provide loving acceptance that lifts you up and out of the dark secret you've been living in.

This is the moment when you learn that if you don't speak the truth of your own lived experience then somebody else will surely tell your story for you and then you'll be forced to live with the conclusions they come to about your life.

The realization shapes who you become. You carefully label the video and store it away knowing you now have proof to give to your son when he gets older ... proof that you have always endeavoured to be true to him and to your own story. A story that nobody else has the right to tell unless they are willing to own their part in its construction and tell it in their own voice. Then it becomes a *different* story. Not yours. But theirs. And that's okay but the distinction must be made and honoured.

This is your story.

And you have the right to tell it.

• • •

You start planning an exit strategy from your own dream albeit unconsciously.

You are so close to completing your degree. Study is effortless and you enjoy the vibe. You and your son are thriving. But you wonder what kind of woman you are when you can enjoy engaging this part of your life while the lovely Arab man, your man, lives thousands of miles away. You dare not think that perhaps he benefits from having you here in Canada. That maybe he's living the life he truly wants, too. That he's constructed it exactly this way because it suits him. No. These are not your thoughts. You convince yourself that the difference you need to make in the world is the difference in the lovely Arab man's life. That nothing else matters – not your education, not your contentment, not your stability, not your artistic fulfillment – if you don't have your man to share it all with. And sharing means living as husband and wife, together, in the same household, raising children together and making a life that everyone can see. This living behind the curtain is nonsense. You want to live out loud and with integrity. It all feels too hidden and obscure. So the part of you that's been content to settle and stabilize your life with your son becomes unsettled again. She is distracted from her studies. She tells herself the academic career doesn't matter as much as being next to the lovely Arab man. It's all been so easy, academically, so really what could it matter? Life is supposed to be a struggle. It's supposed to be hard. And right now you have all the pieces fitting together to make a good life. Why can't you be satisfied by that?

The impulse to leave is so strong that it cannot be ignored. Or so you think. It's as though you've rebuilt your strength and from the strength you are compelled to rocket yourself into the unknown again. But it's not the unknown of your own personal dream of building a career and supporting yourself through your work in the world. No. It's not that. It's the unknown of what this lovely Arab man has in store for you, what he's up to thousands of miles away, who you might become living next to him. And this is where your thinking halts. It doesn't occur to you that you will be putting yourself at risk in some way. You completely trust the lovely Arab man to take care of you and your son. And you feel that is the only honourable thing in the world. To trust your man. Don't question him. Don't hold yourself capable of building your own life so that you might walk alongside him. No. You must make him feel good by being dependent on what he can provide for you. If you become too independent, too strong then how will that make him feel? Because there are moments when you feel like your life could catapult into a new realm of which you can barely imagine from where you are standing. The possibilities keep creeping into your daily life. A professor who sees the promise of your career and encourages you in a specific direction. Friends who gather around you and share the same interests inspire future prospects of building home and life and work right here, right now. On the one hand, it elevates you. On the other hand it threatens to destroy whatever this thing is that you have with the lovely Arab man. And that feels risky. Very risky. So you shut some part of yourself down.

You start to withdraw from your university life. Tell yourself you can always come back and complete your degree at a later date. It's not the top priority in your life. No, it cannot be. Your priority must be your family. You want to live with the lovely Arab man and you want your son to have the experience of living a "normal" life in a "normal" family. You convince yourself that you are not enough for yourself and your son. There must be more.

It you were completely honest with yourself at this juncture in your life, you'd feel the deep sense of loss that is stirred within you when you contemplate walking away from your academic work. You love your studies. You love what you and your son have built together as your home and your community. You're happy here. But there's a voice inside you whispering *everything is nothing unless you have someone to share it with.* You don't ask yourself where that voice comes from and you don't wonder why you're letting it direct your life. You believe it to be true. And it somehow justifies walking away from the safe place you've created, the place your son calls home. It's almost as if you feel it is all too good to be true. Like you can't really let it all in. And shutting off from the possibilities that seem close at hand now means walking toward the lovely Arab man and his life even though you really don't know what awaits you where he is. Maybe it's the mystery of the adventure that lures you away from living your own dream. There is a thrill in leaving even though under the thrill is the dull ache of the work that must be done. Still, you tell yourself you can have it all. You think your life is expanding, getting larger than you are able to imagine from where you sit in your safe home. And what's safe anyway? Surely the safeness is in your relationship with the lovely Arab man. You've learned to not put too much onus on physical location or the stuff of living. You had it all once before. The man died. And everything deconstructed. Through it all, you remained. There was some part of you untouched by the tragedy and the turmoil. You dare to think that that same part maybe thrives on such upheaval. You don't think of it then (you think of it now as you write this) but could it be possible that through that experience of your husband being killed and your life being uprooted that you somehow slipped into a morphic field of drastic change and the only way you feel alive is to keep creating an edge to live off? As though you're addicted to the negative energy of stress and instability.

That's quite a thought.

Not the thought you're thinking now as you tell yourself that the Cordova Bay condo will remain your tether to home until you can build your "real" home with the man you love in the Arabian Peninsula. You talk yourself into believing your son will benefit from travel abroad. You think he'll have better schools in the UAE and you convince yourself that there's really nothing to stay in Canada for. You've defined yourself to everyone here as the woman who has a life somewhere else, that you're only here for a short time and then moving on to better things. It's like an escape hatch just waiting to be used.

• • •

In your mind you are leaving but you can always come back. The escape hatch works both ways. The innocence of your sweet little son keeps you grounded in a strange way. You focus your life around what he needs. That means you spend most of your time organizing and planning and making home. You imagine that when you get all the pieces in their proper places that you'll then have time and space for yourself. So arriving in Abu Dhabi has you step into the flow of the lovely Arab man's world. You know that the minute you arrive, you'll be taken care of. There'll be a driver to take you to the flat he says he's created for you. And there is. And he does. You step into the foyer of your new home and your heart sinks just a bit. It's ever so slight that you might not notice it. It comes when you recognize pieces of furniture that have come from the lovely Arab man's family majlis in Dubai. You look around and realize there are echoes in the things around you of his other life. Bits and pieces borrowed. And then you ask yourself what it was you expected. The man has a wife and children, his own mother, brothers and sisters, and countless employees whom he treats as close family, all of these people he takes care of. You are simply one among many. But you knew that. Maybe you are sensing that this is the flat the lovely Arab man has had his people put together for his mistress. And maybe you are finding it difficult to think that others are watching and knowing and judging.

And that makes you his mistress.

He'd be so angry with you for writing this. But is there any way around the truth of it?

You heart tells you there is not.

You step into the hallway after having tucked your son into his new bed and you are haunted briefly by an insight that lingers. You stand outside the door to the office that has been arranged for whom? There's a big desk. And shelves for books. Is it for you? Or will the lovely Arab man be working from this home? You sense the truth of it there and then. This will be a hollow home. The lovely Arab man will only visit you here. Nothing of his will remain here for long. He is transient. He will come and he will go. In and out. Here and there. Back and forth. You feel your knees buckle. Your head feels light. *I don't want to be here. I want to go home. We don't belong here. He's misleading me and he's lying to himself.* And you resist the urge to curl up next to your son in his bed, whisper in his ear that you won't be staying, you've come to see what you needed to see and now you know. The problem is, however, that you've worked so hard to get here. You've said goodbyes, you've left places and people. How on earth are you to walk back into all that you've left behind and what will you say? The voice who tells you you're here now so you better make the best of it is the one you take directions from. Besides, to walk out of this now would be to admit that the last several years have been a lie. That you're really not building a life with the lovely Arab man. You are fulfilling a role. You tell yourself that he needs you here. And you ignore the fact that he wanted you to stay in Canada and finish your degree. What was your hurry, anyway? Why have you been so determined to get here and see it with your own eyes?

You simply cannot stand living in lies. Truth matters to you. And since Kent died there's been nothing but grey. No black and white answers. No clear right and wrong. The ambiguity of it all is driving you mad. You want to belong. Then to build. To have all the things you were taught you'd have. A home. A family. Security.

Stability. Love. Respect. A way forward in the world. Instead, you just keep bumping up against all these lies that feel like barriers keeping you from living a normal life.

You don't see that you've left the normal life you were building with your son in your own way. You've felt deficient in that life. It's too hard. You need help. And there's the sense that the lovely Arab man has too much power over what he says is your home, the Cordova Bay condo. Because, in fact, it is his. You are living in it. That's all. He also comes and goes there as he pleases. And that just doesn't seem to be enough for you. There is ambition in you but you haven't been wired to manage it very well. Or even to recognize it. You want more. And maybe coming to Abu Dhabi at this point in time is about you not being satisfied with what he's given you. On some level you suspect that the story you are living in with him is a convenient one at best. But if you were to turn and face that possibility now it would unravel the carefully constructed narrative that you've been living. He loves you. He wants a life with you. He'll do whatever it takes to have you know that you are loved and protected and provided for. He is a good man. A loving man. A man committed to taking care of his daughters and his wife. It is she who says their marriage is over. She who refuses to make love with him. She who wants him to have another wife and another life. But if all of this is true then why is she still here in their family home and you are being put away in this flat?

Are you jealous?

Do you want what she has?

If having your heart ache knowing your lover is with his family and not with you is jealousy then you are jealous. But you also have empathy and understanding in you. You can say you really want the best for these two people and their children. They'd decided what was happening between the two of them long before you showed up so it's really not your problem. The lovely Arab man sees things differently than you and you've grown to appreciate the lens through which he sees the world. You trust his sometimes mysterious ways. In fact, it might be the key attraction between you. When Kent died you knew you'd never again be able to live the life the two of you dreamed of. You were done with prairie life and prairie men. You no longer fit into the farm wife and mother dream. You had to leave the pain of that loss far behind. So here you are now. Trying to create a new dream. With new rules. If the lovely Arab man needs you to be his second wife then you'll consider that. You've been his mistress for more than five years so you've clearly demonstrated your loyalty and patience. You've tested his own resolve with hundreds of questions and he's never given you any reason to doubt his sincerity or his intention. You remember the first summer you spent at Seascape when your mom and dad visited. The lovely Arab man was staying with his wife and children in the Locarno Lane house, the home he'd renovated with the help of your brother. He must've had a plan all along. To have you and her in summer homes on the same island so he could be in one place and take care of all his family. The night he came for dinner with your parents, you remember how surprised you were when he promised your mom and dad that he'd take care of you and he'd marry you. It was the traditional approach to marriage that both embarrassed and endeared you to him. You hadn't asked him to make such a bold statement. But there it was. In the middle of the room. He had been openly transparent about his intentions and he wanted you to have dignity and respect.

Really?

You wonder now if maybe the lovely Arab man was overtaken by guilt having your family present in the room with the two of you. In his dark and quiet moments, did he feel he was acting less than honourably in this situation he'd created? Did it only surface for him in the presence of your father? What would he say to his wife's family if they were in the room with you at that time, too?

Shortly after his announcement that evening, he'd said goodnight and you remember walking him to the door. He had to get back to his "real" family.

And you'd stay there with yours.

Now here you are. Back in the UAE in a flat you are telling yourself will be your new home with the lovely Arab man. But something doesn't sit right with you. You feel the tension in your belly. And you remember the astrologer back in Victoria. You went to her for guidance. You were struggling with whether to stay or leave. Her advice was that you needed more information. Why not travel back to the desert and see for yourself exactly where the lovely Arab man's intentions were? So maybe that's the tension in your belly. Standing in this apartment now you know what his intentions are. He will keep you here away from his family. He will visit you and spend nights with you but you will exist on the periphery of his life. If you were to stand in this hallway at this moment and place your hand on your belly, breathe deep and accept what you know then tomorrow morning you'd be calling the airline and booking a ticket back to Canada. You'd sit with your young son, tell him that mama has learned what she came here to learn and you've decided you'd rather go back home to the island. You'd see the delight and relief on his face. You'd feel his little arms reaching out to hug you. You'd hear him say *don't worry mama, sometimes we make mistakes, that's all* and you'd see him shrug his little shoulders, get up off the bed and start packing up his toys and books. He'd want to leave. He's a brave boy. You adore him and long to give him everything he'll ever need to make his way in the world. You worry that when you leave, the lovely Arab man will be angry. How did you ever get yourself in this predicament? On the surface of things you think you know that the lovely Arab man's love for you is unconditional. That no matter what you decide, he'll always help you find your way. Yet deep in the crevice of your still broken heart there is a dark fear that would have you believe that you'll never be able to provide for your boy and yourself on your own. Your life has been damaged and you cannot expect to have a normal life or normal marriage again. You lost that chance. It's over. Now you have this. And this is all you have.

So denial becomes the order of the day.

You know you love the lovely Arab man. He's asked you for time and patience so that is what you'll give him. He'd've been just fine with you staying in Canada. Why did you have to come back here?

Because it's not enough to have half his love and attention. A part of you is angry with being treated this way. Very, very angry. And you want to assert yourself. You want your presence to be known. You will not be fooled with or hidden away. And you are willing to risk whatever you've been able to build to prove something to someone. The impulsiveness of coming here now under these conditions is compromising your soul and you just don't want to be that honest with yourself. You tell yourself that coming here is about getting to the truth of the matter but really, coming here is about you wanting this relationship with the lovely Arab man to be something more than it is. You were forced into being widow. And somehow that's what has made it possible to accept living as mistress. But this isn't how you want your life. This isn't what you dreamed of. So coming back to the UAE is an attempt to reclaim something that you feel has been ripped from you. You want it back. The dignity of your own personhood. And for some reason, the lovely Arab man is holding what was once yours.

• • •

You stay here in Abu Dhabi in the piecemeal flat. It doesn't feel like home and you're not even interested in making it home. You enrol your son in the American School. You focus on creating what he needs to feel he belongs here. You indulge in the time you get with him now. You have a cook and a housekeeper. You are detached from the place in which you live and that liberates you from the mundane to some degree. It's like a vacation. All you need to be is mother and lover. And everything in-between and outside-of is luxurious reading, studying and writing time. You are a perpetual learner. Curious about the culture and the people you are living among. You and the lovely Arab man have long discussions about religion, culture, history, geography, politics … perhaps you sensed you'd get more of an education living here with him than living back in Canada attending university. The surface of things bore you. You like to delve deep and engage, a quality that has always annoyed your father. Probably still does to this day. But here's a man who wants to talk with you. You're guessing that it's your intense listening skill that enhances this part of your relationship. If you were a fly on the wall watching your interaction you'd notice that the lovely Arab man does most of the talking. Whatever this part of your relationship is, it satisfies a hunger in you. This insatiable curiosity is a quality you see in your son but you certainly don't acknowledge it in yourself. You just feel a need to be close to the lovely Arab man. He's unlike any human being you've ever known. Kind to his core. A deep stillness imbues his being. He never seems to rattle. Appears to have no fear. A self-assuredness that magnetizes you. But the deeper your intimate knowledge of him the more you begin to see how he might be susceptible to acting out unconscious patterns that he's inherited from his family experience. It's the ever-present curiosity about the human experience that drives you to consider such things.

His father left his mother while the lovely Arab man was attending an American university, the first generation of young students to leave his country for a foreign education. He completed his scholarship and then needed to return home to take care of his mother and his siblings even though his father was a wealthy man. You remember him asking you *What kind of a man does this to his family?* You suspect this experience was the training that cultivated the lovely Arab man's pattern of taking care of those who've been abandoned by people they thought loved and cared about them. You also know that the lovely Arab man lost a young sister when he was just a boy. She died due to illness. The wound is still visible to you and the main reason why you never interfere with his relationship to his own young daughters now. You imagine that if his American wife were to take his daughters back to her home in the United States that he would be devastated beyond repair. You will not bear being the one to cause such an eventuality. Yet another reason why you stay quiet and hidden as his mistress. You don't want to make her unhappy and you want to help him keep his daughters near.

The lovely Arab man was traumatized by his father's leaving. It changed the course of his life as he understood it. He no longer had the luxury of studying and travelling. He quickly became the sole provider for his family. The pressure motivated him to develop his business acumen. And he succeeded in his pursuit to provide all that was needed to sustain his mother, her home, and her children. The boys and the girls all achieved university educations granted by their brother's financial care. And they developed careers that continue to serve their communities.

You felt proud to be part of such a family dynamic. A man so caring and so creatively capable was surely a risk worth taking.

What exactly was the risk anyway?

The risk was the interior damage being done because you were projecting your own care and creative capacity onto the lovely Arab man rather than developing it in yourself. And the time will come when the walls you've carefully constructed will cave in and you'll get a glimpse of what really is at stake. And you'll need to make a decision that will reset the course of your life.

• • •

You learn soon enough that the flat you are living in was left-over from some business arrangement and the lease comes due in a few short months. So there it is. The lovely Arab man hedging his bets. Maybe she will come and stay for a few months and decide to return to Canada. It is painfully evident that he is not willing to commit to all the things he has been promising to commit to for you and your life together. He is making a small space for you and it remains a quiet, removed space from the rest of his life.

You are even more angry now.

But you dare not express just how angry you are. Not to him and not to yourself. Instead you tell yourself stories that excuse his behaviour and dishonesty. He is a man of integrity after all and who are you to doubt his intentions?

Your way of coping with the truth of the situation is to make another story. You want to move out of this place and make a new place with the lovely Arab man. You deserve to have a fresh and real start for your life together and you convince him that when the lease comes due, you must move out and into a new flat, one that you and he find together. It'll be a proper home and you'll be happy there. Together. All alone.

In this new story, you become Maha. It is the name the lovely Arab man bestows on you in a quietly intense moment of lovemaking. He takes pride in being your lover. He practices extended sexual orgasm, something he's learned from a book. Sometimes you feel like his laboratory. And the most important thing to him seems to be to bring you pleasure. He offers it up through guiding your bodies in a dance he is definitely in charge of. He explores you with such curiosity that you learn new things about yourself. You're an intuitive animal and so is he. But his virility has the capacity to hold you in a place where you can allow yourself to completely let go of all inhibitions. In your shared bedroom, he is a larger-than-life-sized man even though in physical reality he's only a bit taller than you and weighs about the same weight. Making love to you he is transformed into a creature seeking transcendence unlike the practical, logical, problem-solving guy he is in the world outside your bedroom. The magnetic pull between you is so powerful that simply walking by one another in the hallway is enough to trigger a secluded moment in the nearest room and make him late for his scheduled meeting for which he is infamous. Being late for meetings. He says you're like the character in an Arab story passed down through the ages. You cannot remember the tale but you have a clear image of it in your head, the image seeded there by his storytelling. You see making love with him in a tent out in the desert on soft, silken rugs and sand while warring factions of men and horses rage outside the sex chamber. He is the army's commander. But he is wholly distracted by you, his mistress, and he cannot command his forces outside the tent. So war rages on without direction. Chaos and fighting reigns in the desert as the army commander tends to the business of pleasuring the woman in the tent.

You are a bit put off by this story he tells you.

Is this what I am to you, a distraction?

He is silent. And smiling. There is a brief crack in reality as you've been constructing it. Something bigger dares to make itself known to you. But you are quick to gloss over the revelation and attribute the momentary lapse to the games lovers play.

Decades later, however, you reflect on such moments and wonder why you couldn't see the truth of the matter.

When truth hurts, it's amazing to what lengths we'll go to avoid knowing it.

• • •

A few months later, the lovely Arab man takes you to the flat he's found for the two of you to move into. So the fact is that you didn't go looking for it together. The fact is that he sent his right-hand-man to find it for you. And when the legwork has been done, then the two of you get to waltz into this new location. The fact is you've been told this is where you will be moving to.

You are delighted.

It's definitely an upgrade.

You'll be living in the newly built Baynunah Tower. It is a paragon of luxury. Home of the Hilton Hotel. Swimming pool, hot tub, sauna and spa. Rooftop tennis court and helipad. Marble floors, floor-to-ceiling windows for entire walls. A picture perfect view of the Corniche along the Arabian Sea. Replete with 24-hour concierge in addition to your cook and driver. It is a lifestyle you feel fit to enjoy. How'd you get here? The lovely Arab man is teaching you to be worthy of grandeur. He takes his promise to lavish you with pleasure seriously. A commitment he never wavers from. He wants you to trust that all your needs are provided for. You'll not be a slave in the kitchen nor will you trouble yourself with any other domestic details. He has people hired to manage the stuff of your life.

You spend many hours talking to the people he has hired. You enjoy their company and they tell you wonderful stories about their families back home in India and the Philippines. They help you learn the Arab culture from their perspective. You also learn from their stories the darker side of what appears to be true and good and beautiful in this desert land. There is an underbelly of life existing just beneath the surface of things. Women and men in trouble. Domestic disputes. Deportations. Drama that some part of you is drawn to and wants to help.

You vow to finish your university degree and return to this place to make a difference. You've had an experience that you imagine other expat women may be vulnerable to as well. There are no transition houses here for women and children looking for safety. When you talk about this to the lovely Arab man, he supports your vision. He is a human helper, too. He is one people come to when they are in need. And he extends himself in service of others all the time. You remind yourself that it is how he found you. With his guidance, you imagine creating a safe haven for those in trouble.

You will build a transition house and you will provide the services needed for people in strife. This is a way for you to bridge into the community because you are desperate to know what the heck you are doing here. Yes, you are here to be with your lover. But there must be some other reason that you're drawn to this desert land. The lovely Arab man may not need or want you to be anything domestic but he loves to hear you talk about how you imagine your work in the world. He wants you to educate yourself and be of service to others. He takes pride in hearing you have a vision and a purpose to fulfill. He wants you to have everything you could possibly need to step fully into the woman you are becoming. It is a grace emanating from his soul and it makes him the most beautiful man on the planet to you. It draws you closer to him and to your own dream.

You reflect on how fortunate you are to have found him. Or to have had him find you. You marvel at the way the universe seems to work. You are convinced there are no accidents even though your first husband was killed in one. You sense there is a Divine Plan and everything is unfolding as it should. And you really have no idea what your role is in the Divine Plan to make it all come to be. So you wait. And watch. Witness to the small miracles of everything you now have access to. The lovely Arab man empowers you in the world because you know he loves and adores you. But sometimes you are overcome with the need to be a real part of his family. You have come to know his mother, sisters and brothers through his stories about them. Yet he's not taken you to meet them. He says it is because he wants to handle the situation delicately. His family loves his first wife and their daughters. He thinks they all need a bit of time to ease into the transition of realizing he has a second wife, another North American woman who will surely be welcome because she is a widow and she has a small son. Because the Arab way is to look after widows and their children. And he is convinced that if he does this with deep care, then the family will open its arms to you and the integration will be seamless. But it's too soon. He needs more time. He reassures you constantly and asks that you trust him.

And really, is that too much to ask?

He's done so much for you. He loves you so completely. He provides for your every need. And clearly, he is a respectable and well-loved man.

So you are patient.

You spend your time reading and writing and being the best mother you know how to be. You take long walks with your son along the Corniche. You also read and study Qu'ran. You research writers and stories about Arab history and culture. You are drawn into the beauty of Islam. You take refuge in books written by Fatima Mernissi, Leila Ahmed and Nawal El Saadawi, strong feminist voices about women in Islam. You watch women carefully, all women. The UAE population being 85% expat means you are living in a cosmopolitan society yet you are drawn mostly to the local culture and the small 15% that your lovely Arab man belongs to. It is here that you want to find sanctuary. It is here that you long to be a part of too. You are educating yourself about everything that will assist you in being accepted here. You begin covering your head with hijab and draping your body with an abaya when you go out into public. You pray five times a day. You discover a mosque for women just a short walk from the Baynunah Tower but you are reluctant to go in alone. You wish that the lovely Arab man's sisters would become your sisters and you might attend this all female gathering together. This is what you dream of now. Of being folded into this place and its people. Part of your soul is so at home here that you can't help but wonder if you've had this life before. The only thing that helps you make sense of the familiarity you experience here is the notion of reincarnation and past lives. How else to explain the knowingness you hold inside of yourself? You are a girl from the Canadian prairies yet that part of you feels foreign to you now. But there is tension in your life here because you are being hidden away and you are not being welcomed in the way you feel you ought to be. How can this be home when you are being rendered invisible? It is a strange disconnect. And it has you encased in a glass bubble that you want to shatter and liberate yourself from.

You stay here in the Baynunah Tower. He spends most of his nights with you now. When he visits his family, he goes alone. The cook knows when he will be eating with you and when he'll be eating at the family home with his mother and siblings. You are not to bother yourself with those details. When he's in Abu Dhabi, he's generally with you so you figure this is progress. When he's in Dubai, you know that he is with his first wife and their children. You practice not being jealous or feeling left out. Circumstances are forcing you to become a bigger person. And as long as you feel he is being true to you, then you have enormous capacity to be that bigger person. You are surprised at how able you are to embrace these new ways of being. Where'd you learn to be so gracious and understanding? Of course, you attribute these qualities to the lovely Arab man rather than owning them as yours. He is surely the reason you've been made to suffer so much in your life. Everything that happened to get you here now makes sense. He is the gift and the reward. You've been banished from the prairie life because you no longer fit there and you never will. Trouble is, you don't yet fit here in this life with the lovely Arab man either and you long to belong. Somewhere. Anywhere. Back on the west coast in your beautiful seascape retreat, going to school, being a present mother, building community around you all felt like the potential of home with something missing. And you attribute the missing-ness to the absence of the lovely Arab man. But he'd never fit there in that life with you so you must be here to fit in this life with him. Otherwise you're just on the periphery of things floating and waiting, waiting and floating. For what you are waiting is hard to know.

It must be marriage that'll make it all make sense again.

Yes, that's it. You need to marry the lovely Arab man and live openly, respectably.

Yet he tells you over and over and over again that you are respected. By him. *What else matters?* he asks.

What you really hear him saying is that he is respected and respectable and therefore he lends to you his respect and by default you have a larger respect from his unseen family and the culture you are living in. You don't need your own respect. You have his. Rest assured. You'll get everything you desire. Just be patient. So it must be your impatience and imperfection that have you feeling badly. Work on that, you think. Focus on bettering yourself so you are worthy of all this respect coming your way.

You gaze out the floor to ceiling windows from the fourteenth floor apartment. You see below you the British Embassy. During the week you watch Brits in white shorts playing tennis in the heat of the day. It is winter here and it feels like a warm summer on Vancouver Island. On Fridays you watch the men at mosque from these windows. They look like a bunch of ants scurrying to the centre of something that feeds and nourishes them. It's a ritual you take pleasure in, watching these men. Hearing the call to prayer. The fervour of the Imam disturbing you a bit. Too vehement. No love in that voice. It leaves you wondering where all the women are on these Friday mornings. It takes you awhile to adjust the focus of your attention to allow yourself to see that just as you are a woman staring out the window into the world below, there are other women with faces pressed against apartment windows on Friday mornings in buildings surrounding the Baynunah Tower. You wonder if they can see you. And you wonder if they're thinking what you're thinking. Who among them feels as shut away as you do from what must be the centre of life happening outside these walls?

• • •

There is a moment in the San Diego airport. The lovely Arab man is there to greet you. You have a full week together. It is summer. You've gone home to Canada for the hot desert months while he continues to travel between the UAE and North America. His first wife and their daughters are with her family in the United States. He's come from being with them to be with you now. And the sweetest moments are the first glimpses of each other in airports. You're learning to master the rituals of goodbyes and hellos.

He notices a friend there in the airport, a Sheikh from the UAE. You are standing next to him as the Sheikh approaches. The Sheikh is holding the hand of his young son. The men greet each other with warmth and connection. You wonder what you should do. Focus on the luggage carousel or join the lovely Arab man with his friend. You stand a bit to the side not knowing what is expected of you. Much to your surprise, the lovely Arab man introduces you as Maha and it feels as though this is coded in a way that lets the Sheikh understand exactly who you are to the lovely Arab man. The Sheikh is respectful and kind. You are included in their conversation. You are drawn to watch the young son. He might be six years old. And at this young age he already has a striking elegance. It has little to do with the beauty of his physical features and more to do with his presence. He is likewise drawn to you and you eye one another carefully. You are lifted from the chaos of the airport environment into what feels like a calm ocean. A voice in your inner ear beckons to you. You imagine no one noticing the way you tilt your head and look skyward, to the right. Some guidance is there. Your intuition holds you still. And you hear the voice proclaim that this is the reason you are with the lovely Arab man. You will bear his son. He will be a beautiful boy. And for a moment you feel as though the boy standing in front of you now is your son. As though whatever force field is holding this reality together slightly shifts for a split second and a veil is lifted to reveal what has already happened in a parallel reality. This shape shifting has happened to you before. The first time when you were ten years old and you watched from the kitchen window as your grandmother was driven out of the farmyard by your grandfather in their black four-door car and the voice told you to say goodbye to your grandmother because you'd not see her again, she would die. So you silently say a prayer for her and bid her farewell. You never see her alive again. Then the big black letters above Kent's head – ACCIDENT – the day he left you standing in the kitchen doorway. Another moment when you were sitting with Sophie, your best friend after Kent died, and for a moment she became an old Native woman with sacred feathers in her hair. As though ripples in time reveal other layers of living not before, not later, but now. Like time itself is illusory. Actually standing still. Holding all the possibilities for who we are and who we are becoming all at once.

Now you know in your deepest vision for your life that you will have a son with the lovely Arab man. But the knowing is forgotten. You must carry it around with you somewhere because where could it go? Maybe it just falls asleep within you until the moment is right and the knowing comes to pass. However it works, you forget this insight into why you are here and what you are doing with these men in this place. Your attention shifts back into being in conversation while standing in front of the baggage carousel in the San Diego airport.

• • •

While enjoying the luxury of being in San Diego with the lovely Arab man, he tells you about his friend Sultan who is staying a few doors down from where you are in this dockside waterfront community of beautiful homes, boats and marinas. In the middle of the night, while his wife lies sleeping in their bed next to him and his children are fast asleep in their rooms down the hall, the Sheikh dons his swimming shorts, slips out the dining room sliding glass door onto the patio, walks down the dock and dives into the midnight waters. He swims across the marina. Climbs out of the water onto the dock. Runs a few yards. Lets himself into the sliding glass door of the bedroom where his young American girlfriend lies waiting in bed for him.

You are stunned at the audacity and strategic planning of such an encounter.

The lovely Arab man laughs when he tells you this story. You know Sultan has confided details of his sexual prowess to the lovely Arab man. You can't help but notice that the lovely Arab man seems a bit envious of his friend. Or maybe he's simply taking notes and imagining what might be possible for his own life. Maybe he wishes he could be so daring. But he is not, he assures you. You are his biggest dare. And you are not his girlfriend nor his wife. He will never treat you with such disrespect. You are his lover and the one woman he is committed to. He only wants his one woman. And she is you.

You hear the lovely Arab man's words. And you want more than anything to believe him. To trust him. Yet the still small voice inside of you is saying *Pay Attention!*

The lovely Arab man is amused and entertained by his friend. This shared story now connects you to Sultan and his young American girlfriend without you realizing it because you don't put yourself in the same league as the two of them and what they're up to. One night, in the not so faraway future, you and the lovely Arab man will host a dinner by the pool in the Dubai house. You will notice that the only women attending are the young American girlfriend, a friend of hers and yourself. There are no wives. And you wonder if you are considered to be in the same category as the young American girlfriend. You cannot bear the thought. She seems like a kid to you. How old can she be? Not even twenty yet, you surmise.

So you convince yourself that it cannot possibly be true. The lovely Arab man wouldn't do such a thing to you. He is a man of integrity. He is honest. And frankly, he just doesn't seem driven by the same egoic confidence. His soul demands alignment with values that the two of you share. At least this is what you tell yourself. It might be your survival mechanism. Otherwise how could you possibly exist in this space of ambiguity? How could you tolerate those nights when he dresses in his Western clothes to attend a party hosted by Western friends and business colleagues but leaves you at home because it wouldn't be appropriate for an Emirati man to bring his Western woman along? He'd be breaking the code of his culture. The woman he loves is not to be shared with other men. But his woman isn't from his culture. She is of the very Western culture that now exists within his Arab culture and the blurring of cultural codes is confusing to you. You watch how he adapts himself to easily flow between and within both cultures while in the land of his birth. He also does it well as a resident of the rest of the world. He is a well-traveled being. A highly educated man. And he has brought you into his world by calculated choice. But somehow, and you cannot quite name how, you are expected to carry the code of his culture not only in the land of his birth but also in your own homeland. You are not allowed to flow between and within. There are silent and unspoken restrictions for you. You are expected to learn these limits and live according to these rules.

You don't understand it yet, but what you are learning is how to navigate the fine line between creating your life through the choices you make and following Divine guidance. You have this powerful force of your own will through which you've discovered you can make just about anything happen. You will yourself to live there or to live here. And based on what you decide, you make it happen. You push through obstacles. You pull your weight around. Things move to accommodate your desire. You try to push yourself into being seen as the lovely Arab man's woman, even though it looks like you are placating his desire and playing by all his rules, you are actually testing your own will. You want to be a part of his family. He tells you he wants that, too. So, by god you're going to make that happen!

But you're not living by God at all.

You are being driven by the erroneous belief that you can muscle yourself through life based on what you've been conditioned to think is yours to have. Just because a man makes love to you doesn't mean you need to marry him and make happily ever after!

You don't know your own power yet. And you are being pushed and pulled around by lies ... the ingredients of your conditioned self. Every now and then you hear the still, small voice within you that tells you what is wrong and how to make it right but the lies are deeply ingrained in you and they drown out the music of your own soul.

The music of our own soul is easier to access when you are in your homeland. But here, in the lovely Arab man's culture, it is not so accessible. Doubt and confusion move in as permanent tenants. Your innate curiosity is hijacked by compliance. You are flattered by the fact that part of why the lovely Arab man loves you is because you are a Western woman. He has talked at length about how a "local" woman could never meet his needs. The two of you together break down the cultural barriers in what feels like your sacred connection. You are intellectually, emotionally, sexually, psychologically attracted to each other. There is a common ground of effortless ease on which you stand side by side. But it's as though it only exists in this sub-culture you call your couple. You are a couple composed of kindness and good-will. Unless the dominate cultures outside your cocoon interfere, all is well.

Soon enough you'll come to know that all really isn't well. And you're putting your very life at risk.

The question will become *Are you willing to lose it all?*

• • •

You are sitting in the corner of the bedroom you share with the lovely Arab man. A book in your lap. You are gently rocking in the cream coloured leather chair he has bought for you. The baby has been moved into his own room, the room where once his sister slept before her mother took her to America, but your son will never meet his sister or be acknowledged as her brother. His presence will never be known by the lovely Arab man's family here in the desert land and the pain of that fact will be the straw that breaks your camel's back even though you promised your son's father to never take his child away from him, to never cause him the anguish that he is in this very moment because he has lost both of his daughters due to their mother's decision to take them back to her homeland. You are acutely aware of the fact that you've stepped into another woman's life by being in this house and it feels weird. You are a women's studies scholar. You know how Patriarchy has been constructed and you see that you are living within its walls. You want to break free. Reach out. Connect with the lovely Arab man's wife and daughters. Have a conversation with them. You are willing to embrace whatever cultural rules might help you all to find peace and live in love. Why can't it be possible? The lovely Arab man promises you that it is possible but you need to trust him to create the pathways over time. So you let go. And you trust him. But a bigger part of you wonders how this will all play out. You long for the female company of his sisters and mother. You want your sons to be welcomed into the lovely Arab man's family. You feel pride in presenting this family with the lovely Arab man's only son. They have a grandson, a nephew. You want them to know this. You want them to teach your boy the Arab way. You want to belong here in this desert land.

The lovely Arab man has promised you he'd never leave you alone to raise another son. He knows how hard it has been for you. He wants to make your life easier.

When you discovered you were pregnant again it was such a shock that you fell out of the Nissan Pathfinder you had just parked, landing on the sand like a sack of potatoes and broke your arm.

The lovely Arab man took you to the American clinic after you called him for help. Sitting in the doctor's treatment room, you hear the lovely Arab man talking business on the phone out in the waiting room while the doctor injects a needle into your elbow to drain the sagging bag of flesh filled with blood. It's more painful than anything you've ever known. You focus on the lovely Arab man's voice in the waiting room. The sweet sound of his Arabic. It's funny how just writing this opens your heart to him again. You actually miss all that he once was to you. It's hard to believe considering all that has happened since that moment. When the doctor completes the procedure, he sits down directly in front of you. He looks serious. Clearly, he has something to say. And he says it. *There are ways to make an abortion available to you.*

And you are right back to the beginning. Your first pregnancy. The doctor in Swift Current telling you that *God will forgive you the first time but not the second.*

• • •

You were so fearful of being left to parent alone a second time that you felt you had to have an abortion. Because the fear of being responsible for another human being without the cradle of a secure marriage terrified you more than the prospect of ending the pregnancy. You knew it was just too hard to be a lone mother. You weren't willing to go back to where you started and do it all over again. This time with an older boy whom you were so psychically and emotionally entangled with that you couldn't imagine having any love or energy left over to give to another child. You felt that if not for some indescribable grace having gotten you this far with your first boy, you'd be buried alive in hopelessness. But the lovely Arab man begged and pleaded with you to keep the baby. He swore to always love and support both of you. He'd never let anything hurt or harm you. You'd have the best of everything he could give you. If only you could trust his sincerity and put your life in his hands.

It was clearly another one of those moments of choosing and letting go. You told yourself you were choosing to trust and you were learning to let go. What were you trusting? That life was different now. That you weren't stepping back in time and recreating the same circumstances you'd just lived through. That this child was grace embodied and you'd need to grow out of your fears of not being looked after so you might be better able to look after him. What were you letting go of? The need to control the events in your life. Surely this was an honourable endeavour, to trust something bigger than yourself and to trust the lovely Arab man. Upon reflection you could detect a deep-seated fear from adolescence. The fear of pregnancy outside of marriage. You grew up believing that to get pregnant outside of marriage would be the biggest disgrace and it was a mistake you were terrified of making. Looking back it was probably a big factor in choosing to get married the first time. Your relationship with Kent had awakened you sexually and the only way to stay safe would be to get married. So you thought. So you did.

Fast forward a decade and here you are in the very position you feared as a teenager. Pregnant and unmarried.

So, you agree to carry this child in your womb and bring him into the lovely Arab man's world of promises. But you have one condition. You will be married to the father of your child. It is the only way you can change fate and not repeat your past.

He agrees. He will marry you. He always intended to but this is the reason to do it sooner rather than later. He will take care of the details. You are not to think another moment about any of this. You are to focus on yourself, your son and your unborn child. Life will get simpler now. You will belong. You will be loved and protected. You will have home, husband and children. A sanctuary. A sweet, sweet sanctuary. You are not to worry about a thing. Not one thing.

• • •

You are in the Baynunah Tower apartment. It's June 20, 1995, and you are waiting for the men to arrive. You wonder at the serendipity of this moment. Exactly 14 years ago, you were in the Saskatchewan Cypress Hills with your beloved Kent getting married for the first time under the shade of a tree which still bares your initials K.S. & M.B. as he carved them there in a heart. He imagined the two of you visiting every year and renewing your vows there on that spot. He was going to love you forever.

Now it's 1995 and you are waiting for the men.

You sit in your son's bedroom with him watching *Star Trek*. You've explained to him that you are getting married this afternoon. It means that he must stay in his room while Mama goes into the majlis with the men when she is called.

What men, Mama?

With the lovely Arab man, there will be The Judge from Sharia Court. He is coming into your home so you will have privacy, or at least that is what you are told. (Maybe the lovely Arab man just wants to keep the lid on his secret mistress.) Ibrahim will also be present. He is the man who will act as your own father were he to be present. Ibrahim has been appointed to look out for your best interests. To be your voice. To protect and guide you. (You wonder what your dad would think of this.)

As you explain it to your young son, you recall the other day when you told him you were pregnant. He listened to you with wide eyes that soon became filled with tears. He touched your belly and then lay his head down on you as he cried.

No, no, no Mama ... I want it to be just you and me!

You tried to console him and excite him, too. He was going to have a baby brother or sister. He would never be alone.

But you've always wanted a brother or sister. Remember? You've always wanted this. You should be happy.

You couldn't change his mood. He was sad. And he clung to you as though he feared he was losing you. And it made you feel like you just wanted to go home to Canada. You wanted to get out of this place. You needed your beloved Vancouver Island. Until you were there, you wouldn't really know what to do. You needed the island air and the Pacific Ocean. And the balm of the gray west coast days to soften the blow of all that was happening to you.

You heard the men arrive.

Soon, the lovely Arab man would come into your son's bedroom to bring you into the majlis. Deep inside you was the urge to laugh out loud. How could you take any of this seriously? It's outrageous! Yet another part of yourself watched as you played your role. What a performance! And there was still another part of you who was clear and deliberate. You wanted to make sure the lovely Arab man would be held accountable for the part he'd agreed to play. You needed to know he was accepting his role as father to this unborn child. You would not do this alone and the only way to make sure he wouldn't leave you would be to marry him.

So, marry him you did.

After it was done, you walked back into the sanctuary of your son's bedroom where you laughed until you cried. What a hideous ritual you subjected yourself to! Sitting in the majlis with the men. Nobody making eye contact with you. Not allowed to speak unless spoken to. And then only to answer questions The Judge asked you through Ibrahim. When you had performed your part, the men asked you to leave.

You remember wanting to roar with laughter. A witchy-like cackle rising from the depths of your Wise Woman being. Her spirit expanding so large as to swallow all the air, the men, the furniture, the walls, the windows, the building itself and the city beyond. She would swallow the whole leaded hoax into her being, transmute it into fiery gold wings, fiercely envelop both Her children and fly far, far away from the maniacal ruse!

But you restrained yourself.

The disobedient woman in you was not going to take any of this seriously. As far as she was concerned, you were already wed to the lovely Arab man and had been for more than six years. This whole legal dance was just a way to secure your son's rightful place in his father's life. It didn't change a thing between you and the lovely Arab man. Except now he was bound to fold you into his family life here. He was surely going to drop the veils of silence and seclusion around your shared life. You would be seen. You would be accepted. You would belong here and have a place here and your children would be proud of the life you were all going to live with the lovely Arab man. This vision alone contained the witchy-wise disobedient woman in you as you agreed to act respectfully and do as you were told. You believed it was for the good of all of you. This was the only way forward.

That night, the night you were married to the lovely Arab man, he never returned to the Baynunah apartment after the marriage contract had been ritualized. He left with Ibrahim and The Judge.

And the fact that you were spending your "wedding night" alone wasn't lost on you. It was an echo from the past. You remembered your second marriage. On your wedding night on the Queen Mary in California you'd shared a bed in a state room with your new husband but he never touched you. That marriage had not been consummated on that night. Then returning to Canada you thought how that fact might be your saving grace; you could have the marriage annulled. Your new husband had returned to his studies in Ontario while you remained on the prairies for several weeks and you didn't see each other for more than a month after that wedding night. It would have been the right thing to do, have that marriage annulled. But you didn't do that. You waited for him to return. Then you packed up your life and moved with him to live here in the desert. Now you were marrying another man. A third marriage. The insanity of it all threatened to overcome you. It was like you were lost in a vortex of mistake-making that you had to play out to its own mysterious conclusion. You were walking around dazed in a labyrinth and you couldn't sense your way out.

You rationalized your sadness on this third wedding night by saying to yourself that this was a different culture with different customs and you couldn't project your own cultural program onto the episode you were living in now. You had to accept what was before you and trust life was leading you where you needed to go. But after you tucked your son into his bed for the night, and returned to your own bedroom, you couldn't help but feel a new kind of loneliness. You were officially a pregnant married woman. And there was no-one there to share it with. Except your beloved little boy whom you suspected could see and know you in ways that no other being could. He was your guardian angel. A divine witness so you could remember you were still alive.

How the hell did I get here? was the mantra that took you into sleep that night. In the morning, you would start packing for your return to Canada. You and your children were flying home.

• • •

Home.

You and your children are home on Vancouver Island.

The moment the plane lands on the tarmac you feel your whole being open. You breathe deep and easy.

When you walk into your Seascape home along Cordova Bay it feels like you never left. You drop more than your bags at the door. All the perceived burdens melt away as you look out your kitchen window to see open sky, Juan de Fuca islands and miles of beautiful ocean. There's no place like this place anywhere else on the planet for you. You belong here. You feel like yourself here.

Your son has his beach shoes on. He's out the door, down the more than one hundred wooden steps and hunting for geoduck clams before you can even suggest there might be anything else to do first. He feels as much at home here as you do. Such relief!

Home.

• • •

It's mid-summer. Time to meet with the lovely Arab man. He'll be in Philadelphia and then New York so that's where you're going to go. But first to the farm where your son will stay with his grandparents.

Another airport scene with the lovely Arab man. You arrive in Philadelphia and he is there to greet you. He seems surprised by the fact that you are now looking pregnant. As though he didn't fully grasp the reality of your predicament. You announce to him that your suitcase is empty because you need to shop for maternity clothes. He agrees. You will do it together.

The sweet romance of seeing each other again feels delicious and right. You are now a married couple. You've made all the announcements to your family. Everyone knows. At least everyone on your continent. His side of the world is a whole different story. But you are here now with him. And that's what matters. Now with him here.

You shop with the lovely Arab man. And it's great fun. He's relaxed and generous. He feels proud to be with you. It's an experience you've not had before. Walking arm in arm with the man you love while carrying his unborn child in your womb. He protects you. Cares about you. Cherishes and nourishes you. You feel loved. And hopeful for your future.

Then it is time for you to return to Canada. And for him to head back to the UAE.

Parting is never easy.

And it feels particularly difficult on this day.

Could it be that some part of you knows you'll not see him again for many, many months? That you are one decision and one assumption away from turning your whole world of safety and care upside down?

If this part of you who senses this is here with you now then why doesn't she better prepare you for what is about to happen? Why does she insist on living in this fantasy that you will return to Dubai in a few weeks, prepare for the birth of your child and build a future with the lovely Arab man? How does she keep herself from seeing that what you really want to do is stay home in Canada where you know you'll have control over the birth of this baby with the support of your family, especially your mother and your sister? Is she even the slightest bit aware of the fact that you are terrified of what this birth might mean for your life? Does she understand that when you make the phone call to tell the lovely Arab man you've decided to stay in your Seascape home so your mother and your sister can be near you for the birth that he will hang up on you and refuse to speak to you during the entire first year of your new son's life?

Because it'll all come to pass.

As though written in the stars.

Yet you'll be dumbstruck. You'll refuse to believe the lovely Arab man can be capable of such cruel behaviour. You'll keep waiting for him to show up on your doorstep. You'll keep assuming he'll not abandon you when you need him most.

You are strong and decisive when you make the call. You tell him you know what you need to bring this child into the world. You ask him to trust you. You want to be home. You want your mother and your sister. You want your husband. You want this baby to be welcomed into loving circumstances. This is the foundation upon which you stand when you make the call.

But the lovely Arab man is shape-shifted by his unjustified anger.

You assume he'll get over himself. You assume he'll be here for you when you need him. You assume you're not asking too much. You just want to be in your home country for the birth of your second son. You just want to enjoy the fourth trimester in the security of your familiar home with your family around you. You assume he will keep his promises to you. You assume he would never compromise his integrity.

You've been wrong in your life before, but never as wrong as you are now.

The lovely Arab man withdraws from you completely. He doesn't call. And he doesn't answer your calls. You leave messages with Ibrahim but you never get responses. You have such anxiety and sadness rising in you that you don't recognize your own reflection in the mirror.

You turn to your yoga teacher, a wise woman in your life for more than a decade. She teaches you Transcendental Meditation. You slip into a daily TM practice like a duck to water. The practice makes perfect sense to you. You want out of this realm of consciousness. Life has become too painful to sustain. Hanging out in these lower energies just won't do you anymore. If you stay here you're going to die. You've got to find another way to be in relationship to life. You've got to wake up and learn how it is you keep putting yourself in these relationships with men.

Easy for the writer to say as she tells this story. Not so easy for the woman facing the edge of her life again.

Because the worst was yet to come.

• • •

You sit on the deck overlooking the bay. In the fullness of summer you feel yourself blossoming with life. New life. When you are still and in your home with your son it feels like you'll be okay. That life is good and right and true. You love being pregnant. You feel most at home in your body when you are carrying new life. You know that you glow. Even when your face looks sad. And you wonder if other people notice the sadness or if it is only noticeable to you.

You watch your son play on the beach from where you are sitting on your deck. He is happy. Brimming with playful joy. He

builds castles in the sand. He digs moats. He moves water. He sings
and dances without a care in the world. Nothing makes you more
content than when you are witness to his exuberance. Next to him
you feel you must be dull. But he breathes life into your presence
and it buoys you.

He waves up to you. "Mama! Look!"

You smile and wave back. He carries a long stick. He is spelling
out words in the sand for you. He keeps looking up to make sure
you are looking down.

And then there's magic.

You see the words "Birth House" written on the beach. Your
whole body smiles. You know this is guidance from the unseen
world. You feel as though you are basking in light and love. You let
your gaze float out to the waters beyond and into the sky above.
You let the beauty of it all fill your heart.

Then it registers in your mind what you've just seen. So, you
look again. Just to be sure. And there it is. "Birth House." You
acknowledge to the Divine that you've heard the message and you
will heed the guidance. You will not leave Canada. This child will
be born here on your beloved island.

And as you continue to gaze into the words on the beach, they
dissolve.

Gone.

This all happens in an instant. Like Time adjusts herself to allow
you to see spirit's message. Something opens. You have profound
clarity. You are mystified. But you rest in ease, too. As though a
wrinkle in reality shifted just long enough for you to know what it
is you must do. And the experience is enough to hold you steady in
the months to come. You've been given your orders.

Now, you don't feel alone at all.

Everything is right and true and good.

You know in your heart that you were always meant to
conceive this child in the Arabian Peninsula. How you know is
beyond you. And now you know you are meant to birth him here
in Canada.

The words your boy has spelled out in the sand for you are
clearly "I love you."

All is well. And all will be well.
Even though you still have a long, long way to go.

• • •

There are always unseen helping hands waiting even when you think everything in your life is turning out all wrong. The trick is to not believe everything you think. To not turn your life choices over to the voice in you that is constantly scanning the horizon to see if you're safe or not.

Being on the island in your home next to the ocean where you glimpse whales passing by and eagles flying over is where you source your peace now. Every morning and every night you meditate. And most days in the afternoon, too. In fact, the place you can touch in your meditations brings you such ease that you long to be there rather than here.

But you have a son who needs you.

And another boy on his way.

Your guardians, that's what these boys are to you. They keep you in your life. Otherwise you might be tempted to slip away because life on Planet Earth has turned out to be a gruelling trial.

Endurance must be a grace.

Forbearance a quality of soul.

If not, you might just die trying to accept what feels unacceptable.

One day you meet a friend in the local store down the road. The owner, Mary, a woman who loves to tell stories and serve folks, knows you are home from Dubai where there is a husband waiting for you. She also knows another woman who lives up the hill in her home here who also has a husband in Dubai. So she takes it upon herself to introduce the two of you. And there you are. A new friend who can understand your dilemma and appreciate the context of your life.

Sabine becomes that longed-for dear friend. In the years that follow, she will remember every birthday, she will share beautiful gifts on every special occasion, and she will always be a steady hand to help, a shoulder to cry on, and a listening heart to understand what has become your life. With Sabine, you are seen. And having just this one dear friend who has an inside track to what you are experiencing is enough to keep you putting one foot in front of the other. You don't quit. You keep doing what must be done. Even though there are days when you wonder if you'll ever have enough strength in you to face another challenge.

As your birthing date draws near, you have something new to worry about. A strange man knocks on your door one day. He says he's here to assess the property. You refuse to let him in. He leaves but not before you feel your knees start to buckle with fear. *Now what?*

The lovely Arab man, who is now your husband and the father of your unborn child, paid cash for your Seascape home and gifted it to you. He wanted you to know that no matter what happened in life, you had the security of your home. It was your insurance policy. He never wanted you to ever worry about not having a place to live and feel safe. It never occurred to you that you ask he put the property in your name … until now.

You sense you are being threatened. You wonder if the lovely Arab man is considering selling your home. *Why would he do this to me? I'm weeks away from giving birth!*

You are resistant to seeing this as a ploy to scare you into returning to the UAE. You don't want to assume the worst based on your past experience. But there's a new level of fear operating in your life now. It's not until you agree to sell your beloved Seascape home some 18 months from now that you'll discover it's been mortgaged.

But you're not there yet.

You're still here about to give birth. You make arrangements with your mom to be with you. And there's a chance that your best friend Sophie will arrive around the time the baby is due.

Life colludes to make it all happen. Your son is delighted to have his grandmother near and Sophie arrives with her daughter so your son has a playmate, too.

Your mother's presence fills your home. She bakes with the kids. Plays with them on the beach. Keeps them happy and entertained. It is the greatest gift she has ever given you. Peace of mind. It is when she is with your son that you are released to focus on the demands of labour and delivery. You don't spend one minute worrying about home or boy because you know your mother has it covered. It's such a relief! You mother never fails to be unconditional love and acceptance for your children. They are better human beings because of her. And right now, you have the opportunity to be the best mother you can be because you are free to focus on the task at hand which is to usher this unborn child into the world.

And it is time.

Your labour contractions started this morning. It's now mid afternoon. Sophie suggests she take you to the hospital which is a 15-minute drive away.

She drives you there. Parks the car. Takes you to the front desk. Into the elevator up to the labour and delivery floor of the hospital. You tell the nurses you are ready. They get your details and assure you that you have a while to go. You disagree. You want a room now. They are hesitant to believe you. But there is one nurse who looks you in the eye and says: "Honey, you trust what you need. If you say you're ready, then you're ready!"

Sophie is by your side. And your friend Sandy is here, too. You feel protected by their Wise Woman presence. They reassure you. They witness your strength and forbearance. It is time to bring this little one forth.

They say you make it look easy.

You push this child out into the world as though life itself depends on your ability to do so. You feel the ease of letting go and allowing a force beyond you to instruct your body on what is needed next. You become a vessel for the miracle of life.

It happens so fast that the doctor doesn't arrive in time.

It's you and a roomful of wise women who catch this little one.

There is a deep silence the moment you glimpse his face for the first time. You feel strangely detached from him. *Who are you? Where have you come from?*

It's a curious fact that the first people to see him and hold him have called him an angel.

He looks very old to you. His face a thousand faces.

And you are glad he is here.

You feel rejuvenated. As though you've stepped into a parallel life and everything has suddenly and without explanation changed. Forever. Nothing is as it was.

In the next few hours, you'll be thrust into the harsh reality of being alone with another baby. You'll see husbands in the hallway carrying pillows for their expectant wives and you wonder why you don't have the same care and attention from the father of your child. You'll have a sleepless night of wondering how to name this child. You can scarcely get your head around the fact that the lovely Arab man is not here. He has taken a stand against you. You feel strangely elated and punished at the same time.

There is one moment you'll not ever forget.

A moment of such intimate beauty that it hurts your heart.

A few moments after he is born, Sandy takes this new baby of a thousand faces, holds him close to one cheek and then the other while whispering something in each of his ears. He grows still and quiet. Then she sings in full volume the Muslim call to prayer, her voice ancient and deeply feminine. You can hear a thousand angel wings rising and lifting the air in the room. Nurses stop in their tracks. The vibration meant for your son's inner ear is heard throughout every doorway on the maternity floor. A ripple of light and energy clears the space of a thousand rooms.

Later, one of the nurses asks you, *What was that beautiful song?*

And you reply, *It is the song of this child's soul sung to him by his guardian mother.*

Then you cry a thousand tears.

For a thousand years.

Or so it seems.

• • •

The abandonment is beyond belief. The experience doesn't move through your being. It gets stuck and it's sticky and you hold more pain than you know at this time in your body. You'll hold it for many years to come. And somewhere in the future you will feel safe enough to let it pass through you so your body can heal. For now though, you have two reasons to stay open to love and to life. You watch how the newborn son grows every day and you sense that it is you who are breathing life into his very being. You have a new awareness around what it means to be a mother. It's easy to get pregnant, to labour and to birth compared to what it is to hold a child in your arms every day in every way through hunger, distress and need. You sense he will wither and die if you don't nurture the life force in him. Your older son marvels at the arrival of his new brother. It changes him just as it changes you. The love connection between the three of you expands exponentially. So even though the lovely Arab man has abandoned you and your sons, life demands you lift yourself out of the muck. You simply don't need to live there. And being needed as a mother pulls you into a new reality where you develop a fierce strength that is fully maternal and supports all of your life.

But make no mistake. You are alone. You are more alone than you've ever been in your entire life. And the truth that begs to be faced is one you glimpse only in your dreams while you sleep. Because you sure as hell cannot muster what it would take to accept the truth in your waking life.

The lovely Arab man's love for you is conditional.

When you were his mistress, he loved the disobedient woman in you. He thought she was sexy. But as his wife, he will not tolerate you making decisions on your own. According to his psychology, you've shamed him by choosing to birth your child in Canada. You tried to explain that the decision really had nothing to do with him, that it was what you needed to do for you. But he wasn't having any of it. You are his wife now. And you have disobeyed not only him, but some code you somehow assumed wouldn't be applicable to you.

You had taken him for his word. You really believed that he meant it when he said he'd protect you and provide for you and your children not only now but for always. And that belief freed you to make a decision that you felt guided to make. Yet the experience of following your intuition and good sense has led you to see a part of the lovely Arab man that he has, till now, not revealed to you. As though another veil has been lifted. The courage that it takes to see what lies beneath the veil will only come from the maternal strength you are forced to develop.

There are moments when you feel your heart is going to break so far open that you'll lose all connection with the world that your sons inhabit. How do you stay with them? How do you not succumb to the pathos and literally check-out of this reality for good? Your boys need you so you cannot kill yourself. You wouldn't be your mother and father's daughter if you did that.

You will not leave these boys motherless.

You're going to need to write a different ending to this story.

You stayed in Canada to birth your son. Your decision inflamed the lovely Arab man and made apparent an operating system in his psyche that you'd not had the chance to see before. Some part of you feels that maybe you've just dodged a bullet. Because the longer you stay where you stand, the more the lovely Arab man reveals the truth of who he is. He offers no assurances to you whatsoever. You never know if you'll have money in your bank account to buy groceries to feed yourself and your children. He never answers your calls. He doesn't even receive the news of his son's birth from you. He hears it from Ibrahim.

Obviously, you cannot turn to the lovely Arab man for anything anymore.

So this should be the end of the story, correct? Right here, right now, the end.

Nope.

Not that easy.

You still need to be willing to see the truth of what's been revealed to you.

A few years from now you'll hear Maya Angelou talking on *Oprah*. She'll say this: *When someone shows you the truth of who they are, believe them the first time.*

Too bad you didn't hear it before the next chapter of this story was written. Perhaps you could've avoided what was about to happen next.

• • •

The lovely Arab man arrives just in time for his son's first birthday.

One year. It took him one full year to take a step toward you. One full fucking year.

The woman who is writing this now can scarcely believe this to be true. You must've missed some part of the story somewhere along the line. Something must've been said or done that you forgot or didn't see clearly or just plain misunderstood. How could a man who said he loved you and would protect you for your entire life just simply disappear for the first year of your son's life? What kind of reasoning would possibly make any of this okay? Who could do this? What kind of man can walk away from his family like this? What does it say about who he really is and what he values?

Even though you've lived this story and you are writing it now, you still cannot come to grips with the truth of it. Surely, it didn't happen this way. And if it did then why the hell didn't you see it coming? Were you so fast asleep that you missed all the clues that must've been available to warn you of the heartache ahead? Did you misread the signs along the road you'd taken and turn south when you thought you were heading north?

It didn't make sense then.

And it doesn't make sense now.

Maybe this is why you haven't been able to write this story. You keep thinking one day you'll understand what happened but the clarity never comes. It never makes any sense.

Maybe it's the writer's job to tell the story of no sense. Because none of it made sense then and none of it makes sense now. And if the writer doesn't write, she dies.

So you decide to live.

You live to tell the story.

The lovely Arab man has learned somewhere along the way that to withhold and withdraw is the ultimate source of his masculine power. And you have learned somewhere along the way that to disobey means sure death – death of stability, security and belonging.

You feel in your body the experience of your second marriage. Of losing your home and your bank account and your means of feeling secure. Only this time, you're in the house with the kids and wondering how the hell you're going to get through the month. You can't help but think the past has come to harmonize itself. There's something you've left undone and unlearned and now's your chance to get all the pieces back in order.

The part that you don't understand yet is the fact that your order is Divinely Orchestrated and is not dependent on the lovely Arab man. You are looking for the right pieces but in the wrong places. You need to remember that you have all that you require inside of you to meet these challenges which means you could, at this point in the story, if you really understood spiritual law and who you really are, say goodbye and good riddance to the lovely Arab man and get on with your life.

But you're not there yet.

You're still in the part of the story that believes it is the right thing to negotiate a way forward *with* the lovely Arab man.

So, you do.

Negotiate a way forward.

You agree to meet him in Seattle. With your son. Even though there are alarm bells going off in your head. *Why won't he come to Canada? Is he going to try and take my son away from me?*

You get a lawyer's advice.

She says he'll never get the child out of the country without your son's passport. So as long as you protect your son's passport, there is no problem.

Still, you've never looked at the lovely Arab man through this lens before. The lens of mistrust. And it feels weird. Because he is the man who saved you from your second marriage and through his love and care, you've come to trust yourself again. How could it be that you now have to second-guess his intentions?

You are resistant to the idea.

You much prefer to see him as your knight in shining armour. You want him to be your lover, protector and bringer of all good things.

It turns out that you need to choose denial in order to feel like you are trusting life. But that's the way denial works, isn't it? You talk yourself into what you want to believe is true. When, in fact, you're denying the very truth that is rising from the depths of your soul.

You tell yourself you will meet him in Seattle so he can meet his son. And you tell yourself that you'll know when you're in his presence whether or not you are willing to move forward in this marriage. You tell yourself this while every cell in your body is screaming *no!*

No, no, no, no, no!

Still, you go.

Now you are in the Seattle airport and something extremely strange happens.

The two of you meet.

And the shapeshifting happens again!

Everything seems to move in slow motion. You seem to stop in your tracks as the edges of so-called reality become watery. In the blur of the moment, the lovely Arab man becomes Dan, your second husband, right before your eyes.

Another crack in reality.

Fractal turbulence.

You freeze in the phenomenon. You hear yourself saying inside your own head *What the fuck?*

You instantly get the answer. It arrives like a bolt of lightning, flash and all.

This man is not good for you. You are done. Go home. And never look back.

For a moment you actually consider what it might take to get on the next plane back to Canada.

Then you rationalize how ridiculous that would be.

You tell yourself there is nothing to fear and you are simply reacting based on your past experiences. You convince yourself that to trust yourself means following this man out to a taxi, getting into the car with him and your son, driving to the hotel where he has booked you into a suite, allowing him to make love to you that night while your son sleeps in his crib in the next room, waking up the next morning and agreeing to move back to Dubai so you can be a family again.

Part of you panics in the taxi back to the airport. So you assert yourself and tell the lovely Arab man that you have one condition. You want him to be fully accountable to the situation you are creating together. He needs to declare himself the father of your son so if something happens then you have legal recourse in your home country. You ask him to give your son an Arabic name. If you're going to move back to Dubai with your sons then you want assurances that you'll be living as a family and accepted into the culture. To that end, you believe an Arabic name for your son will lend itself more to that reality. And to make it legal, the lovely Arab man will need to visit you on Vancouver Island so the two of you can go to the Vital Statistics Canada office in Victoria to do the required paperwork to have his name legally changed. You believe having the lovely Arab man's name on your son's birth certificate will secure something for his and your future. It'll be proof that the lovely Arab man is his father. Proof that you are not in this alone.

It turns out to be one of the dumbest mistakes of your life. Which is an understatement, of course. Because this choice sets so many wheels in motion that it'll take you a decade to recover.

Trying to manipulate circumstances into something that seems more palpable so you can feel secure in the world is a dangerous game. But you feel so powerless in the presence of the lovely Arab man that you are grasping at anything to regain your composure. You'd expected that having agreed to bring this child into the world had elevated you in some way. You believed his promises. You dreamed of living freely as his equal partner. You assumed you had the right to choose where to give birth. You assumed he'd be there when you most needed him. You assumed that when he said he loved you that it meant all the same things to him as it does to you.

But it didn't. You've never been so wrong in your life.

You believed you needed the lovely Arab man in order to be secure in the world. You had two sons to raise and you were not prepared to go it alone. You'd made that clear to him the moment you discovered you were pregnant. So now you are trying to be smart, trying to think ahead, trying to hold him accountable to his part of the contract. But as you go down this road, what you tell yourself within yourself is actually wishful thinking, fantasy and farce.

The only way to stay safe in the world is to listen to your own soul.

Trouble is, you don't know how the soul speaks. So when it does, you aren't listening. But She *will* get your attention. And you *will* learn to listen. Because when you're not being honest with yourself, your soul will crush you like a bug.

• • •

You've worked hard to get yourself and your boys back to the UAE. A journey you could no longer avoid once the lovely Arab man had been to Canada and signed all the necessary documentation to have your son's name changed legally.

It's official now.

The lovely Arab man declared parentage so you've got what you need to feel secure in moving forward.

Or so you tell yourself.

And he tells you that he'll be happy to have you in the Dubai family home. His American wife has left and returned to the United States with their daughters. So there is no need to get a different place. Home is ready for you and your sons. She has moved out. You're to move in.

If you could've been honest with yourself at this point, you'd have felt how creepy it was to be stepping into another woman's home. But you didn't allow yourself to feel it, at least not for too long. You'd quickly brush it aside and convince yourself that this was destiny. That the way had been cleared for you and the lovely Arab man to finally live openly.

You now know the difference between destiny and fate.

You'd chosen this road you were on. And when the road was blocked, you pushed through it by denying what was trying to rise up from within you. But those road blocks were actually sign posts leading you away from danger.

You didn't know how to read the signs.

What you did know how to do was take control of details and events. And taking control was the way you felt empowered. You manipulated the story inside your own head to make what was happening seem more palpable. The storyline that served you well was this one: *I must respect the lovely Arab man's culture and his different ways even when it means denying what I know to be true for me.*

You mistook compliance for wisdom.

You adapted yourself to his needs even after he'd abandoned you during what was, for you, the most important time in your relationship.

You simply let it all go. You forgave him. All in the name of love.

You thought this was what it meant to really love someone. And because your someone came from and lived in a culture different from yours, you always gave him the benefit of any doubt. The problem with your adaptability and compliance though is that you've been pulled so far off your own centre that you really don't know who you are anymore. You are not being pulled by destiny because you are projecting your highest possibilities onto your husband. You are not aligned with the Divine course for your own life.

So fate is having her way with you.

And it's just going to keep getting harder.

• • •

You toss and turn in the bed you are now sharing with the lovely Arab man, your husband, and the father to your sons. This is the bed he shared with his American wife. This is the bedroom he shared with her, too. You are now surrounded by things she has left behind. You clean out stuff she's left in drawers to make room for your things. Your side of the bathroom vanity is full of her make-up and perfumes. You find all of this deeply disturbing but you say nothing. You don't want to upset your husband. You know it is difficult for him, too. So it becomes your mission to clear the space and make way for the life you intend to share with the lovely Arab man.

You see yourself as strong. And you are willing to adapt to any circumstances. In fact, you pride yourself in your ability to make home wherever you are. The lovely Arab man is relieved to have you here beside him. He's been waiting for this, he says. And so you've taken all this on with a kind of grace that you're sure is aligning you with all the right things for your life and the lives of everyone in your family. You're a hard worker. A devoted care-giver. And a brilliant home-maker.

You continue to toss and turn in bed at night. You don't understand the disturbance. You've never had problems sleeping. Sleep has always been your refuge. Especially since Kent died. It is the one state where you feel liberated from all the challenges of living. You often think how pleasant it will be to die. You look forward to slipping out of your skin. You have absolutely no fear of death. It is living that is hard for you. Dying will be a breeze! If you weren't a mother, you imagine you'd have found a way to death by now. But your sons need you and you cannot imagine leaving them motherless. So you stay in this life. You persevere for them. When they're independent and well on their way, then you'll be free to consider whether or not it is time to leave.

For now, you are here.

And for the life of you it makes no sense that you are sleeplessly tossing and turning in this bed! You decide it must be the bed itself. When you are in it, you feel like dozens of internal burrs ignite a flame that starts to burn in the middle of your back radiating outward from your spine and upward toward your neck. You scratch. You rub. But there is no relief. You try to describe it to your husband. You just can't get in and under your flesh to address the burn.

It is when Sabine is having tea with you one afternoon that you share with her what you're experiencing. You laughingly tell her that maybe the bed is cursed and trying to get rid of you! You also tell her you've noticed a kind of rash under your arms. You show her a couple of vesicular spots that burn when you touch or scratch them.

She is startled.

She says she thinks it looks like shingles.

"What are shingles?" you ask.

You find out from the doctor you see at the American Hospital the next morning that you have the worst case of shingles he has ever seen. Most usually the outbreak of the rash will be on one side of the spine but yours follows the nerve root path on *both* sides. You tell him that you had chicken pox twice as a kid. The first time as a toddler and then later as a ten year old which was an experience you remember because every inch of your body seemed to itch and ache with chicken pox! Your mother recalled that when you were a toddler, you only had a few spots. And she reasoned that maybe that was why you got it a second time ... the first time was too mild a case.

The doctor tells you that the shingles virus is called herpes zoster and it is a relative of chicken pox. There is no treatment, nothing he can do. He says that after you have chicken pox, the virus lies dormant in your spine until something triggers it. He asks if you have any stress in your life.

"No, not really, none that I can think of."

He glares at you. He knows you are lying.

"Well, I suppose I have some stress. I did just move here from Canada. It's been a hard year, I guess. But everything is getting easier now. My husband is with me now and I have his help."

Blah, blah, blah, blah, blah ...

There's a part of you that is losing patience with your willingness to conceal the truth of what you are really experiencing. You don't think of yourself as lying. You're just coping with life. But your body knows better. She's had enough. And she is screaming from the depths of your nerve roots for you to get a grip on what is happening to you.

You do your own research once you leave the doctor's office. You learn that shingles affects people when their immune system is already weakened. It affects the collection of nerve cells supplying a given nerve root. The nerve root path is commonly along the chest but it can also occur in the sciatic nerve or into the face. If it's really bad (the doctor says yours is really bad) then it can cause blindness. For some folks, the post-herpetic pain which is a peculiar, internal burning can be totally incapacitating and never go away.

Shit. What have I done?

You turn to your beloved teacher, Caroline Myss. You've read everything she's ever written and you know that if there is something here for you to get a grip on then she's the one who'll help you get it.

You read her energy analysis of shingles and you learn that it is a disorder created through the experience of chronic anxiety. In particular, an irritation due to feeling overwhelmed by the circumstances or demands of one's environment. It is an anxiety generated because a person feels physically, financially or materially insecure or vulnerable. It may be stimulated by an event or a stressor but it is actually a chronic anxiety. So there's a history. A long history. And it's come home to roost.

The roots of your nerves have been deeply disturbed by the uprooting of your life over and over and over again. You've warehoused the traumatic episodes of financial and physical insecurities and burned your nerve endings out. Your body is speaking because she cannot lie. The body never lies. And she is saying *What the fuck are you doing? Get me out of here! I don't belong here nor do I want to be here. Take me home!*

So, do you book the next flights out of the country homeward bound?

Hell, no.

Somewhere in you, that feels like defeat. Another failed marriage.

Sabine is an aromatherapist. She does her research. She sources the essential oils you need. Her treatment is your only relief. And it is the beginning of your life-long love affair with pure essential oils. It's Sabine's wisdom that eases the pain. She visits you every day. She listens to you talk. She helps your kids. It takes weeks to recover. But you do, eventually. Because you are one tough broad. As you tell this part of your story today, you realize that even when you make the worst mistakes, heaven is here providing help so you might knit your way out of trouble.

There is one thing you know for sure.

Sabine is a godsend.

• • •

The next thing you do is agree to sell your beloved Seascape.

Seems easy enough to do while you're living here in Dubai some ten thousand miles away. The lovely Arab man convinces you that it's time to let it go. You are here with him now. You don't need a home in Canada.

You wonder now as you write this why you didn't question his motive. Didn't it seem strange to you that he now wanted to sell the home you'd invested so much love and time and energy into? It was your sanctuary. And that's what he'd always said he wanted for you. So why aren't you at least a little curious about his suggestion that you sell? Where are your powers of suspicion? Do you not have the ability to see beneath the veiled illusion of making a home in the Arabian Peninsula and living happily ever after?

He does share a secret with you. One that you must not divulge to anyone until the project has been implemented. He shows you a video that has been produced to sell the idea he has generated.

You will have a new home.

On the Arabian sea.

In fact, he's going to build an entire island.

He shows you the floor plan of your particular villa which stands among many in his uniquely designed project – a man-made island in the shape of a date palm in Jumeirah. Sand will be dredged. Villas will be built. A whole community with a world-class hotel, shops and venues. All to give you the home you have dreamed of having ... a home with private beach and beautiful inner space. You are speechless. The immensity of the project stuns you. He is amazing. And he really is, you aren't just saying that. You see his creative brilliance. He is a builder of worlds. A man of great vision. He wants peace and prosperity for all. He extends himself beyond himself to aid when aid is needed. He's built companies and now he tells you that he will build "The Palm" project because you've inspired him. This is for you.

You are deeply moved.

The least you can do is sell your beloved Seascape. Declare your loyalty to live here in the desert with the lovely Arab man.

The realtor is given instruction. Within days a buyer makes an offer. You tell yourself it's just a condo. Let it go. You're good at letting stuff go. You've learned that people, places and things go all the time. If it wasn't meant to go then there'd be no buyer. But there is a buyer so it must mean it's right to let it go.

Your beloved Seascape is sold.

You plan to return early in the summer to clear it out, put your things in storage and spend your west coast summer in a hotel on the inner harbour of Victoria. Your sister plans to join you and help. When you finally arrive on the island and walk in the door of your beloved Seascape, you are instantly overwhelmed by what this decision means to you. First, your brother has been staying in the condo and everything has been changed. Your bed and bookcases have been moved. Your son's bedroom has been rearranged. Nobody said anything to you about making these changes and the affect hits you hard. It's like you've had the wind knocked out of you. You sit in your bedroom and feel insulted by the fact that it is no longer yours. You call the lovely Arab man to tell him. He reassures you. You know what you must do now. It's time to leave. This part of your life is over. And a new part has already begun. But you are so saddened by the sudden change that you feel like you're standing on quicksand. The Seascape condo has been your bedrock for a decade. It's been the place from which you steer your life. Now it's all gone. And a part of you is terrified. Yet under the terror there is a still, small voice that says you are lucky to get out of here alive.

What do you mean? This is my home.

You will not understand until many months later that you've actually dodged another bullet. That the condo will undergo an assessment that will cost its owners thousands of dollars of which your husband would be unwilling to pay. Had you not sold, you would've been stuck with the condo for months while the whole exterior is being reconstructed. And what turns out to be your wisest financial investment would've become a big debt and financial burden overnight.

Growth is never comfortable.

Seascape had been the sacred space where you were able to withdraw from the world and heal yourself. Now life pulls you out of your cocoon. It feels as though you are being forced to expand your domain. Part of you wants to remain hidden in this beautiful home. But another part of you wants to grow beyond the walls you've built to protect yourself from experiencing more pain.

You reflect on the number of times circumstances in your life have forced you to detach from whole life settings and people associated with them. You think you might be crazy. Nobody you know has ever lived what you're living. Time and time and time again you are detaching. Maybe you are here in earth school just to learn how to detach? Maybe this is your life's purpose? Maybe you're right on track during these times when you feel like you're going to die from heartache? Because time and time and time again, just when the pain threatens to overcome you, something shifts and you're on a new path in a new place with new people.

So this is your life.

The pain of change is the engine that drives you.

Some years later you'll be hired as a Learning Coach at University Canada West in Victoria. You'll enter the classroom where the communications professor, who is your professor and second reader for your masters thesis, is teaching business students about the rapidly expanding field of communications technology. On a big screen at the front of the room there will be an image being streamed from the internet. Your knees will go weak. You'll feel lightheaded. You'll want to vomit. Because up there on that screen will be an image you've seen in a video animation. But it's no video. It's a google image of a real place. A place that looks like a palm tree in parts completely surrounded by water.

Your heart will do a somersault.

It's been built. The thing you inspired has been made manifest.

You'll want to run from the room so you might collect yourself. But instead you'll sit down. Quietly. And hope nobody notices that you are shaking. Actually vibrating. How can you possibly tell anyone anything that will let them into your inner world of knowing? The Palm Villas were to be your home. Yet here you are earning $20/hour as a Learning Coach in a Vancouver Island university and wondering every day how you'll make your way forward taking care of your boys and making a home as a lone mother with no money. Who would ever believe that you stepped away from the elaborate wealth of the desert Arabs and their oil?

You mustn't say a word. Keep it inside you. What was once a secret shared with the lovely Arab man is now a world-class destination. You are now on the outside looking in and what you see is all you've ever seen … the need to fight for your own and your children's independence and freedom.

No one will ever get it though. Including your children who will judge you as a bit crazy.

Why would you choose to make us poor?

Because I feared for our lives.

The woman writing this today in the summer of 2013 does a quick online search to see a visual of the Palm Villas in Jumeriah. An article in *The Telegraph* headlines "Trouble in paradise as plumbing problems hit Dubai's Palm island."

Ha!

• • •

It is the thing you'll be most grateful for in relationship to your sister. That she is willing to come to the island and get you moved. Without her organizing and doing the proverbial heavy lifting, you would crash and burn. You wonder about this third husband of yours. Sending you to clean out your home, move all your things into storage while taking care of your two sons. What was to be his contribution? He also gives you power of attorney and charges you with taking care of all the paperwork.

You see a pattern now, looking back. You Bowyer girls are beyond self-sustaining. You know what it is to step in and take care of everything in every way. You build the home. You feed the kids. You work the job. You manage the money. You give the care to all in need. What a job description you've grown into! How'd you get here? And where are your men?

Well, that's exactly the point, isn't it? The men are missing. They are off in their own corners doing their own things. They let you take care of everything they deem to be less important than whatever it is that has their attention. And they have little or no caregiving skills at all. They look to the Mother in you, all of you. Your grandmother, mother, your sister, yourself. They sit at the table and wait for their food. They instruct your kids to do the dishes while they step away and back into whatever it is that feeds their crippled masculinity. They are not real partners to any of you. They hang back. They lack the confidence to assert themselves in service for their wives and children. But they don't see it that way. They feed their egos with the knowledge that they have a family as though they own their family and having it in their possession is enough to make them feel like they've made something. They haven't made anything at all though. The women around them have created the lives they are living in and the women sustain it. The men act like visitors and they expect to be treated as honorary guests. When the women talk too much, be they mother or daughter, they are told to quieten down. The men sit in bathtubs and call out to their wives in the kitchen to come and scrub their backs while the children sit at the table eating the food their mother has made for them.

When does she get to sit down?

When does she get to rest?

At the end of the day when everyone else is tucked into their beds, she tiptoes into the bedroom where her sleeping husband snores so loudly that her only hope of getting to sleep herself is to put a pillow over her head.

She is suffocating. She cannot breathe. She will die in here with all this noise and all these expectations. You remember your mother laying diagonally on her bed in the middle of the afternoon sobbing loudly and you knew she was trying to get somebody's attention but nobody was listening as they just shook their heads and shrugged their shoulders going about their own business and closing her door so nobody would have to listen. You were always the one to go into the room and give your mom a hug and tell her how much you love her and she would eventually come back out into the kitchen and resume her duties and life would go on.

Now you are that woman.

You want to throw your hands into the air, land on your bed and cry so hard that the sobs will shake the house that is no longer yours. You are giving it up. You are going away. You are doing whatever it is you have to do to keep your family safe and fed.

Then something occurs to you.

Your third husband has already spent his half of your house. You now know that he mortgaged the house he'd called yours for business reasons. And he did so without telling you. He's never lied to you, he says. But he lies by omission all the time and you know it.

A still, small voice in the deepest part of you urges you to secure your half of the house. You've invested a decade of your life in this marriage and this home. He's made promises that he hasn't kept and you've got to wake up to the fact that you now have two sons to feed, house, clothe and educate. Can you depend on the lovely Arab man to do the things he has promised you he'd do? You are beginning to doubt it. Just beginning. And the still, small voice deep within you whispers *be smart*.

You have everything you need to be smart. Everything. Including power of attorney.

So your beloved Seascape is sold. The funds arrive. You meet with your financial advisor and investment broker. You hear yourself giving instructions about where the money is to be invested. You tuck it all away. You secure the proceeds from the sale in your name. And while you're talking like you know exactly what you're doing, another part of you is watching how smart you are. You also notice that you feel like you're trying to fly under the radar. As though you are doing something that you shouldn't. Which doesn't make sense if you are indeed in a full-partnership marriage and this was your house as gifted by the lovely Arab man. But maybe these things are not true. And maybe that's why you are feeling as though you are doing something that might cause problems between you and the lovely Arab man. A tiny crack is beginning to show the truth of what you've gotten yourself into.

The truth is that he thinks you are his puppet. The truth is that he plays you for innocent and perhaps a bit stupid in your innocence. The truth is that he is in financial difficulty and he is willing to jeopardize your home to relieve something for himself and he hasn't been honest with you. Again, he hasn't lied. He just lies by omission. Most people know this to be a form of manipulation but you can't yet get your head around that notion. You are not ready to see how you are being played. But you are ready to listen to that still, small voice because you sense she is all about being able to take care of her kids.

I will not be rendered useless and caged as mother to my sons!

Suddenly it occurs to you that the young daughter in you sees her mother as being trapped in a life she did not want. And you are now fighting for your own right to life on your own terms. You've discovered a key to the cage. You are using the key, then tucking the key safely away out of reach.

It is done.

You sit in your car outside the bank where you've enacted all the necessary transactions with your financial advisor whom you come to know as one of your guardian angels. Willie facilitates things that shouldn't be possible in the months to come. You will call him from Dubai and tell him what you need and he'll provide it along with assurances that all is well. *How much do you need and when do you need it?* His voice on the other end of the phone will be balm to your soul. He will help you knit parachutes out of the increasingly complex situation you've walked into. You will wonder who the heck he really is. And then you'll be overwhelmed with a sense of calm appreciation for his presence. He walks you out of the mess and into safety. And all you ever have of him is his voice. His ten thousand mile voice.

• • •

The summer is both sad and liberating. Walking away from your beloved Seascape is hard. A decade of your life in this place. Beautiful memories of peace and tranquility in this place. Deep thinking and creating in this place. Every other place you live will be compared to Seascape. Something about the energy of the rock and the ocean healed you here. The winter wind had the power to unsettle you. The waves crashing beneath the floor of your house made you feel open and vulnerable. And you were exactly that. But you held a vision of being protected by the lovely Arab man and it steadied you. The idea that someone cared only for you and would do anything to protect you. The idea of love even though you were asked to live apart. Have you ever known anyone to have the endurance that you have?

Then again, have you ever known anyone who could've found the sweetness in such an arrangement?

Be honest now.

You liked it.

A man who might show up in the middle of the night, walk into your bedroom, lay down by your side while slipping his hands under the covers, seeking warmth on your belly. The way you would know it was him. Smell his breath on your face. Seek the moistness of his lips on yours in the middle of your dreamworld because you're not fully awake. Maybe if you'd had an aunt or a mother or a woman of any relation whom you trusted say to you that this is a perfectly acceptable way to be in relationship with a man you might've been empowered enough to enjoy what he was offering you AND continue to build your own life based on your own dreams. But you didn't have that. What you had were puritan notions of what it means to be married and to be in a family. What is it they call it? The nuclear family? The basic social unit of which you've never been a part.

The way you see it now, you had it all.

The only thing you needed to do was build your own life. Be a good mom. Finish your education. Create your home in harmony. And the only thing the lovely Arab man asked of you was to be there when he arrived. Meet him where he was which meant fabulous world travel for you. What was hard about this arrangement?

Nothing!

You loved it and you wanted it.

But there was a voice in you telling you that this kind of arrangement made you less of a woman. You'd never be the wife. You'd never be part of his family. You know now that being a part of a man's family is overrated. There are expectations for you to take care of others and do things for others and fit into their customs and celebrate their holidays. You remember when you first married Kent and the sense of betrayal you felt to your own family when you needed to share holiday time between both families. Certain traditions needed to be changed or blended. It was all a bit confusing. Now all these years later you see that this basic social building block isn't all that it's made out to be. It has its fault lines and limitations.

If only you'd had just one person say to you that what you were creating with the lovely Arab man was a good thing, a right thing and a blessed thing.

Instead you felt judged in every way by everyone.

Now you wonder if the lovely Arab man was the more forward thinking one of you two. If maybe he was more progressive and assertive than you'd taken him to be. What if you were the backward one? What if you were stuck in a set of cultural expectations that were restraining you from living in the beauty of the moment. A loving relationship with a man is a beautiful thing regardless of what the packaging around it is. Why must we constrain ourselves so? What will it take for us to feel liberated enough to create whatever kinds of marriages work for us?

These are not the questions you are asking yourself as you board the plane on your way to meet the lovely Arab man in London. This is your rendezvous after a few weeks apart, a summer of selling your home and storing your things to enable you to pack up your boys and head to the desert to make a proper home with your third husband.

You wonder how he'll ask for the proceeds of the sale.

You wonder how you'll tell him the money is invested in your name.

You'll not need to wonder long because it is the first thing on his mind when you meet.

You steel yourself.

You reach for your voice, hoping it will be clear and strong.

You know you've given him the promise of your life by selling Seascape, packing up your children and coming home to him. It is an act of faith. And an act of love.

You also know you've drawn a clear line in the sand of your marriage for the first time. *This money will be mine*, you are saying. *You said the house was mine*, you are saying. *You promised to protect and secure me*, you are saying. *You assured me we are equal partners*, you are saying. *This is your chance to show me the truth of who you are*, you are saying.

Show me the truth of who you are.

This is the real risk you are taking.

That he will show you the truth of who he is.

And he does.

And you are shocked beyond repair.

When you tell him that you've secured your half of the proceeds from the sale of the house in investments under your name, he is livid.

And there you are.

In London with your kids.

With no home in Canada to fly back to.

This is what vulnerability feels like.

Then you remember you have some money invested in your name that he'll never be able to touch. And you stand just a little bit taller. And your voice reaches just a little bit deeper.

Watch me, you say.

I'm not as dumb as you think I am, you say.

Don't mess with my ability to care for my sons, you say.

If you're not going to love me and treat me fairly then say it now or forever hold your peace as you watch me walk out the door of this so-called marriage. Because you are done, done, done with messing around with men who pretend to be one thing but then turn out to be another thing altogether.

That still, small voice that led you to let go of your beloved Seascape is now leading you to locate an inner strength that you've been hiding. The truth is that the only way to stay safe in the world is to listen to your own soul. And your soul doesn't speak in words ... it speaks in volume. It is a powerful space that occupies the great Truth of your own life.

• • •

How do you make home in someone else's land when you have one foot out the door before you even build the house?

The thing you have glimpsed about the lovely Arab man and who you might be to him has rocked your inner world. As though a veil has been lifted and now you get to see something that if you'd seen it in the beginning then you would have made different choices. It worries you that you didn't see this. How could you not have seen this? There must be something deeply skewed about your perceptual skill. Seems you continually miss key traits about the men you draw into your life. What is it with you, anyway? Just when you think you've built the life you're dreaming of everything comes crashing around you. How much more disappointment can you possibly bear?

You feel the weight of all the choices you've ever made since you turned 18 and were supposedly ready to be an adult in the world. You see now that you knew nothing. And nothing you did know could ever have prepared you for what you were about to live. Yet at the same time there is a realization that you wouldn't have done anything differently knowing only what you knew when you made any given choice. It feels like a grand paradox. The decisions you made while you were making those decisions always felt like the right decisions.

Or did they?

Let's get real and honest here. As honest as you've ever been in your life. Right here. Right now. You always felt you were making the *only* decision that would save you from the deep fear you felt about whatever was facing you at the time.

It's high school graduation. You long to go to college. You are acutely aware of the fact that your parents do not have money to send you to college. So you get married. While it never occurs to you to work for your own dream. Get a job. Go to school. Trust you have what you need to find your own way.

Then your husband dies. And the first thing that comes to your mind when the dust clears is that now you can go to college. So, you do. And while there you meet a man whose intellect and creativity draws you into his life and him into yours. It's fun. And that's all you want it to be. But he gets serious. Sticks to you and your home and you cannot get rid of him even after he hits you. He literally lurks his way back into your life. But wait a minute! Where *are* you? How did this guy get through your boundaries? Well, there's the key, isn't it? Your boundaries were penetrable. Your first thought was always your right thought. When he hit you, the first thought was to kick him out of your house. First thought, right thought. But then weeks later after being the subject of what now would be called stalking, you let him back in. Because you gave him the power to make you feel guilty about having right first thoughts. When he returned to your home, self-doubt walked through the door with him. Then the Saboteur took over the driver's seat of your life while you tried to ignore her self-destructive behaviour. You told yourself it was the way to grow and change. But it wasn't. You see now that you were terrified of the real growth and change that was possible if you kept that man out of your house, completed your university education, nurtured your son with the confidence that you were all he needed to develop into his best life and trusted the path that was opening for you. The Saboteur whispered in your ear that you were nothing if not with this man, that you should not turn away from a man who wanted to be father to your boy, husband to you. The Saboteur laughed in your face. *Who do you think you are? You can't do any of this on your own!* And thus began the descent into your low self-esteem.

From there the Victim decided to visit again even though you had tossed her out onto the street when you'd decided to leave the life that you and your first husband had envisioned for yourselves. You walked away from that community because they no longer wanted you there. You were their widow, someone to be pitied and then you were the single mother who was estranged from their experience. They shamed you out of their town. They were all terrified of you lest their carefully constructed lives unravel in some tragedy they couldn't see coming. But you still had an ounce of self-esteem then, enough to get you out of Dodge. You were determined to make a life that you and your son could be proud to call your own. And so you stepped up and away with whatever grace had carried you through that dark and lonely time.

It only seemed fitting then that when you let that second marriage happen you would be opening the door for the Victim to come live with you again. She bugged you a lot. You hated the way she made you feel. But she was tenacious and she didn't take no for an answer when you were feeling vulnerable. Her sister the Prostitute took you totally by surprise and in some insidious way became your closet ally when you were yourself tossed out onto the street by the very man who begged to come back into your life. When he locked you out of your own home in the Arabian Gulf desert, threw your son's toys out into the yard, your soul knew that he had orchestrated the whole affair in order to get back at you. This was his revenge. He was beyond angry. He wanted to harm your chances for ever having a normal life. He resented everything about you. The fact that you had a good job, made good money, had good friends all seemed to make him feel like less of a man. His self-esteem so low from whatever life experience had harmed him that he couldn't strengthen his inner structures on his own. He needed to project the pain onto you and it came with a force you simply hadn't seen coming. The shock landed you in front of the man who would become your third husband. A man you trusted with your life and your son's life. A man you agreed to share a second son with. A man whom you were now beginning to see in a different life. Another shock wave rising up in your awareness bringing nausea and vertigo along with it.

The Prostitute was here to teach you integrity. *Where are you trading your body and your spirit for security and safety?*

With the lovely Arab man.

Yet you don't know this until the veil lifts. The veil that reveals how angry he is with you for taking your half of the condo even though he'd gifted you with the whole property. He does not like that you've made this decision on your own. He feels betrayed. He withdraws his love as he retreats into his hurt. He is wounded. And this is when you glimpse the Prostitute within. You see how she was acutely aware of the lovely Arab man's power over her. How she was quietly orchestrating her own security and safety because she sensed he had an agenda lurking behind his actions. She was smart enough to sense the danger and she knew she needed to survive the shock wave when it hit. It's a curious and mysterious position to be in. One part of you so open and vulnerable and available for love. Another part of you on the alert and waiting for the signal that your house of cards is about to fall.

Whenever anything doesn't turn out the way you expect it to, you will do well in the future to remember this: You need to examine your relationship to Truth!

• • •

History repeats itself. Stephen King writes that the past harmonizes. Churning to bring up all kinds of questions about who we are, where we've been, what we've lived.

Every man you married felt like a familiar in the first moments of meeting. As though you already knew each other in some intimate way. It never once occurred to you that that kind of connection meant you could still say no, that you still had a choice. Just because he felt familiar didn't mean you should be swept away by what you interpreted the moment was demanding from you.

Yet, here you are. Back in the Persian Gulf prepared to live the honourable life ... as a wife. You have it all, you tell yourself. The man. The children. The home. The lifestyle. You fine tune the routines to keep it all moving forward like a well oiled machine. You have staff in your house now so some of your time is spent managing people. It fits beautifully with your dream of writing. Each morning you walk to the second floor apartment in the guest house across the yard while the nanny, housekeeper, cooks and driver tend to the children, the house and the yard. As you sit at your desk writing, you gaze out the second storey window to see the nanny playing with your toddler son by the pool and you think to yourself that finally, finally you have a life. A good life. You knew you were capable of creating this reality and here it is with you in it.

But you are restless.

You pace the elegant apartment with bougainvillaea running along the window ledges. You cannot settle down, keep your ass in the chair. When you try to focus on the words that want to pour from your heart through your arms into the tips of your fingers and onto the page you are overwhelmed with an anxiety rising from your core. And the only thing that stills your racing mind is running out to the yard, picking up your son, gazing into his beautiful face and holding him close to your chest. Then you remember who you are. You are mother. Your breathing softens. Your body relaxes. And you tell yourself that tomorrow you will write. *Bukra ensha'allah.*

All the tomorrows add up to yesterday. And the story you want to tell just cannot find its way to the written page. It trembles inside you like a vibration whose echo reminds you that you are still alive and still have a dream to live.

Because this reality that you are bumping around in is not the dream of your life. There is something seriously wrong here. You can't put your finger on it. You can't find the words to describe it. If not for your children, perhaps you could locate the truth in you. But for now, their needs keep you distracted enough from yourself that you think you are providing all they need by filling up the routine of the day with meals and school and entertainment and beach and play and swimming and friends and round and round and round the day spins into the night back into day and along the way you notice that the lovely Arab man starts to sleep in his bedroom down the hall. He isolates a part of himself from you. He stays out late at night coming home when you are already in bed and he doesn't join you there. In the morning your life revs up and his bedroom door is still closed. You open it a crack to see him sound asleep in a pile of pillows. You leave him sleeping. You field the phone calls from downstairs that ask where is Boss and when is Boss coming for breakfast and why is Boss missing his morning meetings and you don't know what to tell everyone so you just tell the truth. Boss is sleeping. And you don't know the answers to their questions. And you notice over the coming weeks a pattern of unraveling within the lovely Arab man's psyche. He is worried about his health. He senses there is something wrong in his body so he travels to Europe and America to see the finest doctors and they all tell him there is nothing evident from his blood tests. But both you and he live with the darkness that has taken over his inner world. You over-extend yourself in service to making him feel better. It means an inordinate time alone, quiet and together. He is lost in himself and has little to give to you or the boys. You sense his heartache is the missing of his daughters. He only comes to life when he is travelling to America to visit them. Or when they make their annual visit to stay with him and you and the boys here in the house they once called home.

Your heart breaks for all of them.

And no matter how much you are willing to suffer on behalf of their pain, your life doesn't budge one inch.

You are stuck.

In mud as thick as clay.

The loam of your life gets heavier and darker even though you are in the Arabian desert with sun and sand and sea all around you.

The light is not bright enough to illuminate the truth of what you have chosen.

The message from both your second and third husbands is *be obedient and you'll have love, security and belonging, do as I say, don't ask questions.* You want to tell them to go fuck themselves but you feel dependent.

You keep on pushing to make it all be what you need it to be.

And it keeps pushing you back into the only place you are allowed to be. Alone. You've never felt more alone than when you're in bed with a man lying next to you whose heart is closed and unavailable. It's been the heartbreak of your life in these two marriages. You want so bad to have it be another way but it is what it is and you will eventually learn that you cannot make things what they are not.

So here you are in a place where the lovely Arab man has turned into the distant husband. Your second husband exercised his lack of self-esteem by powering over you and taking all your material possessions away. Your third husband showers you with material things, wanting to prove his love for you but he is still acting from a low self-esteem. When you argue or disagree, he withdraws from you. He will not stay in the conversation. He leaves. So you learn what to say, how to say it and when to say it. Because if you don't, he takes his power over you one step further. He withdraws from your children. The first time he does this you are simply baffled. *Why would he ignore the boys?* Then you make it worse by making excuses for the man they call father in an effort to protect their innocent hearts. But they see something you do not. Over time they withdraw their affection from him. They stop trying to get his attention. They leave him alone. And this dynamic creates an estrangement that lives under the surface of things. You begin to see that your husband withdraws from the children to hurt you. It's actually his way of bringing you back to him. Indirect. Manipulative. *What kind of man does this?* A man who doesn't have a strong self-esteem. A man who for all his seeming power in the external world feels utterly powerless within himself.

It comes as such a shock when you see this as clearly as you see it now. Because in the beginning you were attracted to the power this man exuded in his life. He appeared confident and able to manifest anything he desired. Which begs the question, *what part of me felt so insecure that I needed to draw on his power?*

Now that's a question.

And the answer is ... *your low self-esteem!*

• • •

You seek the help of an osteopath who practices from his home and is rumoured to be Sheikh Muhammad's personal physician. You soon learn it's not a rumour. It is, in fact, true. And everyone is quiet about it. The Sheikh's Osteopath turns out to be the healer who really helps you. When you reflect on your life you realize there are always healers around to help you. Whether or not you call them in is up to you. But you have this uncanny ability to build support around you wherever you go. You don't realize it until later, but seeking treatment from the Sheikh's Osteopath is the step you take to open up a way out of the mess you've created. The minute you walk into his home-clinic, you enter a different orbit and the more you visit, the more influence it has on you. The woman who makes your appointments, takes your payment, sees you in and out of the treatment room becomes your guardian. Turns out she is the Sheikh's Osteopath's Lover and Life Partner. And everyone is quiet about it. That's the way things are here. There's always a story under the story, an invisible reality that holds up what is seen. And you're never quite sure what the right thing to do or the right thing to say is but you fumble along being polite and kind which has always gotten you in good with folks. You're genuine and sweet and a whole lot of naive.

So, it turns out that the Sheikh's Osteopath's Lover & Life Partner is a physiotherapist and she is completing her Phd in Transpersonal Psychology. She quietly works with folks as a counsellor. And it's inevitable that you will be in a room with her, sitting in a chair across from her, pouring out your life story so far. There are times you see that you are putting her to sleep with your story and you will later learn as a counsellor yourself that this is a sure sign that the ego has hijacked the people in the room and is commanding the energy which is heavy and hard to slog through.

She stays right there with you. Slogging through the heavy.
The Counsellor becomes your beacon of light.

But it ain't easy.

She has you sit in front of a mirror. Full body. You can't see the image reflected back to you without any sense of loathing. You hate the way you look. Your hair. Your body. Your clothes. Your expression. You look like one big lump of sad ... pathetic! The Counsellor holds you steady in front of that mirror and all you want to do is look away. While you look away, you wonder what part of you is watching you look away. And you wonder why it is so unsettling to see yourself. There is a disconnect and it scares the hell out of you. You're not who you think you are. But then who are you?

The Counsellor holds a space for folks who want to show up in the early morning hours for meditation. She lives only a few blocks from your Jumeriah home so it becomes your safe refuge. Between the Sheikh's Osteopath and the Counsellor you are being groomed for the next stage of your life. You've since learned that life always supports you even when you can't see what is unfolding. There it is. Clear as day *after* you've survived the trauma. But when you're in the muck and mire of it, all you're capable of doing is sensing what makes you feel better. You've since learned that that's your soul guiding you forward into a new reality. When you visit this healing place with the Sheikh's Osteopath and the Counsellor, you begin to imagine a different way of being oriented to your life. And the day the Counsellor shares a piece of her story with you is the day the dam breaks in your imagination. *I was married to a man from here and we have four children together,* she says.

All the air seems to escape from the softly hued room you're sitting in with her. Your blood runs cold. This is not who you thought she was. How did she get here? Did she leave her children? Is that why everyone is quiet about these people and this place? And you immediately realize you are in exactly the right room with exactly the right woman to learn exactly what you need to know to get out of the horror that has become your life.

Relief.

Instant relief.

The Counsellor knows exactly what you're living through because she, too, has lived it. This means you are not alone in your stupid mistakes. This means you are not alone in this painful place. This means you are not alone in the worry and the horror. This means there is a way out.

A way out.

You are here talking to the Counsellor looking for your way out.

The fact that she is here talking to you from another life that she has created for herself means that she found a way out and her story will reveal to you what that way out is.

Hallelujah!

There is hope.

And this is where it lives. In *her* story.

A decade later when you are writing this story for your readers you will be enlightened by the very simplicity of what it takes to transform. It requires you reach out. Share your story. Listen to other stories. Then you find your balance. You begin to heal. Then transformation is inevitable. And you never ever ever get there on your own. That is why a decade later when you are writing this story for your readers you will be filled with the deepest sense of appreciation and love for the Sheikh's Osteopath and the Counsellor. They were your earthly angels. They bridged you into new possibilities for your life. And you realize there are no coincidences in this life. It is all a divine orchestration.

You begin to study Transpersonal Psychology. And one day in the not so distant future you, too, will be enrolled in the Phd program. But for now, you are here talking to the Counsellor. This is a gruelling process. Yet the two of you sit and talk and sit and talk and one day you get up and you know that you are knitting parachutes out of this marriage with the lovely Arab man.

Deepak Chopra comes to Dubai. You buy a ticket. You go to the event expecting to learn something more to help you out of this fix you are in. You sit at a table directly in front of the stage upon which Chopra stands talking. He is only a few feet away from you for the entire day. You are transfixed. Words pour through you as questions and realizations onto the pages of your journal there in front of you while you sit there in front of Deepak Chopra and you have so much you want to say to this man and so much you want to hear him say to you. Every sentence he speaks now makes it feel as though he is talking only to you. At the end of the day you go home and you write more and think more and process more. You create a card of gratitude with a carefully constructed message for Deepak Chopra. You want to thank him for shining so much light onto what until now has eluded you. You have new understanding and you are freshly inspired. The next day at the end of the first session you approach the stage, you stand before Deepak Chopra, you gaze into his eyes and you shake his hand while giving him your card. You say something. You cannot remember quite what you say. Because you are overwhelmed with the sensation of darkness. It's all dark standing here on the stage with him. Everything is heavy and shadowy and slowed down like mud. It is confusing to you. You wonder why all you experience now up close and personal with Deepak Chopra is this darkness. It takes you years to realize what is happening in this moment. Much later in your life you reflect on this meeting and you get it. You suddenly get it. Like the brightest flash of light you understand instantly that the darkness you saw that day standing in front of Deepak Chopra was your own shadow because his light of awareness is so penetrating that he enables you to see exactly what you are standing in at that moment in your life. You are, in fact, immersed in the darkest night of your own soul and it's only when the most beautiful of human radiance stands before you that it becomes apparent. He has shone awareness into your pain body and when he does that you become aware of something you have not known about yourself and you will not know about yourself until much farther down the road. All you know is that something inside of you shifts. You are disturbed by the shadowy presence and you don't yet realize it's your own projection. But in your quest to free yourself from the pain you're experiencing, you seek more guidance. You will eventually learn it is your own unillumined state that has you perceive the radiance of Deepak Chopra in this way. Mystical teachings refer to it as the "shining darkness."

Someone somewhere lets you know there is a guy in Dubai who'll do a reading for you and you must ask for Tim when you call because that is code for him to understand what you are calling him about and he'll set up a time and you will meet him in his beautiful home with so many cushions on the expansive sofa that you cannot find a place to sit comfortably while you wait for him to take you into the candlelit room filled with deep male voices chanting sacred text.

Your beloved first husband is here in this room with you. He has things he wants to say to you. He speaks through Tim.

There is no love around you. Why are you here?

You are dumbfounded.

You are here because life wants you to be here and you've sold everything and taken a leap of faith and you have two sons and you want to provide for them all the good life they deserve and you love the lovely Arab man.

There is no love around you. Why are you here?

You know the minute these words are spoken that they are true. Well, some wee small part of you knows but she's so deeply buried under that larger part of you that is driving your life that you dare not hear her speak because that would mean everything needs to change. Again.

But everything is already changing because those words spoken give rise to a new reality that is brewing in your deep awareness. Tim is the conduit bringing forth your own wisdom. Drawing it out of you like a deep breath drawing liquid from a straw.

You walk away from that first session with Tim feeling gutted. A bubble has burst. And you are left standing in the middle of an open field with mines buried just under the surface of the desert sand upon which you must only dare to tread if you take your life seriously.

I am not loved. What am I doing here?

You see things differently now. You smile inside yourself knowing that Kent has never left you. You have an angel you know. You stop efforting so much to make things into something that they are not. You have new eyes to see with, new ears to hear with. You have different clarity. And you wonder why you couldn't sense it all like this before. You negotiate with the lovely Arab man. You need to move out of his family home. *There is no love around you. Why are you here?*

For the first time in your relationship with the lovely Arab man, you start flying under the radar. You visit Tim regularly. He is an extraordinary man living in a country that is not his home, a country whose laws will imprison him for the truth of who he is – a homosexual. But you sense he has some kind of protection otherwise why would he risk being here? Then you learn that his lover is a local man. And they're part of a larger community of men and women living out the truth of their sexuality under the radar in this Arab country. Everyone here seems to know how to live their real life while appearing as though they are living the only life they are allowed to live. It unsettles you. You can no longer trust what you see because you know there is another reality living just below the surface of things.

But then again, isn't that what you are doing?

You start listening in the gaps of what the lovely Arab man speaks of with you. You start asking pointed questions to test the waters of his transparency. There are parties he attends that you supposedly are not invited to. He claims he goes for business reasons only. When he returns he tells you stories. There are wild and wonky things at these parties according to the lovely Arab man and he speaks of these things as though he never participates because although he is curious, he never subjects himself to such lowly endeavours. There are Russian hookers and drugs and music and entertainment and all things that are forbidden fruits on the surface of his culture. You get the sense that the lovely Arab man sees himself as an innocent caught up in the games of the rich and powerful and in order for his ideas and his businesses to thrive, he must be seen as willing to be among the less than tasteful aspects of the underworld.

You actually believe him.

You experience him as light and purity. You don't see darkness in him which makes you wonder just how whole a human being he actually is. Does he dwell in naiveté? Is this what you most have in common with this man? He certainly treats you as though you need to be protected. He once said you were a precious gem to him and that it was his job to make sure nothing rubbed up against you that might scratch and blemish your perfect qualities. The notion that he finds you flawless is seductive because all the folks at home have judged you harshly, albeit in silence, as a wicked widow impregnated by another woman's husband. You wear that judgment among those people there and it is perhaps the greatest reason why you've left them and your home. They've made you feel unwelcome and undeserving. In contrast, the lovely Arab man sees your purity and your innocence. He wants to save you for himself and no other as though you've never been with any other man. He calls you his own and wipes clean the slate of your sordid history. It is what you most love about being here. You get a do-over. He has married you. He has taken full responsibility for your eldest son in the eyes of the law, promised to always provide for him as his own father should have. He has made it his mission to restore your dignity and it feels divinely right to you. Because this is how you've always seen yourself. As a woman of integrity driven by divine impulses. There is a denial of all things dark in you so, it seems, you're not unlike the lovely Arab man at all. You believe you can move among the less than faithful and they will not destroy or damage your life. It is a dangerous dance with the devil. Unwilling and unable to see your own shadow, you are fated to live out its bidding.

But life will continue to conspire to wake you up.

The stories about westerners having their teenage children locked up in prisons because they were discovered at a party or hanging out with girls. The stories about western women being flown to places under the pretences that they were going to be safe in their home countries with their children, but in fact, are taken to some desert prison where they'll not have access to their children ever again. The stories of local Arab men using their influence in the courts to divorce non-local wives and get full custody of their children and banishing the women to destitute lives. Stories all around you. And no matter how hard you try to not hear the stories or how hard you try to tell yourself these stories have no relationship to you, because the lovely Arab man provides assurances all the time that you don't live where those people in those stories live, it unravels something within you. According to him, you have his protection and that's all you need to know. But the stories follow you around in your head and lurk in the corners of your imagination. Surely, these things could never happen to you! You can trust the lovely Arab man, can't you? You even worry that your son could be drafted into the army. The lovely Arab man laughs at you. But you've lived here through the Gulf War. You've seen things. You hear what's happening around you. But the lovely Arab man treats you like some kind of innocent which causes you to doubt what your soul is trying to warn you about.

Get out! she says.

Go home! she says.

You don't want to live another moment as a self-endangering innocent.[12]

You start living another life in your head. You don't share every thought you think with your husband. You start to hold back pieces of yourself. You learn to become more calculating in the everyday decisions you are making. You are taking back parts of yourself and building a new way of being again. You accept that your marriage to the lovely Arab man needs to look different from what you'd hoped it to be. You begin to notice there might be times when he's not completely honest with you. He never lies. No. He wouldn't be that transparent. What he does is far more insidious. He withholds information in strategic ways. And you find yourself having conversations within conversations with him – you speak something out loud, assess his response, talk the way you know he needs you to talk while speaking to yourself in your own head in a very different way. It allows you to learn discernment in the face of things that are unsettling to you. You are no longer willing to be so open, naive and vulnerable with the lovely Arab man. It is a strange and foreign way to be for a woman whose natural state is openness. But you sense your life now depends on you becoming more discerning. You need some street smarts. Not everyone in this world is who they say they are. People are full of contradictions, shadows and survival instincts. And you are no exception.

---

[12] concept from Elizabeth Gilbert's novel *The Signature of All Things* p.96

You find a newly built villa in a complex with a pool and a gym. The Wind Tower Villa with its traditional desert design and beautiful indoor outdoor flow will be a home where you can hang your own pictures and plant your own flowers and make your own space free and clear of the love that is not around you. You will make this a loving home and the lovely Arab man may grow into the space with you if he likes or not. (The naive part of you is still operating most of the time despite your efforts to see the truth of your situation.) All you know is that you need love around you and if there is no love around you then by jove you're going to create some.

You work so hard. Again. To make another home. It is now a life skill. Your determination to provide your sons with home and stability and love is the one constant in your life.

It is a beautiful home.

You are a creative force when it comes to making home. You notice how important it is to express the feelings you have inside of you about home. It matters. It brings you immense pleasure to provide a place and a space where you and your boys and anyone you love and welcome into your place and your space will feel that love and protection. It's the very thing you always depended on as a kid and it's the very thing you can still depend on from your own parents. Home is home. Wherever you are in the world, you have that feeling of home inside of you because your mother and your father gave it to you and in fact, still give it to you. They are home. And you, as their daughter, have always been and will always be welcome in the home they provide for you. To this day, they still remain living where you grew up. To this day, you can still go home and touch the very things that grew you up. To this day, you belong there. It's a prayer for your life that your parents continue to keep for you. So, why is it then that you are wandering the planet wondering where you belong?

You recall when you realized you wanted to devote your life to writing. You stood in the middle of your bedroom in Seascape gazing out the bay window at the ocean and the mountains beyond. *How can I be a writer when I have nothing to write about? I need to see more of the world. I need to find a story.*

You didn't understand then that the world awaiting you was your inner sanctum. You literally aspired to venture forth and create adventure so you'd have something to write about! You also didn't understand that when you'd decided to leave the University of Victoria to join the lovely Arab man in the Persian Gulf (that being your idea of adventure), you did so not knowing the value your own education. Because while you were a student, you were writing a lot. When you left your studies, you stopped writing. You didn't appreciate that the hollowness from which you believed you had nothing to write about was actually a result of not being replenished intellectually and artistically. You were hungry for connection with deep thought and contemplation. You wanted to know yourself and the world you were marching in but nobody told you that you didn't need to leave the country and risk your children's lives so that one day you could call yourself a writer. You were, in that very moment, already a writer and a thinker and a storyteller. You just didn't have the self-esteem to locate yourself in your own stability and let the world generate itself around you. Instead you went searching outside of yourself because you had no idea that everything you ever needed as a writer was already at your fingertips. Story was pulsing through you and around you and calling you to capture it, tell it, share it. Is it possible that some part of you did see and know this but another part had yet to wake up to it, own it and be strong enough to allow it to show you the way for your life? Truth is, and here it is, the truth, so listen up and pay attention. Truth is you were afraid. You had fear in you. You resisted knowing the truth of yourself because of what it might mean for your life. You sensed you had a reason and a mission and you just didn't have the faith to believe in yourself and believe in your dream enough to stay in your own truth and create your own life. You thought you needed someone else to do it for you. How could you possibly be enough for all that you desired?

You were too big for you.

You didn't appreciate that every time you created home, you actually established the foundation you needed to allow yourself to flow into your writing life one word at a time, one page at a time, one story at a time. That it's sorta like walking. You just need to put one foot in front of the other and when you've been walking for awhile then pretty soon you can begin to sprint and jog and run.

Your first son built communities from milk cartons, boxes and lego in that Seascape home. Entire cities with trains on tracks and farms with animals in barns and yards with trees and birds. He would build for hours. He'd beg you not to vacuum the floors so nothing would be moved and you'd not vacuum the floors so nothing would be moved. But then one day he'd destroy it all with great fanfare. A hurricane or tornado or earthquake or tsunami would blow through him and it'd all come crashing down. You'd watch from a distance. You'd feel the pain of loss. You'd tell him not to destroy everything. He'd shrug his shoulders, furl his lower lip. *It's okay Mama, that's life!*

Then he'd start the building process all over again.

It's never occurred to you until now, *how did I not see this,* that he was reflecting back to you the life experience you were generating for him. By the time he was four years old, the two of you had moved eight times! Which means you created home in eight different places on two continents in two countries and three provinces. The only stability in that boy's life was your connection to your own childhood and the insatiable need to be home. That drew him into you and you held him close. Wherever you landed, you created ritual to provide home. And when you were in-between homes, or when you were in doubt about what would come next, you would pack him up and take him to the farm where your parents, his grandparents, would welcome you with the predictability of their life and home and once again the two of you would know you belonged somewhere and people loved you. You'd stay and replenish yourselves until it was time again to venture forth. Why in hell didn't anyone sit you down and say for god's sake woman get a grip and come home to yourself before you grow so weary on the journey that you lose both yourself and your boy?

Nobody did. (Or maybe they did and you just weren't listening?)

And some part of you thought you were living your adventure.

You now ache for that little boy. Why on earth didn't you feel like you were enough for him and for you? He was your tether. In his loving need for you as his mother, he grounded you in ways that allowed you to know how to make home, how to provide for his daily needs, how to stay emotionally connected to his well being even though you never saw until the moment you are writing this that you were also generating inner chaos for him. And his child wisdom found expression due in large part to your ability to hold a space for him to connect with his own wisdom. You must redeem yourself here. And release any guilt for all the things you now see you could've done differently. Because in the end, it was your mothering observation that had you decide to make one more home on Vancouver Island. And the lovely Arab man provided the bridge for you and your boy to make your way back to Canada the first time. To find Seascape. To enrol in university. To make a life pattern that was harmonious to your soul.

It was really a grand and grace-full gesture.

As though the lovely Arab man was another earthly angel bringing you home to yourself.

Maybe you called him in.

Maybe that's what we do here in earth school.

We get lost. We reach out for help. Help comes in the form of relationship. We take the ride. Find a new land. Make another home. Tell a different story.

When you look at the artwork on your walls from that time you see images of strong goddess-like women beating drums and paddling canoes. Perhaps you were seeking your own feminine strength. If that's the case then both the boy and the lovely Arab man have been guardians on your path.

The path that has brought you to the Wind Tower Villa.

Both of your boys seem happy here. They each have their own rooms. Gone are the reminders of little girls who have been taken from their dad. Every room has a door or a window opening onto the outside garden splashed with bright bougainvillea and persimmon. Your music reverberates through the space making it feel sacred. You feel free to express yourself here. You hadn't realized how trapped you were in the big family home with all the stuff around you that wasn't yours nor was it an expression of you. It all belonged to someone else. To another time. To another family. And you were and would forever be a visitor in that space.

It wasn't that you hadn't tried.

You'd made every effort to make it home for you and the lovely Arab man. But too much had already been lived there to make that possible. You recall an event in the family home around the dining room table. Your good friend Sabine is over for lunch. The lovely Arab man and Ibrahim have joined you at the table. You and Sabine love each other's company. You share many lunches and tea times together. But having the lovely Arab man and Ibrahim with you changes everything. Conversation is disjointed. An unease is in the room. With Sabine watching you closely, you sense how different you are behaving. She is your witness. And her reflection leaves you feeling nervous and uneasy. The lovely Arab man and Ibrahim clearly do not approve of your Canadian friend and they have an almost imperceptible way of expressing their displeasure. You are aware of the fact that she is dressed as a western woman in the presence of these Arab men. Of course she is! She has no interest in being someone she's not. How is it that you are now uncomfortable because Sabine's arms are bare in her short-sleeved blouse and her legs exposed in her knee-length skirt? When has this become a problem for you? You feel as though you are sitting between two cultures. The tension emanates from the fact that you don't know anymore to which one you pledge allegiance. You belong to neither and to both. You are hovering somewhere between and extending yourself to both parties in an effort to bring some kind of harmony. Why do you do this to yourself? Why do you think you need to facilitate anything at all here? Where is your clarity and confidence? Have they fallen along the wayside because you've sold your soul for something you thought was security and belonging? If so, then that's the saddest part of this whole tale.

You felt lost.

You belonged nowhere.

Neither here nor there.

The only thing you have ever known for sure is that you are the mother of your children. And you've always had a sense of your own value as mother which in the end turns out to be your best and biggest saving grace.

But besides being mom, you notice now that the only thing on your own calendar are weekly appointments to the spa where you spend so much of your time getting pedicures and manicures and hair colours. It doesn't feel luxurious. It feels like a responsibility. As though you have internalized the lovely Arab man's need for you to be perfectly groomed and ready as his lover and bedmate. You are sure he has never suggested such a thing yet you have read this into your relationship. Is it possible that you feel you've prostituted yourself? That you feel used? It seems the only real communication you have with this man anymore is through your sexuality. You've tested the ground in other domains. You've wanted to grow alongside him in every way. You've tried to insert yourself into the conversation about finances. What to invest? Where to invest it? What long term goals did the two of you want to aim for?

You were abruptly dismissed by a haughty laugh that let you know in no uncertain terms that you'd advanced yourself into a domain that he was unwilling to share with you. This was not yours to think about nor talk about. You remember the heat in your face as surely as he'd given you a back-handed slap. You also remember thinking to yourself *See this! See the Truth of this! He thinks you are less than he is.*

His culture runs through his blood.

It is bone deep.

And now that you are married to the lovely Arab man, the rules seem to have shifted. You could be the independent Western woman when you were his mistress. In fact, he demanded you be her. That's who he was attracted to and that's who he wanted in his bed. But there must have been some fine print in the marriage contract that you didn't bother to read. Or perhaps it was only stated in the Arabic language of which you will forever be enamoured but wholly inadequate with when it comes to speaking and understanding its nuances.

It's becoming clear to you.

You are not to be the free-thinking, independent Western woman any longer.

There are rules that you are expected to accept and adhere to. Trouble is, you don't have anyone telling you what the rules are. So the lovely Arab man must be in some kind of denial himself to expect that you will learn without anyone guiding you. Or maybe he knows you only too well (he should) and suspects that if he were to lay it all out in front of you that you'd run in the opposite direction because the thing he's most liked about you in the past has been your disobedience to your own culture. He admires that. He probably relates to it in an unconscious way because of the man he is or wants to be. He himself pushes up against everything he is supposed to be. There's a part of him that is proud of having married not one but two North American women. His family teases him about his wives and assures him that if he only married a local woman all his troubles would cease because she'd know exactly how to take care of him.

And this is why he doesn't invite you to his family home and have you introduced properly as the wife that you are or even tell his family that he is the father of his son. None of this is revealed. None of it. He repeatedly convinces you that when the time is right, he'll come out in the open. Until then, he demands you be patient with him. Meanwhile, you are supposed to understand the rules of this new game. Being his mistress was much easier and much more in alignment with the values you prefer to live by.

Things are changing. You sense him watching your every movement now.

Your comings and your goings.

He questions the way you wear your abaya. He wonders why you wear it at all. You know it's your feeble attempt at trying to belong. You defend your right to wear it the way you want to wear it. He sees you mimicking other Western women trying to blend into the Arab culture and you sense a kind of distaste in his comments to you. It hurts you deeply that he is making no effort to fold you into his life in a real way and yet he takes the liberty to criticize the inroads you are attempting to travel on what you hope will be your way into the heart of his family and his culture.

It's really sad what this does to you. And how little he cares about what this does to you.

So bloody sad.

It's going to be just another layer of sadness for you to carry when you march yourself back home to a land you understand and have the possibility to thrive in. But for now, you are here and there is nowhere else to go.

One day, he pushes you too far. And you surprise yourself by the reaction that rises up from inside of you. You invoke the power of your own family in a moment when you realize that you are somebody, too. You also have people you have come from and people who love you. You might not belong in this land but by God there is a place where you do belong. And the words well up and through you with such force that you feel yourself standing taller than you've ever stood in this desert land: *I stand before you as the daughter of Wayne and Margaret, the sister of Brent and Murray and Jody, the mother of Matthew and Gabriel and you best know that when you are talking to me, you are talking to my family!*

You then storm out of the house in your abaya on your way to anywhere but here.

You hear him murmur something about how much you are changing. And you think to yourself that he best pay attention to how you are changing if he wants to keep up because you've about had enough of being treated like a second-class citizen. You are somebody, damn it.

You've surprised yourself by the fierceness of your own voice.

You've invoked the names of your family to find power. Living in this place you are absorbing new ways of being that don't necessarily feel authentic to you but they are becoming your survival strategies. Tribal language is a language the lovely Arab man relates to and you've used it to get under his defences. It's the first time in a long while that you've felt empowered while standing before him. It occurs to you that you hadn't realized you were being disempowered. How exactly has that happened without you even noticing?

Not long after, you are sitting at the table feeding your toddler his lunch on a Friday. The household staff have Fridays off so you are on your own with your kids. And the lovely Arab man is travelling abroad on business. So you are surprised when the back kitchen door opens and a man clad in dishdasha and guttra walks through to the dining room where you are sitting.

It's the lovely Arab man's brother.

He is surprised that you are there. *Where the hell else would I be?* you dare to think to yourself more angry than you realize. How do you tell this guy that you actually live here? This is your home now? You knew this day would come and you are embarrassed to be seen as living some kind of secret. The lovely Arab man has put you in a precarious position.

The lovely Arab man's brother recovers quickly and makes a polite enough greeting and you fall all over yourself trying to make him welcome without getting up from your chair. You fear that if you stand up, you might just fall over in the shock of it all because you immediately realize the guy doesn't even know his eldest brother has a son and here you sit feeding the boy. Furthermore, you remember that this brother also has a son a little younger than the lovely Arab man's son which means if the guy puts two and two together he'll know that he, in fact, does not have the first born son in the family ... his brother does and here sits the boy.

Here sits the boy not even knowing that he is in the presence of his Uncle. *This is too fucking sad to bear.* You watch a shadow come across the guy's face when you introduce him to your son. You hold steady as you witness his brain making the computations.

Silence.

You don't know what you expect the lovely Arab man's brother to do or to say. Maybe you are hoping that at last it is all out in the open and he'll welcome you into his arms as a sister and he'll be ecstatic to meet his beautiful nephew and regardless of the lovely Arab man's fears it will now be all over and you'll be one big happy family. Finally, one big happy family.

But it doesn't work that way.

Not even close.

The dude becomes cold like an ice-cube. You feel him retreating. And he is quick to turn away and walk out the kitchen door. There is no doubt in your mind at this point that you and your son simply are not welcome and certainly not important enough for him to acknowledge in a real way. It's as though you are seen but then purposefully not seen. As though the lovely Arab man has license to live whatever he wants to live in his private moments and if those private moments spill out into a place where they don't belong then they will be neatly tucked back into the corners where they're not to be seen and life will roll on as though nothing has changed.

The lovely Arab man's brother leaves the house indicating in a silent language that nothing he has witnessed here changes anything. Life remains as it is until the lovely Arab man himself decides that there is something to change the way it all appears to be. He acts politely but you read the subtext. You are nobody and nothing and neither is your son.

He is gone.

You are devastated.

What the hell am I doing here?

• • •

You begin to plan your escape.

But there's nothing conscious about the planning.

You notice quiet whispering intuitions nudging you toward things. A teacher appears. His name is Cyrus. You are drawn to study Reiki with him and you convince your friend Sabine to join you. It is a small gathering of people, some of whom fall asleep during the teachings which perplexes you because you just cannot get enough of the energy work and the knowledge. You drink it up as though you are dying of thirst in the desert. Wait a minute! Maybe that's exactly what you are feeling. Dying for connection, for replenishment, for life and love and beauty and hope and peace and healing.

You find all these qualities in Cyrus' teachings. You are enormously relieved and inspired. The feedback you get from this group of people is that you are strong with potential and wise beyond your thinking. You know in your heart that this kind of learning and pursuing will change the game of your life. That you've said yes to something that will now transform how you show up for the decisions in your life. Deep internal shifts are happening and there is no fear for you because it all just feels so good!

But there's fear in the lovely Arab man.

You feel him observing you. He sees you changing. It worries him. And the fact that it worries him mystifies you. If he loves you then why can't he encourage you growing strong within yourself?

Well, that's a dumb question now, isn't it?

He's worried because he feels threatened by your development. And this is a theme you recognize in your life. *Don't shine your light too brightly cause you might make others feel bad.*

What if you were to step fully into your own strength and wisdom? What then? Who would still love you? And want to be with you?

It's incredibly painful to imagine that the people you love only love you because you agree to not outrun them. That they are invested in keeping you small and weak and in need of whatever they provide for you. What a confusing notion! You know that you want the best and the brightest for everyone you love and even for those you don't know. You have this innate care for the world and for the beings in the world. You imagine that everyone possesses this charism – a quality you learn about through the teachings of Caroline Myss. You don't yet see that you are here in Earth School as a healer and it is this sacred contract that you have with life that makes you the kind of human that you are. You don't yet understand how to manage the power of your charism which is your personal divinity, your special grace. This assumption you make about the people in your world is what keeps you naive. You just keep thinking that everyone else is looking out for your best interests in the same way that you are looking out for their best interests. Some would call this stupidity. Others would be kind and call it naiveté, which really isn't that kind at all. Either way, it's how you navigate your world even though you keep getting bruised by the belief.

Your memory floats you back a few months ago when you are in Palo Alto for the residency part of your graduate school program. Across the street from the hotel you were staying in there was a sign on a home advertising "Psychic Services." You were drawn into that home and into a conversation with an elderly woman. She told you that if you left the lovely Arab man, he'd give you nothing and you'd be alone for many years. You don't remember asking if you should leave the desert and the lovely Arab man. And you wondered where she got the idea that you might want to. You left her house feeling somewhat deflated. There was nothing in her reading that confirmed for you anything that you imagined you were creating in your life. The path that she described you being on didn't feel like your path at all. The disconnect was unsettling. But a few hours later when you were in the back seat of the taxi on your way to seminar, you were struck still by a fleeting thought that seemed to speak in your inner ear. A clear and present voice said to you: *You can break free. You have a money nest from the sale of Seascape. It is protected and waiting for you to use. It'll get you home.*

Time stood still.

Mind space opened.

A lightness of being flooded through you. You felt yourself smile. And in that interlude you could feel the freedom of returning to Vancouver Island with your sons and taking back your life. It was the sweetest sensation. The deepest knowing. As though it were already true.

And then you knew.

The way had been opened.

Now all you needed to do was put one foot in front of the other, listen to your intuition and follow the guidance to get you back to where you belonged. You had no idea how you were going to make it happen. But what you did have was an unwavering soul knowing that you were already home. It was already written somewhere in the pages of your destiny. The mere fact of this soul knowing would be all you would have in the days and weeks and months to come. This ineffable feeling that it was already so. Is this what it means to have faith? You would surely find out. Because something deep within shifted. Your interior was reorganized and reoriented. You were now pointed in the direction of freedom. And there would be no turning back from this moment in the back seat of the taxi on the streets of Palo Alto, California. Just when you think all might be lost, you discover that you've never been lost at all. There is a force of love all around you at all times holding the precise GPS coordinates of your soul location.

You are never too far from home.

When all else fails, ask for guidance. And guidance will come.

The only question left remaining is will you have the courage needed to do what you know must be done?

• • •

The plan lives in your imagination every day in every way. It's never too far out of reach yet you wonder if you're conscious of it at all. It takes up residence in your mindspace and claims a handle on every decision you make. When you're shopping, you consider whether or not it's really something you need and will you be taking it with you when you go? You don't know. But every little detail of your life is now to be considered in this way. Will it stay or will it go? It's a gradual process of inner detachment from all you've grown to love about living here in this culture. You are also distancing yourself from the idea that has been driving your life here for years ... that you can find a way to belong and make home and be happy here among these people. Your radar picks up on what is really unfolding. The lovely Arab man makes mention that his son will be "arabized" and you are struck by the absurdity of such a notion. What exactly will that mean? How will it come about? Who will be involved? Your interior is flooded with fear because you know you have little say about anything of any import. That you are in no position to deny or demand anything when it comes to your young son. And you notice with deeper perception that your older son is feeling more and more removed from the family and the culture. He's losing his sparkle. The lovely Arab man seems to be deliberately distancing himself from the older boy and you don't know why. But it causes you deep distress. You sense a division developing between your sons. Not of their making. And maybe that's the very reason you feel a rise in your defences. You feel you must protect these boys and who they are to each other. And your mother radar is relentless when in service to their innocence. It's one domain where you know your strength and power. And maybe you wonder if that, too, is at risk. There is some kind of undercurrent of something that is at work and you can't quite put your finger on it. So you are constantly scanning your environment to read where the danger might be.

Is the fear residing in you?

Are you generating problems where there are none?

Or are you waking up to the truth of your life?

Only time will allow you to learn how to discern your interior markers. Right Instinct is built through experience. Your inner radar is signalling to you that you're in a danger zone and it's time to go back home.

• • •

When you start trying to figure out a man and a marriage, it's actually you avoiding the fact that it's simply not working ... for *you*. Your needs are not being met. But your focus shines toward *him* as you try to make *him* happy rather than getting honest with yourself. It's hard to look a man in the eye and tell him that whatever the two of you are doing together, ain't *it* for you.

Somewhere along the line you learned that you were always the one doing something wrong if things weren't working out. When you're not getting your needs met in the marriage, you simply start giving more. Until you get so tired and so depleted that you have to pull back into yourself or die. At that stage there is a death of sorts. A piece of you *is* dying. The question is what piece? Then to save your life, you start moving in another direction, discreetly. And here's a telling truth: *he doesn't even notice.*

Herstorically, no man has been willing to follow you, walk alongside you, fully partner with you since your first marriage. They've each tried to pull you down and away from yourself. It's painful. But you seem to have an extraordinarily high threshold for pain. What does this cost you? How does it force you to grow?

• • •

You think what's needed is a real conversation.

So, you give it a go.

In a restaurant over lunch with the lovely Arab man who is your third husband. The man who rescued you from your crazy second marriage. The man who has been your lover and knight in shining armour for more than a decade. You retreat to the place inside yourself that truly trusts and admires all that he's been to you in your life. All the ways that he's extended himself to you and your family. You've been nothing less that true to him and his love for you. You have built a life on his promises. You expect that your loyalty and devotion will provide you with an abundant life. You expect you will be treated with fairness. That the lovely Arab man is a just man, a wise man, a loving man. His benevolence gives meaning to every decision you've made to bring you to this place alongside him as his wife. You expect he will fulfill his promise to shower you with all things good and beautiful. That he'll always love and protect you. That he'll never desert you and your sons. You expect that you've secured your place on Planet Earth and that all will be well. So all of this gives you the courage to speak truthfully on this day over this lunch with this lovely Arab man, your third husband.

Well, at least that is your intention. To speak truthfully. But very soon into the conversation you notice yourself being censored. You are censoring yourself. Or being cautious which eclipses the courage you had starting the dialogue. It's as though a part of you is watching you be all sweet and open and true while another part of you is holding something back, poking and prodding a bit because she senses that truth is no longer possible with the lovely Arab man. That something remains hidden. You can't quite put your finger on the pulse of untruth but it's as though you're stumbling around in a dark room full of furniture. You know the furniture is there even though you cannot see it so you walk with the clear intention to avoid hurting yourself. But this part of you is getting mighty tired of tip-toeing around truth and you are ready for a face-off. You know you are capable of a face-off. But you are also keenly aware of where you are and who you are in this desert land. You believe the lovely Arab man is the source of your safety and security here and so there are also alarm bells ringing in your head. You want the truth but you also want to be safe.

You are testing yourself and you are testing him.

"Here's what's true," you say to him, "I've been here with you a long time. I've tried living in your family home with you. It could've worked for me if it could've worked for you. I tried to make that house our home but you are stuck in some in-between place. You've kept me and my children away from your family. We're married yet I remain hidden. So if the traditional way is not open to me then I've asked you to help me create my own way here. I've moved out of your family home. I've created a new home with my children and one that I'm dreaming you'll one day step into as my present husband. But the truth is you only visit. You spend the night. Then you leave. The boys wonder why you are not with us and I wonder why you are not with us, too. I've been patient. I've watched you suffer through a hard divorce. I've been nothing less than loving and kind. And I know you will be angry when I say this but you are not treating us very well. And I cannot continue to live like this."

Silence.

The truth hangs in the air like a dark cloud above your couple.

You can see how difficult it is for him to hear what you are saying but you are now on fire with truth and there is no going back to pretending that you are fine with the way you've been living.

"I am your wife yet you behave as though I am your mistress!"

Now you've crossed the invisible line of what's acceptable to say out loud and what is not acceptable to say out loud. You know this is the hottest button to push and you know you'll have unlocked the lovely Arab man's wrath. Because he himself cannot bear to think that he is treating you like a mistress. You are too kind and sweet and patient and loving which makes it nearly impossible for him to face his own shadow. That he has parts of himself that are less than kind and honourable is just something he is not willing to see.

Then you do something that you've never done in all the years of loving the lovely Arab man. You stand up.

"I am so done with all of this," you say.

Then you walk out of the restaurant leaving him dumbfounded at the table. You know you've crossed another line now. And your legs begin to quiver. You feel light-headed. A bit buoyant. You are rising up to meet yourself where your dignity lives. There is a different quality to the air where you are headed, and your body feels a deep relief, even a light-heartedness. It feels so good to just walk away.

You hail a cab. And just as you're opening the door to get into the car, you feel him behind you.

"Please don't leave. Come with me. Come with me, now," he says.

You hesitate momentarily. You turn to meet his gaze. He looks sad and tired. You decide to turn toward him this one last time.

You close the car door and wave the driver on. Then you walk with the lovely Arab man to his car. He opens the passenger door for you and you get in. He gets in the driver's seat, starts the car and drives out of the parking lot. And you think to yourself that the silence is no longer acceptable. You tell the lovely Arab man that the two of you must keep talking, that there are things to say out loud.

Then he says something that reignites the fire burning in your soul.

He says he wants you to return to Canada. To leave. To go home.

You tell him to pull the car over. That he best stop driving. So he pulls into the parking lot of the nearest shopping mall. When the car comes to a halt, you start to talk.

"You want me to go home to Canada? For how long?"

"I want you to leave here. Take your sons to Canada and make a life without me," he says.

Your world stops spinning. There's a ringing in your ears. Of all the places you've been with the lovely Arab man, you never for one moment dreamt that he'd have you repeat the very nightmare you were living when he swooped into your life to save you. He's sending you home.

Or is he?

Because your world has stopped spinning and because your ears are ringing you are forced into your interior where deep silence fills every fibre of your being. And suddenly you know that he's using your past to trigger your present in his attempt to manipulate you into obedience. In a split second you see the truth. It blinds you. You no longer have access to what you've been telling yourself all these years. All that you'd built this reality on dissolves in an instant. You are emptied out. Gutted.

Then a voice rises from inside of you so strong and clear that you have no choice but to be carried along on its vibration through the conversation that follows.

"And what of your son?" you ask.

"He'll be better off without me. Take him to your home. Live as though I have died."

You think you might just implode.

"As though you have died?!"

Rage rises from within you, takes you over and speaks.

"What kind of bullshit is this that you are saying? You begged me to bring him into this world! You promised to never leave us, to always take care of us. You promised I'd never repeat having to raise a son on my own. I trusted you and I made decisions based on your promises. And now you think you can just send us away? What foolishness is this? I take this boy and I'm supposed to live as though you are dead yet every day I'll be face-to-face with your image in him, every day I'll hear you in his voice, every day I'll see you in his movements. Why would you torture me so? Why? What has changed in you that you are no longer willing to be the man you promised you would be?"

The lovely Arab man is shamed into silence. He has never witnessed you like this before. And never have you felt so right and so strong and so clear in his presence. But even though it sounds like you are making a case for staying, there's a part of you that has glimpsed a truth that will demand you leave. There's no going back from this awareness. Another veil has lifted.

And both of you know it in your hearts.

But only one of you will have the courage it takes to make the break. The kind of courage that trumps love yet is in sacred service to Love.

The lovely Arab man leaves you sitting in the car while he goes into the shopping mall. With him absent, you regain your grounded breath and you sense that something significant has happened. You don't move. The stillness comforts you. You open the car window to the soft breeze and sweet sunshine that is characteristic of the winter months in the Arabian Peninsula. The tension in your body melts away and you talk yourself into staying present for whatever wants to happen next.

But what happens next is so painful for you to remember that you don't want to write about it here.

It's embarrassing.

It reveals a trait in the lovely Arab man that you just don't want to look at. You are much more attuned to his soul than to his personality. So it is shocking when he succumbs to his lesser self yet he is merely human, isn't he? What does this response of yours say about you?

That you have changed.

You arrived in this desert land fragmented. The pieces of your broken heart have been messengers and magnets sending out unconscious shadowy fragments to draw in the people and the experiences to help you wake up.

Waking up now is out-of-this-world pain-full because you are faced with the chaos you've created through your un-clear choices. How are you ever going to get back to wholeness?

The lovely Arab man comes back to the car, opens the door and sits next to you. He places a small box in the palm of your hand. You frown and meet his gaze.

"What is this?"

"It's for you."

You open the box to find an exquisite diamond pendant on a gold chain.

Another veil lifts.

He thinks this makes it all okay. He thinks this is the appropriate response to the dialogue you've just shared. He thinks this is what is required of him in order to keep you near. You feel sick. But you don't let him see that. Instead you smile warmly, close the box and say thank you.

Things will never be the same from this moment forward.

He knows it, too, but is unwilling to face it. He once said to you that *a drowning man has no fear of getting his pants wet* in reference to making sense of the craziness that your second husband was generating for himself and for you. You wonder now if the lovely Arab man knows his own fear. Because you've actually glimpsed it in this exchange between you. He fears that you will, in fact, do the thing he has demanded you do – leave.

And it is the one thing that you've promised him you'd never do because you can't bear the thought of taking his son away from him nor do you imagine you have any power to do so. Yet you cannot help but feel a gateway has opened on this warm winter afternoon. An initiation. Something invisible has been made visible.

How will you process the deep disappointment of not being able to fulfill your own expectations and of not having your expectations met?

You don't know this now but you will. All expectations are a projection of your lesser self and an act of fear. Your expectations of others work to shield you from having to surrender and trust the Divine thrust of your own life. The expectations that you have projected onto the lovely Arab man are your fragments lost and looking for wholeness. They are a reflection of an ego spirituality. You fail to trust the Divine in yourself so you project your fear onto him and trust what you see to be the Divine in him. And then you tell yourself that you are trusting the Divine Plan for your life. Your proof? You make fearless decisions. That is, you make decisions that ignore your own fears. You don't understand that the fear in you is actually a friendly signal telling you to listen to your own needs. It's your body's response to wrong choices. You try to talk yourself into things that you really don't want to do. You never really wanted to leave Vancouver Island. You never really wanted to move into the lovely Arab man's family home. You never really wanted to marry the man. But the cultural buzz where you come from in the Western world is about feeling the fear and doing it anyway so you translate that to mean not trusting the big feelings that your body emits in order to guide you along your way. You have this incredibly sensitive intuitive system and you haven't been taught how to navigate its wisdom. But you'll learn. In fact, you are learning through all of this hard experience just what it costs you to ignore your interior signals.

There will be years of meditation and contemplation and yoga and affirmative prayer and cognitive self-care and sacred service to teach you precisely what your ego looks like. This ego of yours, this little self, is a skilled trickster.

Your soul is a strong, Prairie Wise Woman. When your first husband died, you became untethered from Her. This story you tell now is her healing in progress.

You and you alone created the chaos in your life through the unclarity of your own choices.

It's that simple.

And every choice generated a consequence. And consequences eventually come into balance.

You know now that you're already who you need to be. You are already you. There are no big decisions to be made. None. The thing you notice today is that your soul is the part of you that you've always felt at home with. It's been here all along. And it's your ego that drove you into places, both internal and external, where you didn't really want to go. It was your ego telling you that it wasn't enough to just be content and easy and free. It was your ego that had you choose the option that made you uneasy. You must never forget this about yourself.

Know thyself and you know the Universe.

Your soul is easy and natural. Your ego generates chaos and problems.

You're learning to own your own power by connecting to your own Divinity. And your Grace has been your refusal to be obedient to a man. It has been both the ruination and divination in your life because it has been the path through which you've discovered your dharma – your learning agenda.

Your last few months in the Arabian Peninsula are embodied in the wise Arab proverb that says to *Trust Allah but tie your camels!*

• • •

You are sitting down for dinner with your sons. And suddenly you feel light-headed, dizzy. Your arms and hands so weak that you cannot pick up your plate. You feel as though blood is draining from your body, down through your legs and out the soles of your feel. You think you must be hungry. Your blood sugar must be low, you reason. You break out into a cold sweat. Sit down and eat, you tell yourself. Just eat and you'll feel better. From the haze of your thoughts, you look at your eldest son sitting across the table from you. You tell him that if you should pass out that he must call Sabine and then Ibrahim because they'll know what to do. He looks puzzled and he doesn't understand the urgency in your voice. You feel as though he is a thousand miles away from you and that you must safe guard him should you leave. It causes you such intense pain to imagine you leaving these boys sitting at this table like this. That they'll wonder what happened to their mother and they won't have your guidance or protection or love. It rips your heart out to think of being separated from them and yet you are slipping away. Right here. Right now. You can feel yourself slipping out of your body. There's spaghetti on the table. You reach for some, put it on your plate and try to eat it quickly thinking it's just food that you need to bring you back to your senses. Even though the food is in your mouth you cannot taste it. You are consumed by the fear of leaving your children and not having anyone to care for them. The fear puffs you up like a helium balloon. It takes your voice. You cannot speak. Your head filled with intense, searing pain. *I don't want to die here ... I cannot die here* are the words rushing through your awareness. The pain of not being able to reach your sons even though you are sitting there before them is so excruciating that you are blinded into oblivion. All of this is happening inside of you and they are eating their dinner as though nothing is happening. You excuse yourself from the table trying hard to not alarm them. You say you just need to do something in your studio and will return shortly. Some part of you watching as you stumble down the hall into your studio. You close the door behind you and sink softly into your recliner chair. Closing your eyes, you pray this will all pass. You pray that you will live. The pain of not being able to reach your children from this cloud of collapse is too much to bear. You feel heavy. Exhausted. You surrender to the sensation now. It takes you over. You drift into spacious space. There is relief here. You are alone. You are dying to the world as you've known it. You are letting go. There is nothing left. It's over. Gone. Done. Goodbye.

But it's not over because you do wake up. It's only been moments but it feels like forever.

And you know with every fibre of your being that if you do not leave this country you will become very ill and you will die here. You have seen clearly how this all ends. You know where you are headed now and there is not another day for you to delude yourself to thinking anything is otherwise. Your death will impact your sons profoundly. Their lives will be torn apart.

In your deep vision you see your eldest son returning to Canada to study and be with your family. Your youngest son will be privy to his father's life in ways you have never been. He will be "arabized" and taken into a life where his brother will not be welcome. Your children will not grow together as brothers. They will be estranged from each other. You will die in a country where you are considered to be a foreigner and your sons will be ripped apart. It will all be very sad. They'll say you never recovered from the death of your first husband. They'll say you were lost to yourself. And they'll be right. And your sons will be abandoned to live like orphans.

This is not the life you intended for yourself. Your dreams slipping away into blackness.

You are shocked by this deep knowing yet it brings you ease to finally see the truth of what you are choosing. This vision of the life path you have chosen has radiated from deep within you as a warning. You want out. You must get out. It will not be easy, you know this. But you also know that if you want to save your sons' lives and reclaim your own then you need to get out of this place.

A prayer emanates from your consciousness. It becomes your mantra just as steady as your breath. *Goddess-God, let me see all there is to see. Show me the way home.*

For days after you suffer with intense headaches. Your eyes are burning tired. You can no longer focus correctly. You keep closing your eyes for relief. Within a week, you have seen an ophthalmologist and been prescribed glasses. He wonders why you haven't had to wear glasses before now because you have a stigma in your right eye. He says you must be adaptable.

You are no longer willing to adapt yourself to everyone else's version of who you should be.

You are hungry for clarity and truth.

Once you've seen the truth of things, once you've awakened to what is really unfolding, you're stronger than you've ever known yourself to be. You will never again go back to living in the foggy haze of delusion.

You are in danger of losing your life and losing your children. This and this alone is what becomes your driving force now.

You recall walking the city streets with your mother in search of a second wedding dress and all the while feeling a sense of dread. Yet you ignored the feeling. You told yourself it was the next thing you had to do even though you really wanted something else. You really wanted to just sit comfortably in the home you had created for yourself and your son, to accept the funding from the provincial government which would allow you to study, to get your degree, to build your life's work. But instead you listened to the voice in your head telling you that you could do none of those things without a man, a husband, a protector. It made you angry to succumb to it but you did nonetheless. What would it have looked like to heed your own intuition rather than undermine it?

You also recall telling your mother and father that you were leaving to live in a country thousands of miles away from all you've ever known to be home. You remember your second husband's sister saying that you were giving up a lot to move and you remember thinking how nice it was to have her acknowledge it out loud. Your mother's tears at the time annoyed you. Didn't she realize you had to make a new life for yourself? Didn't she understand that you were being brave? Being a mother yourself, you now wonder how you could have been so insensitive to her overwhelming feelings of loss. You were taking her only grandson 10,000 miles away ... *I want her to be excited for me, me, me* you said to yourself ... the me always looking for the life she thinks is hers. You were determined to *not* be your mother, to *not* need the things you thought were yours to build like family and stability and belonging. Yet the truth was you had already made a good start at generating those very things for yourself and your son.

And you walked away from it all.

Because you convinced yourself that you wanted something *different*. Trouble was that you had no idea what that was and you were unhinging yourself in hopes that somebody somewhere would give you exactly what you were looking for. You didn't realize yet that your life is a grand adventure and you have everything you will ever need inside of you. And that it's okay to not know exactly how it's all going to unfold. In fact, you can *never* know exactly how it's to be because you are the creator of your own experience. Your inner sensing was correct – you had an adventure to live. But your self-doubt and belief that what you required would come from somebody else was misguided. You let that misguided belief pull you from the path that felt right for you because you told yourself you didn't have enough and you wouldn't have enough and you needed to get more so you could come back to this path someday to do all the things that you actually wanted to do like make a home for yourself, be a good mother, study, read and write. You'd be able to finally do all that when you had enough and then you'd be happy and settled and free. Until then you'd need to pay a price. You'd need to leave home, travel to a country that you had no interest in seeing with a man who seemed to love you enough and who certainly seemed to need you for his own happiness. That would surely be a "real" adventure much more valuable than you staying where you stood. Together you'd be stronger than apart. You could work and earn and save and come home to Canada to build the life you really wanted. You convinced yourself that the fear you felt about leaving was just fear and you needed to ignore it and go anyway. Rather than listening to your intuition, you lied to yourself which set in motion a corruption of your own power. You chose to *not heed* your own interior signals. You chose to *not know* that the so-called fear was actually a clear warning that you were about to step into territory that would cause you distress and distortion. This is your self-endangering innocence. The corruption of your intuition that brings you to this crossroads of choosing to live or to die, to be a mother to your sons or to abandon them.

We come to a crossroads through the chaos we create based on the dis-clarity of our choices when it's time to live more consciously.

It's time to live more consciously!

• • •

It's time.
The time of year when it's time to leave the desert.
It's time.

And in this time it is unbearably hot. Your heart longs for the rain forest balm of Vancouver Island. You want home.

It's time to go home.

And to never return to this place again.

Ever.

You're done here.

It's time.

Yet your heart breaks. Because now you are living dishonestly in relationship with the lovely Arab man. You now have a hidden agenda. Something you've never had before. It feels dangerous and necessary. You wonder to yourself if he might understand if you were to tell him what's on your mind. But there is fear in you. You fear being separated from your sons. You fear losing yourself in this desert land. You fear being held captive to a life that will kill you. All this fear has you navigating your everyday life differently. You are no longer vulnerable and innocent and trusting. You watch the way you plan under the radar. You think about what you'll be able to pack to take with you and what will need to stay behind. None of it really matters that much to you in contrast to having your boys with you safe and sound. Yet you know you'll need to build a new life again and the boys will need things. Things that they already have here. How will they cope when they learn that Mama has left it all behind and they'll need to do without?

To face these realities is too painful.

So you create a new story theme in your mind to get you through the process. You tell yourself that the lovely Arab man will eventually come around after he learns you have no intention of returning to the desert. That he'll demand of himself to be respectful and kind to you even though his anger will surely blind him for awhile. You tell yourself that you just need to get back to Canada and then you can negotiate with him about what you'll need to make home and provide for the children.

No more vulnerability. No more trust. You must be careful and awake now. You must be smart and quiet. On the surface of things it must look as though life is unfolding as it always has. The lovely Arab man is taking his family to New York for a week. Then he'll send you off to see your family in Canada while he goes to visit his daughters in Tennessee. You'll rendezvous in Europe in a few weeks and then make your way back to the desert when the blazing summer is cooling down. That's the ritual. That's the plan. All very ordinary.

You've never done this. Being dishonest makes you feel afraid and alone. You sense your life depends on it though and so you spend much of your time saying silent prayers for protection and guidance.

The thing most difficult to grapple with is the knowledge that you are taking the man's son away from him. How will you live with this? How will you reconcile this within your own soul?

You live this question every moment of every day. It never leaves your awareness. It colours how you see everything around you. You want nothing more than to keep the father and the son together. Well, maybe that's not entirely true. You cannot say you'd rather die than to separate them because you are fighting for your life. Why does it feel like you are fighting for your life? When you look around you, the danger is not visible. It lives in the shadows and you are sensing it but to describe it to others seems impossible. On the surface of things, you have it all. Yet there is some risk lurking just under the precarious surface of what is visibly your life. It has you feeling unsteady. Insecure. You've seen and heard too much to be fooled into silence or apathy. You can feel how guarded you've become. Even cautious. And the false notes that you hit in order to make it look like all is as it's always been causes you inner strain. But you cannot focus on that right now. You just need to get to safety. Get to a place where you can think straight again. And feel grounded. So you go through all the motions as though nothing has changed when in fact, your whole world is turning and tossing and taking you some place where you've never been. And your hope is that you'll be smart enough to get yourself back to yourself.

There's fear. And then there's fear.

The kind of fear you are now experiencing is nothing like you've ever felt before. The one person you've learned to trust unconditionally with your own life and the lives of your sons is now the man you are wanting to escape from. None of it makes sense. Yet you know your life depends on leaving. How can this be so?

The intuitive mind is a different beast altogether from the rational mind.

You are intuiting your way back to where you need to be. And you cannot speak this out loud to anyone. You must trust your inner signals and follow through on your guidance. And so you do.

You do it by lying to the lovely Arab man. But lying to him feels like finally living in alignment with what is now true in you.

It's a direct flight on Malaysian Airlines from Dubai to New York City. There's a hassle at customs when you arrive as you and your boys are allowed to go through while the lovely Arab man is held for questioning. It triggers more fear in you but then you realize you're on North American soil. And that fact comforts you. Yet you are surprised by the intensity of your reaction to the situation. You are deeply afraid.

The verve of New York City feels a bit overwhelming but you allow yourself to be swept up into it and you vow to make it a memorable stay for yourself and your sons. You book Broadway shows and plan shopping sprees. You watch yourself stock your wardrobe as though it's your last opportunity to buy what you need. You notice you are living a split life. And you're doing it deliberately. You take your eldest son to Broadway and delight in his excitement. *Phantom of the Opera, Annie Get Your Gun, Les Miserables* ... he delights in the theatre and it makes him the best company! You know you will treasure these moments in the years to come. You allow yourself to be suspended in the fun of it all ... for him and for you. Back at the apartment the lovely Arab man who is loathe to sit through musicals or theatre makes it known to you that he is feeling less than amused by the fun you and your son are having. You point out the fact that as father he is getting the opportunity to spend time alone with his son. But he is more concerned about missing you and what you are doing without him. And you think to yourself *What the fuck! You're a father, start acting like one and stop feeling sorry for yourself* and then you feel an internal guilt because there's another part of you that is planning to take the man's son away from him. You wonder if maybe this is your way of testing the lovely Arab man. Of giving him a chance to prove to you that he wants to be present for you and the boys. That when you're on "home" ground away from his culture and his world that he will be the man he once was with you. The man who was willing to want a life with you. A real partnership with you. The man who wanted you to thrive and have fun and live carefree. But the look on his face when you walk in the door after enjoying an evening out with your son is not that man. He is angry and sulky.

You let yourself notice this.

The man isn't acting like a father at all. He's acting like he's a babysitter and you owe him something when you get home.

You will always and forever be grateful for the fact that you took the time and had the fun with your son because the memories and the music and the stories will sustain the two of you when you're living the life of a single mother who sells her jewellery to make mortgage payments. The delight on your son's face while you watch him watching what's happening on stage will live in your heart forever. It is magic!

The rest is just bullshit.

And as the days in New York count off the calendar you start to get nervous.

On the morning of departure, you think your heart is going to fragment into a thousand pieces and drop out of your body onto the floor while you stand in front of the lovely Arab man. You cannot make eye contact with him. He will surely see that you are hiding something from him. Maybe he already senses something is different about you and maybe it all confuses him as much as it brings clarity to you.

There is a moment.

When you feel such love and tenderness for all that this man has been to you and done for you.

You stand at the end of the hall and you watch him playing with your young son.

How can I knowingly take this son from his father?

You reassure yourself by telling yourself that you don't know how it'll all unfold. You just need to do your part. You just need to get to safety. Get to your family. Then you'll be able to think clearly. For now, you tell yourself, just stay awake and be grateful and be good.

You walk over to the lovely Arab man as though you are going to walk past him. You slip your hand into his hand which is in his pants pocket. You rest your right cheek on his right cheek. You feel the warm, familiar flesh on your flesh. You're overwhelmed with sadness and love. You dare not look into his face. You close your eyes. Then you trust your voice to whisper into his ear. *No matter what, know that I've always loved you and I always will.*

You squeeze his hand.

Then you walk into the kitchen.

And he continues to play with the boys.

You dare not allow yourself to know that this is how it ends.

The end is now.

• • •

You arrive at JFK. All of you. Your husband is at the check-in desk doing what he always does so well … taking care of the travel details for you and your children. He is the ultimate provider and protector, that's how you like to think of him. You wonder how far he'll stretch himself if you don't return. You've seen changes in him recently and part of you understands that he will only grow so far with you. If you remain in Canada, you may never see him again. You sense this. It makes you sad. And then you start to second-guess yourself. He needs you. You've promised to never leave him or take his child from him. He's lived through that once already and you don't want to do the same thing to him again. You've been his loving place to fall when he felt overwhelmed and depressed. How can you possibly be the one to now inflict that same misery upon him?

It's a tough place where you stand now.

You are faced with saving yourself or saving your perceived sense of who you need to be to another.

You begin to doubt yourself.

Then the Universe responds in an effort to wake you up.

The airline agent informs the lovely Arab man that your flight has, in fact, been cancelled. There is a storm brewing and you can't get to Toronto. Immediately you think the heavens have given you more time with the lovely Arab man. You suggest he delay his own flight and you all go back to the apartment to take a few more days to enjoy being together. But your husband is determined to get to Nashville. He's promised his daughters he'll be there today. He doesn't mince his words. There's no affection in his tone. You can either re-route your journey by leaving JFK now and spend the night in Chicago before departure for Calgary in the morning or you can choose to return to the apartment alone with the boys and delay your departure from New York. Depart when you want to. Either way, he's leaving.

In that very moment another veil is lifted.

He really doesn't care if you stay or if you go.

He will not alter his plans to accommodate your needs.

We're not his priority.

We're not his priority.

We're not his priority.

You feel the shock of it in the centre of your chest. You don't know how your heart remains in your body. Why doesn't it just fall out of you onto the floor where he can step over it on his way out the door?

He wants his daughters more than he wants to be here with you and your sons.

The truth is so crystal clear that it stings your eyes and tastes bitter in your mouth.

You don't want to see this. You don't want to know this. But here it is staring you in the face and ringing loudly in your ears. There is no avoiding the truth of it now.

This moment is *the* moment that will replay in your mind every time you second-guess your decision to take that plane to Chicago. This is the memory you've never shared with anyone. The one you've kept locked up and hidden away. The one that has whispered in your dreams in the middle of the night when you've wondered if you'd made a terrible mistake. The one you'll force yourself to recall whenever you feel guilty for leaving. The thing about truth is that once you've acknowledged it you can never again not know it exists. It changes your orientation to life. It changes who you can become.

It's time.

It's time for you to leave the lovely Arab man.

It's time to go home.

Seats assigned. Boarding passes handed to you. The schedule is tight. You must get through to the gate now. No time to waste. As though the Universe doesn't want you to think another moment about any of it. As though you are being ushered along despite your reservations, despite your self-doubt, despite your guilt.

Get to Chicago. Go!

And a part of you takes over. Puts on a brave face. Pretends this is just another step on the journey. No big deal. You're flying home to see your family. It's summer. Vacation. See you in a few weeks. Say hello to the girls for us. Take care. Call us when you can. Bye for now.

Bye bye.

Bye bye bye.

This isn't goodbye. Just get to Canada. Then you can think.

You are terrified inside. Surely everyone can see how terrified you are inside. Your legs feel week. As though your life energy is draining out from within you with every step you take away from the lovely Arab man. Tears form in the corners of your eyes. You quickly will them back. You want to reach back for him. Take him to where you are going. It's not him that you fear. It's the life built all around him that scares you. It's not yours. You don't belong in it. You love him but you don't belong to him. Years later you wonder if you'd have told him the truth of your desire to return home if he'd have helped you create it. Would he have supported you if you'd have had a frank discussion with him? Was he prepared to follow through on what he'd said about wanting you to return to Canada? What would that have looked like? He'd said he wanted you to go and live as though he were dead. He didn't say he wanted you to go and he'd meet you halfway and collaborate with you to create a life that you both could thrive in. He didn't say he wanted more than anything else in his life to be a good father to his son. He didn't say that he would follow through on his commitment to you and your children to love and protect you regardless of where you wanted to be in the world. You thought these would have been the easiest words in the world to speak if he loved you unconditionally. And you knew yourself to be the kind of woman who could adapt to any lifestyle if it was grounded in love and respect. You knew your capacity to commit. You understood the depth of your own devotion. What was lacking from this marriage was his capacity and his devotion. The truth had revealed to you that this was a crossroads for you now and you needed to decide and you didn't have all day to make your decision.

Keep walking. Keep moving forward. Get to the gate. Get on the plane. Get in your seat.

You arrive at the gate.

The agent checks your boarding passes.

You've made it in time. You are the last passengers to board the aircraft.

You find your seats.

You settle down.

You remember to breathe.

Soon enough the roar of the engines and the force of the plane lifting off the ground give rise to an anxiety churning in your belly. You can feel it leave your body. As if it is melting into the atmosphere all around you. Dissipating. You hold your young son's hand. You glance over to the window where your older boy sits looking out and beyond. He turns his head to meet your eyes. He smiles. And you know that he knows you are leaving for good. But he will forget what he knows in this moment and so will you. There will be plenty of moments of forgetting and feeling lost and alone. Plenty of moments of worry and doubt and fear. But for now there is sweet relief. The three of you are feeling relieved. And from what you don't even really know. It's the feeling that you've just dodged yet another bullet. You've been given another chance to live. Chicago is a short distance away but it's the distance between two worlds – the world you are leaving for the world you have yet to create.

I am coming home.

• • •

A decade later, precisely ten summers after your departure from JFK, your divorce arrives in the mail.

It's official.

You are a free woman.

In an overseas phone call several months prior to receiving your divorce, during the time he was helping you get a passport for your son and arrange your divorce, Ibrahim commented that he knew you and the lovely Arab man had a *real* love. He knew this better than he knew anything, he said.

"You really loved each other."

And you were stunned by the admission.

Finally, after all these years, a witness to your life.

We really loved each other.

Yet you never again set eyes on the lovely Arab man.

EPILOGUE

I have come to know that we are godly by nature. And every challenge we encounter along our path is actually a creative opportunity to reveal the truth of who we are. There is never a moment, not one, when we are separate from the intimate weave of divine love and wisdom of spirit with our soul.

We are guided and guarded every step of the way.

I stepped into the unknown thinking I was known. And I discovered my own unconscious creating the effects of my experience. There was no coercion, only a need for me to stop resisting myself, resisting the call of my own being to follow its nature. There was also the need for me to recognize what my life is about and to acknowledge my spirit has ways of redirecting me in order to support the truth of my own nature.

I've had to excavate every perceived wrong, see things through an impersonal lens, witness the Truth, realize how it changes me and correct the imbalance through right action. This has been my healing process.

"I've been robbed" has been an unconscious narrative thread weaving itself through my life story. Robbed by men whom I willingly gave everything. My money. My body. My dreams. My aspirations. My ambition. My spirit. My desire. My labour. And when I was most vulnerable, a young mother with children to provide for, it was taken away from me.

Why did I generate this experience over and over and over again?

The pattern was activated in my unconscious through my first husband's death. When he died, I felt I'd been robbed of my identity, my home, my family and my community. And on an egoic level, that was indeed the experience I endured.

And then I carried that sense of emptiness into my next two marriages.

The Big Pain in me was a magnet for trouble.

From the moment of Kent's death, I felt a deep sense of isolation. The event thrust me into a dark night of the soul. The world wasn't what I thought it was. I felt I no longer belonged. So it was fitting that I create a situation in a culture on the other side of the world where, in fact, I did not belong. I was not visible in my third marriage, I was kept hidden. I longed for acknowledgement. I felt powerless in a culture where women are, in fact, powerless in many ways. In my powerlessness, I sought personal power through relationship. Being widowed left me feeling powerless and alone and isolated. And these are the very qualities I created for myself in the Persian Gulf. I came home to Canada to reclaim my life when the intense emotional pain of being cut off from my own spirit became too much to bear.

I'd forgotten my wholeness when my heart was shattered through Kent's death. Each fragment was like a little shard of glass that I picked up, held to my eye, and used to see my life through. I remained stuck in the lens of emptiness. So again and again and again I lost everything. Each time I had to learn to detach from material life and all the lies I'd learned about what marriage should be. I got stuck in the same story. Each marriage was a different plot with the same ending. The crossroads I eventually came upon involved two other human beings wholly dependent on me — my sons — and it was for them that I woke up out of my soul sleep, and started picking up the fragments of my heart.

Our true teachers are Inner Beings. No one human teaches another. We only contribute to one another's experiences in ways that draw out of us our own healing, our own knowing, our own wisdom. My husbands contributed to the experiences that led me to my own Inner Teacher. They've helped me to see that the fragments of my life through which I was living were skewed, distorted and incomplete. It was the pain of my marriages that brought me back to myself. And my sons were literally and metaphorically my lifestory guardians. Because it was through the lens of mothering that I re-membered and re-connected with love and care and trust. It was the one lens that remained clear for all time. Mothering became and continues to be my deepest spiritual practice. The energy from this devotion eventually spilled over into every area of my life. It's been the way of shapeshifting. The sacred contracts I have with each of my children have been rudders on rough seas. I decided a long time ago to never compromise my ability to be the best mother I am capable of being. It's been the way I've ordered and prioritized my life. Mother-hood was my initiation into power, depth and self-learning.

Being ripped away from all that I believed was mine, time and time again, has forced me to detach from ego conditioning about what I think I should have or should be. It has allowed me to live more truthfully. It has opened me to allow things to move through me and realize I own nothing. I am but a foot soldier for spirit. It all belongs to quantum consciousness, that which our ancestors have called God. I am but a vessel through which S/he pours.

As I've changed, every man I have loved has become a stranger to me. As though we never met. As though life demands he leave my orbit and I leave his. The bonds between us dissolved. Life carried us onward and away. Yet I know that whatever love was shared between us is eternal.

When Kent died, death didn't happen to me. It was *his* life's journey, not mine. The car accident happened to him. It was wrong for me to be so entangled in that event to cause myself to be lost in something that wasn't mine to begin with. What his death really taught me was to never lose myself in another human being. I belong to me.

I've learned to never fragment myself again based on another soul's journey.

I've learned that when I start running on empty that it's a sign I'm on someone else's road.

And I've learned I have tremendous capacity to self-correct.

Pain is never meant to be avoided. It is meant to be felt. It is feeling with self-awareness that carries us from one state of consciousness to another. Pain is the portal we go through to awaken.

I learned to stop running away so I could go through a full season with myself and learn to hear my Inner Teacher.

A broken heart is an open heart. But when you're THAT open, you must take care to wake up to your inner wisdom and not get stuck in a shard of fragmented lens that is too small through which to view the truth of your life.

In the early morning hours of a fall day in October 2013, I had a dream.

It's winter. And snowing. I'm wanting to walk with my father. I wait. And I wait longer. He is in his truck. It slips off a small cliff onto its side. I watch from a distance. He rolls out of the truck from the driver's seat onto a small ledge of ice. He lay there on his back. I talk to him from below. I ask him what happened? He mumbles something I cannot understand. I sense he is going to fall again because he is precariously perched on the edge of the edge. Sure enough. His body rolls off the ice. I turn away. I cannot bear to see him hit the ground. I am relieved when he lands on his feet. I walk over to him. Face him. Wrap my hands over his. He doesn't want to look me in the eye. And I say, "Father, do not underestimate the healing power of my hands."

When I awaken from the dream, I see how my three husbands have reflected back to me my experience of the Dark Masculine. Each and every man has turned away from my Feminine power. They have been strong soul mates as they've caused me to discover and step more fully into the Truth of the power that runs through me. And to touch that power and become wholly-holy integrated with it has demanded I evolve the immature relational patterns that live in my psyche. Patterns that I refer to as the Dark Feminine. These patterns are not mine personally. They belong to all of us collectively. And we are each called to do the work of the many.

For years I have been wedded to my wounds and I've carried guilt for taking a man's son away from him. Writing this story has been a process of self-forgiveness. I know now that we don't create reality simply by the choices we make but rather by the *intention* that flows from our heart when we choose. The distinction is critical. For every choice ignites wheels of energy spiralling forward in infinite ways to impact the whole of who we are and who we might become. And it is our heart's intention that holds the real power to set the creation in motion.

I can say sincerely that my heart's intention has always been loving.

And I came into this world with an ancient and abiding love in my soul.

All choices have consequences. And all consequences eventually balance. The wisdom of quantum consciousness is working for everyone.

We change constantly. Everything influences us. We must learn to hold our centre. And that requires we be deeply devoted to ourselves so we might learn and expand.

At every crossroads in my life I sensed something about myself that was trying to emerge. Through three marriages, I've developed the courage and the self-esteem to make decisions when decisions are called for. I've been able to let old parts of me die so I might birth anew. When my awareness gave me the insight to act in accordance to something that was wanting to happen, I created new life experience. Above all else, I've done this profoundly well. Otherwise I wouldn't be telling you this story. And I wouldn't comprehend this Truth: *life conditions follow consciousness not the other way around.*

I remember when I realized that I love writing more than anything else. I now understand that that's the Storyteller in me. It is She who longs to tell stories to wake us up from our soul sleep.

I also recall when I thought I needed to leave home and all that I knew myself to be in order to have a great adventure so I'd have something to write about. I'm not so sure I needed to put myself through the conditions that I created in order to have my great adventure but alas this has been my path of evolution.

Whatever the truth is, here's the story. The book of my great adventure. Facing my own humiliation has given me unshakeable courage. The great Christian mystics would say that humiliation brings us back to the ground of our being ... back to humus, the organic component of earth itself made from decomposed life ... back to the stuff of which we are made. It's taken me awhile. But I've been willing to die to myself over and over and over again. Through three marriages, I've learned who I am. And now that I know the truth of who I am, I realize that I knew Her all along!

My sense is that this ever expanding constant unfolding is the only thing I can trust and be sure of now. I am not the same woman today as I was the moment I wrote these words for you or will be as you read them. But the one thing that has remained is my burning desire to see the clarity of Truth. If that's the evolutionary impulse then I am precisely where I need to be doing exactly what I came here to do and learning all the while just exactly who I am. Life *is* a great adventure, to be sure. And I have all that I'll ever need to travel it wisely, within me.

I am love.

I am here to express the Divine Dream that lives in me.

And I must never, ever, ever second-guess myself again!

This story has been living me. I daresay, I was born with this story in me. My ever-present companion, who will I be without this story talking me through the night?

I give it now to you, beloved reader.

May it bring love and light to you and your story.

Blessed Gratitude

With deepest honour and gratitude to Divine Mother. This entire work, my life and all I create belongs to you. You speak to me through the people who have touched my life in perfect ways and for whom I give thanks.

Matthew and Gabriel Bowyer, my sons. It's so obvious to me now that I was destined to be your mother. Everything of value that I have learned about life and about who I am has come to me through our sacred relationship. I could write volumes expressing my gratitude for the two of you. This book is the first instalment.

My beloved teacher, Caroline Myss. You. Light. My. Path. Through your teachings I have come to fully understand that I've had life experiences so I may become spiritually mature, sense the presence of my soul and realize that truth is a force through which I move my life forward.

Mom & Dad for giving me unconditional love and home so I knew how to create it for myself and my own children and I could sense when it was missing in my life. Life conditions follow consciousness. You gave me Home Consciousness. I do not pretend to know what it must have been like for you to watch your eldest daughter's life unfold the way that it has. But I know enough through my own experience of parenting to say it must've been hard. Thank you for never judging and always listening with an open heart. You have been and continue to be my life-line to Cosmic Goodness.

Brother Brent & sister-in-law Janice for opening your home and giving me a soft place to fall when it looked like my life was falling apart, but in fact, it was falling together again. I know it wasn't easy for you to have the three of us land on your doorstep. You not only provided home for us when we were homeless, you embodied loving encouragement and engaged me in strategic conversations that help set our world right side up again.

Brother Murray for our exquisite soul connection. We are the mystics in our family. It's like we share a secret code language. With you, I am never lost.

Sister Jody for being a loving mirror. It is when I look at you that I see a part of myself that is both like and unlike the woman you are becoming. Through the her-story of our mother and our mother's mother, we have the opportunity to reveal and release the emotional patterns that lead us to believe we are trapped in lives we don't want to live. As we lovingly create our lives forward, may we endeavour to liberate the Wise Woman in us all, or as Clarissa Pinkola Estes writes, may we *Untie the Strong Woman*.

Cathie Myers, my "other" sister. You were by my side when I birthed my sons. And you've been midwife to my own potential. Your constant friendship saved my life. We are and always will be soul sisters.

Shari Lainchbury, godmother to me and my sons when we were lost in the desert. You brought us home, both spiritually and literally, through your simple acts of kindness and constant love. You were a channel for grace and I owe you lifetimes of gratitude.

Cody McGowan for taking charge of what needed to be fixed and remodelled to make beautiful the house that would be home so I might be settled enough to write. Don't ever imagine that all you've done for our family ever goes unnoticed or unappreciated.

Stefano Crivelli and Monica Sangberg for your inspiring, soulful friendship and for sharing your beautiful Casa del Pozzo. It was while writing in your loggia that I discovered the voice I needed to tell the story of my third marriage. When I imagine writing my next book, I see myself there, with you, in the Tuscan Hills. I cherish your company and look forward to years of deepening conversation.

David Wasylynko whose healing hands help me process layers of emotional residue in my body from decades of perceived burden and overwhelm.

Richard Bartlett for aligning me with the magic of who I might become without the perceived burden and overwhelm and for lighting the way with Matrix Energetics.

Jimmy Mack. You are a portal to the Divine. And a brother to my soul. I love you for saying to me: "Magi, crank that book out and help as many people as you can!"

Ron Wheatley, my Co-Creative Collaborator. You attune to my inner vision, virtually cast it into form, and communicate it to the world through the online platforms you build for me. I can't imagine trusting the spirit of my business to anyone else.

Sanjay Mohan-Ram for opening the doors to Cross Roads Naturopathic for me so I might meet those I am meant to serve. Kristen Brown and Rob Baron for welcoming me into the clinic and helping me build a practice that not only serves others, but has been the catalyst of healing for me. (Which is how it works, of course.) Your steady stewardship is appreciated beyond words and time.

Jen Cherewaty and Carley Akehurst. Your intuitive wisdom, acupuncture and magical herbs are loving potions I cherish and depend on.

Thank you Melissa Tofsrud, Jessica Buxbaum and our Cross Roads team for all the ways you enhance and facilitate the healing in our clinical environment.

Which brings me to thank every person who has ever sat with me in deep conversation. It is such a privilege to have your trust. Your life has shone a light in my life and helped me to see more clearly who I am and why I am here. Through our intimate connection, we heal each other.

My healing took a quantum leap when I met Divi Chandna, my physician, coach and go-to Wise Woman. Thank you, Divi, for keeping me tuned into the frequency of creation that makes this book possible.

It is one thing to write. It is a wholly-holy different thing to have readers. I am grateful beyond any words for Jessica Buxbaum, Monica Sangberg and Sharon Butala for receiving the story and giving it your loving attention. You helped me find the courage to broaden my spirit and send it out further into the world.

A special note of thanks to Sharon Butala whom I think of as my Writerly Mother. When I wrote the first segment of this story some sixteen years ago, before the age of technology that we are living in now, I mailed it to you from the Persian Gulf for safekeeping. You not only read what I'd written, but you encouraged me to keep writing. That is the greatest gift for any writer. And for me, it was the difference between giving up or giving over to the burning desire in my heart to make this book. I harbour such love and gratitude for the essence of you. Thank you.

And if I have a Writerly Father, it is Eric Maisel with whom I've enjoyed years of creativity coaching and training. There is no doubt in my mind that had I not invested in myself through Eric's guidance this book would never have seen the light of day. In fact, Eric even said as much in a book he recently published to expose what *really* goes on in a coaching conversation. (I had the privilege of being one of the artists that Eric engaged for the research of his book *Secrets of a Creativity Coach.* I'm "Paula" in the chapter "I Prefer Flying Under the Radar.") Thank you, Eric, for all that you do on behalf of all artists. I never had the courage to call myself an artist until I met you.

Reverend Michael Bernard Beckwith and the Agape community. I can't help but think that all the connections I've made in service to sharing this story have come through the field of love that you are. Thank you for being my beloved spiritual home.

Claude Adams. You are my lover, my best friend and my life partner now. We are learning a new model of marriage together. I like to think we are creatively adaptive which is ultimately essential to our individual and collective evolution. We support and nurture each other's interior worlds. We honour each of our soul's calling. And we find ways to still be our Sacred Couple. It is a Fierce Love that binds us. Thank you for accommodating my evolutionary journey and for being large enough to hold the truthful being I am becoming. I've loved you in other lifetimes, I love you now, and our love is eternal come what may.

And finally to Dante, our beloved dog. Some say we rescued you. But that's not true. You've come into our family with gifts of seeing and being. We needed you. You've helped me see this project through to completion. Your heartbeat while you lay at my feet kept me in my chair writing.

May this story be an open portal for
Divine Mother's Grace

THE AUTHOR

Magdalen Bowyer

Magdalen Bowyer was born and raised in Saskatchewan, and she works with a team of practitioners at an integrated health clinic in Vancouver. Most of the people she helps are artists—people who have taught her how creativity flows through and from Spirit, and if that flow is fragmented, how it influences health and well-being. She is the mother of two sons, Matthew and Gabriel, and shares her life and home with TV journalist Claude Adams, and her beloved dog and writing companion, Dante. This is her first book. You can find her at www.magdalen.ca

59503846R10178

Made in the USA
Lexington, KY
07 January 2017